HER WITS
ABOUT HER

D1284829

HER WITS ABOUT HER

Self-Defense Success Stories by Women

Edited by
Denise Caignon and Gail Groves

PERENNIAL LIBRARY

HARPER & ROW, PUBLISHERS, NEW YORK
Cambridge, Philadelphia, San Francisco, Washington
London, Mexico City, São Paulo, Singapore, Sydney

FIRST EDITION

Designer: Erich Hobbing
Copyeditor: Beth Greenfeld

Library of Congress Cataloging-in-Publication Data
Her wits about her.
   1. Self-defense for women. I. Caignon, Denise.
II. Groves, Gail.
   GV1111.5.H47   1987   613.6′6024042   86-46051
   ISBN 0-06-055078-3   87 88 89 90 91 MPC 10 9 8 7 6 5 4 3 2 1
   ISBN 0-06-096172-4 (pbk.)   87 88 89 90 91 MPC 10 9 8 7 6 5 4 3 2 1

To all the women who didn't think they used
self-defense, but who survived to tell the story

Contents

The names used in some of the selections are not real and, accordingly, individual traits and descriptive details of the women, their friends, families and assailants have been altered.

Preface: And He Turned Around and Ran Away

Gail Groves

For six years I worked on a rape hotline in Santa Cruz, a small California central-coast town with an activist spirit. Santa Cruz Women Against Rape, the collective that runs the hotline, is known for propagating the idea that direct confrontation of rapists is a way to exert community control over men's behavior. The group prides itself on its political, rather than service, orientation. The rape calls we got were not unusual, from what I know about rape hotlines in the state and the nation. One year, the hotline received six hundred calls, while local police got only seventeen.

One of the most surprising aspects of these calls was the fact that so many women got away without being raped. Over the years, a consistent picture began to emerge of women effectively resisting, paying attention to clues about a potential attack, and escaping by many different means. We told each other success stories at our group meetings, partly to bolster ourselves for another night of waiting for the phone to ring.

I had been working the hotline for six months, when one day, at a meeting, someone was talking about her boyfriend in high school pressuring her to have sex. Suddenly, I remembered that I had been raped once and had fought off a second rape attempt by the time I was twenty—both times by acquaintances in "social" situations. I had blocked them entirely out of my memory. As you read this book, you may find yourself remembering incidents you wish you had forgotten, too, but perhaps you will also remember how you got away.

The knock on the glass apartment door startled me. It was late; it wasn't my house. Strains of the Jefferson Airplane and my quiet thoughts were disturbed by this person at the door. It was a foggy San Francisco night, and my boyfriend had already taken a bus back to his mother's house across town.

The clear glass door revealed a large man in his mid-thirties, with a beard and bushy dark hair.

"Who are you?" I said.

"I'm a friend of Cherri's," he said, smiling at me with large, perfect teeth. Cherri Black, my friend who rented this flat, was across the bay at the time with her boyfriend. I felt uneasy, confused by conflicting values and messages. I knew I should not let the man in.

"What's your name?" I asked.

"I'm T. J. Broderick. See?" There, on his expensive patchwork corduroy shirt, were his embroidered initials: T. J. An expansive, egocentric man, he was sure I wanted him to come in.

"Why don't you let me in, and we can talk for a few minutes?" he said.

"Cherri isn't here right now," I said suspiciously. And not likely to come back after 11:00 P.M. either, I thought. But I had been raised to be polite, and he was a very smooth talker, very nice. Why not, after all, let him in? What if I was a scared seventeen-year-old who had never had sex. He just wanted to talk. After a few more of his persuasive assurances, I let him in.

We walked into the living room. My body stiffened. I knew this wasn't right, but my upbringing had not prepared me to rebuff the friendly approach. We talked, or rather I listened and nodded.

"I write scripts for television. Cherri has known me for years. I'm surprised she never told you—I drop in on her all the time. What's your name?"

"Gail," I said numbly. This man wanted me to trust him. What was I going to do? I was slight next to his huge man's body. He talked on and on. I felt uncomfortable, aware of sexual overtones, afraid of rape.

"Here, come sit over here with me." He planted himself on Cherri's couch-bed, leaning back against the pseudo-Victorian wallpaper.

"No, I don't want to," I said, sitting across the room. But he hadn't hurt me yet. He had only talked me into passivity.

"What's the matter? I won't hurt you. I just want to talk. Come on over here." Unconsciously, he mimicked my thoughts. I got up woodenly, walked to where he sat, and sat down at the far end of the settee, near his legs. I allowed him to manipulate my body into a half-lying position at his side. He tried to kiss me. I fended him off. My entire body was stiff, unyielding.

I kept thinking over and over, You can do this, but I am not going to feel anything. You can touch me, but you can't really get to me. My only defense was this unfeeling rigidity.

He stroked my back, kept talking.

"There now, that's not so bad. Look, I won't hurt you. A pretty little girl like you should have a boyfriend." I wouldn't tell him how old I was, and contemplated telling him my boyfriend would be right back, but didn't. I didn't want him to think I had had sex.

He kept stroking my back, over and over again. Lost in my thoughts, trying to absent myself, I fought to stay stiff. Then, for a crucial moment, I relaxed. I have always hated myself for that "guilty" moment. I shocked myself back into awareness, and finally began to react.

"I want you to go away," I said tentatively. "I don't want to do this." We talked a little while longer. I began to feel shaky, tired of resisting. Finally, he let me go. I got up, moved away, and since his only weapon was persuasion, he could not force me back. Finally, hours after I had answered the door, when I was obviously, if passively, continuing to resist, he left.

"Give Cherri my best regards," he finished amiably as I shut the door in his face. He could have raped me. At that moment, I had no idea why he hadn't. I looked out the window, watched him leave, began to shake, still feeling numb. I called my boyfriend's house. His mother answered.

"May I speak to Tim?" I asked.

"He's gone to bed." His mother never slept. She was a suspicious, prudish woman who had raised Tim alone after his father abandoned them.

"Look, Mrs. Drummond, I was almost raped, and I want to talk to your son," I gasped angrily at her.

He came to the house. I told him what had happened, cried, made tea. It was over.

But I never forgave myself for that moment in which I relaxed; I felt in that moment I gave in and betrayed myself. Now, I see that I also successfully avoided rape.

Eight years later, I took an eight-week self-defense class, wanting to finally break free from some of the fear that gripped me whenever I walked alone, that compelled me to look in all the closets whenever I came home to an empty house. These were my private nightmares then. Now I see them as common to the everyday terror of having been born female. I began to question limits I had previously accepted.

I was fascinated by self-defense. After years of living in a cage, I had been given a key—skills and attitudes that could change my approach to life. My teacher, Kathy Quinn, helped me see that I had power, and that I could learn to use my mind and body to sense an impending attack and to deflect it. I *could* fight back effectively, no holds barred.

I apprenticed myself to her, and within a year found myself studying joshi (women's) judo, and teaching one-day self-defense workshops for women and girls at the YWCA.

Part of my motivation for learning to teach self-defense was fear. I was afraid to walk home from the bus stop. I was afraid of someone breaking in through my bedroom window. I was furious at the restrictions that had been put on me and other women.

When I felt it safe to do so, I began to experiment. On my way home, instead of running breathlessly with blinders on down the long road by the ocean to my house, I would stop. I would stand still by the side of the road, or sometimes in the middle of it, and listen in the dark. I would look to see how far away someone was when I could first sense they were there. The first thing I learned was that I was not afraid of the dark. If I was alone in the dark, I was fine. I was afraid of people in the dark.

My limit was about twenty yards. If people were out there and I was listening and looking for them, even if they stood relatively still, I could still tell where they were. If they made any sound at all, I could spot them immediately. This was a revelation. After all, I too had seen all the movies in which the woman walks down the street while the rapist lurks in the (rustling!) bushes, then suddenly jumps out, and, wham, it's all over, she's been raped. The more I studied rape, the more I concluded that this thirty-second fantasy was born out of the necessities of half-hour TV shows and two-hour movies. Most rapes in real life take longer than that. In real life, for someone to get close enough to rape you, he must first be far away. Then either he sneaks over the last twenty yards, or he runs them, giving you lots of warning. Or the person is an acquaintance and you let him come near, even if you feel uncomfortable. Paying attention to, rather than ignoring, those uncomfortable feelings became the norm for me rather than the exception. I began to enjoy my nighttime walks a great deal more.

Fear plays a special role in learning about self-defense. One of the most effective ways to teach self-defense is to have students act out situations they are afraid of, using other students—telling the "attacker" what to do, and then seeing what the defender's options are. Now fear is a tool for me—it helps me see areas of my life where I need more skills to handle situations.

One way to deal with particular fears and to learn realistic self-defense is through dreams. I used to be extremely afraid of someone breaking in through my bedroom window. Early in my second year of teaching, I had a series of nine dreams about this. In the first dream, I was paralyzed, and somehow the attacker disappeared by magic. In the second dream, I struggled and pushed him out the door. In the third dream, I picked up a flowerpot and hit him over the head. During my waking life, I began to look around my room for available weapons. I practiced throwing someone off me while I was under the covers, and I learned how to deal with a knife from that position. Finally, in the ninth dream, after each previous dream's defense had become more effective and realistic, I killed the man. That was the end of the dreams, and signaled some resolution of this particular fear.

Fear becomes more and more a pointer to areas where I need to learn skills, and thus a useful tool. Many students tell of dream sequences in which they cannot scream or move, but as the class goes on, they find their dreams changing to include more effective, skilled responses.

Contrary to images on TV and in movies, when you make a situation real in your mind, there are always options for the defender—ways she can damage the attacker, verbal points she can gain through negotiation, strategies that will work. Self-defense means looking for these openings, having the faith that there will be one at some point, and then trying something, and not giving up.

The more I taught, the more self-defense stories I heard. Initially, I found that women in classes and workshops used me as a place to dump all the horror stories they had ever heard. After some workshops, I would need to go have a good cry, staggered by the ugly, brutal violence against women I heard about. I think my students assumed that because I was a self-defense teacher, it was all right to talk to me about all the terrible things they were afraid of, about all the stories they had heard on television. They thought I could handle it. More and more, I found I couldn't. The stories upset me and brought down the positive mood of an empowerment workshop. I found I had to shield myself from the stories, to cut myself off from the pain associated with them. My empathy was working against me.

In an effort to focus on the positive in these classes, I began to collect success stories informally. All self-defense teachers have them. These were stories of both the simplest and the most convoluted escapes. The woman who rolled out of a car going fifty miles per hour to escape a kidnapping. The woman who, hearing two men talking behind her about what they were going to do to her, began punching air, only to see them turn and run. The man who pulled his frightened face back from me when I stuck a fistful of keys in it to stop him from approaching. The woman who took care of her attacker with one hand and her knee while not breaking the cookies she was taking home for her children in the other hand. The woman at the bus stop who answered the man who said he was going to rape her with ''No, you're not!'' He turned away, mumbling vaguely, ''I guess you're right.''

These were not the kind of stories I saw on the nightly news. The crime report in the local paper abounded with stories of women brutally raped. Regional and national news were excruciating with their tales of horrors done to women. Santa Cruz itself had been named ''Murder Capital of the World'' by the media, for a series of rape-murders that Edmund Kemper committed here in 1971 and 1972. Later would come David Carpenter, the ''Trailside Killer.''

During the time I worked on the rape line, I stopped watching television and rarely learned about world events. When you hear the real stories on the phone every night, the sensationalized versions are overkill.

At best, the media would report on spectacular defenses, like the woman in Berkeley, California, who pulled a bayonet out of her closet and stabbed her attacker with it. But these unusual stories did nothing to alleviate the fears of the average woman on the street.

Few people believed that women could protect themselves or stop an attacker. Instead, they believed that women lied about rape, that all men were stronger than all women, and that no woman ever got away. Gradually, through my involvement with self-defense and the rape hotline, the belief began to build in me that these ideas simply were not true. Women did get away before rapes were completed. They did fight back—and they did win. In fact, most of the women I talked to on the phone had done something to stop the rape, or to make the situation safer for themselves. They were not paralyzed by fear. They acted.

Most women who are attacked remember feeling a hunch, an intuition, a nonverbal perception before something physical happens— the feeling that something is wrong. The sooner women act on this intuition, the more likely they are to be safe in the end. Ninety percent of an effective defense is the recognition that yes, this person is attacking me. This feeling is especially important with people we have reason to trust, but who take advantage of that trust. Over 75 percent of all attacks on women are committed by men who know them, at least on a first-name basis. Acquaintance rape and rape in marriage are not uncommon.

One in three girls and one in six boys are attacked sexually in this country by the age of eighteen; the majority of these are attacked by a family member or friend. Yet even very small children, like those who have been trained by the Child Assault Prevention Program in Columbus, Ohio, can learn to defend themselves.

Dr. Pauline Bart, a renowned sociologist from the University of Illinois, began to publish the results of her studies about effective rape avoidance in 1980. Bart established that women who fight back get away more often than women who are passive. For the first time, a reputable scientist was contradicting the advice of the police "not to resist, you'll just get hurt." Too many women had gone into court after following that advice, only to be told that it was not rape if they didn't fight back.

Dr. Bart's results were extremely interesting. She found that the more strategies a woman uses, the more likely she is to escape with minimal injuries. Strategies include yelling, fleeing, reasoning with the attacker, pleading, and physically fighting back—kicking, hitting, biting, using the body as a weapon. Verbal strategies alone were not particularly effective unless used with other strategies. Pleading and acting passive actually seemed to *increase* chances that the rape would be completed. Her reports included exciting stories, many about women who had escaped from armed attackers.

Dr. Bart's findings were borne out by the stories we collected. These women used their wits and their incredible nerve, even when terrified, to figure out what to do in life-threatening situations. Even in some of the most brutal attacks we heard about, women tried strategy after strategy until something worked. They used their wits to negotiate with or outwit their attackers. At times carrying out split-second physical decisions, these women fought back physically, ran, reasoned, and yelled with vigor until their attackers gave up. They have made true the maxim: Your own will to defend yourself is stronger than the attacker's will to hurt you. Dr. Bart's results were recently published in *Stopping Rape: Successful Survival Strategies* (co-authored by Patricia O'Brien, New York: Pergamon Press, 1985), which we recommend.

Women Who Resist: The Self-Defense Success Story Project is the result of my work with Denise Caignon, first in studying judo together, then in teaching self-defense as founding members of the Santa Cruz Women's Self-Defense Teaching Cooperative, and now in writing and editing this book.

The conviction has grown in us that many women do successfully defend themselves. Furthermore, we believe that women use success stories and their knowledge of other women's strategies to create new defenses in unknown situations. This project comes out of our joint desire to share the stories we knew existed with as many women as possible.

There are not ten easy steps to perfect self-defense. Good self-defense is whatever works. The defenses women use are as varied as the women themselves. Each woman uses intuition not only to gauge the danger of the situation, but also to plan her own unique response, geared to her perceptions and abilities. No one can teach you exactly what to do in every possible situation. But in a self-defense class you can learn skills and attitudes that you can combine, should the situation arise, in appropriate ways. The idea is to give women more control and more options. Part of this means unlearning inappropriate responses, originally modeled by actresses on television or in movies—like panic, helplessly screaming with your head thrown back, or pounding on someone's chest, which happens to be one of the strongest parts of the body.

Sometimes the most unexpected strategies work. One woman, guessing that her attacker was Catholic, told him that the Baby Jesus would hate him if he did this to her, and that Mother Mary would condemn him and hate him. He burst into tears and took her home.

Another woman said, yes, it sounded fine with her, but she needed to get her sweater and purse inside at the party first, and then they could go somewhere comfortable. Inside, she screamed and got help.

Two young girls were being followed by two men in a car. When one of the men got out of the car to lure them in, they began to beat him up. The other attacker jumped out of the car to help his buddy escape. The girls' parents, both karate teachers, had taught them some good blows and kicks.

One woman, trapped between two men in the backseat of a car, grabbed the knife one attacker was holding and broke it over her knee. She cut her hands badly, but the attackers apparently thought she was crazy and let her out.

The women that get away are as diverse as their stories. Black women, Latinas, Asian-Americans, white women, fat women, young girls, teens, women in wheelchairs, women with canes, deaf women, married women, mothers, women with cerebral palsy, lesbians, old women. I think of the eighty-six-year-old woman who told me she grabbed and pulled on a man's testicles after he dropped his pants and began to assault her. He ran away crying.

Many attackers can be discouraged verbally at the outset. Lots of assailants begin with a verbal attack, asking personal questions, or becoming obscene. If the woman seems intimidated, or goes along with them, the attack may become physical. The verbal attack is a form of testing, like teasing, that is aimed at the weak points in a woman's self-esteem.

Attackers are not looking for equal partners to fight with when they pick women to attack. Men do not begin an attack on a woman thinking, I'm going to attack her, and then she's going to hurt me. Rather, they see women and girls as easy targets, weak and helpless. There is some evidence, from interviews with rapists in prison, that they look for women who exhibit little confidence, who use minimal eye contact, and who are hunched in posture and taking relatively small steps. They often choose to attack women who seem physically infirm in some way, or who react in passive rather than self-respecting ways.

Most of us women have been taught to be polite, to smile at everyone so that people will like us. Girls learn that they should be seen but not heard, and that they should truthfully answer questions put to them by adults, even strangers. Many of us have been told not to talk to strangers, but were not taught what to do when we don't want to talk to people we know, or if a stranger tries to talk to us or to touch us. These passive patterns make women and girls less likely to resist and easier to rape. And the patterns are often cemented through years of reinforcement and are difficult to unlearn.

Women have been seen for years as weak, helpless *victims*. I used to cringe every time I heard someone in the rape crisis movement say that word, which literally means "sacrifice unto death." In the past few years, many groups in the rape crisis movement have begun to question the use of that word to describe a woman who was raped. I have changed my vocabulary. I now refer to women who have been attacked, whether a rape was completed or not, as *survivors*.

Perhaps as more and more men are injured by the women they have attacked, another truth about women's strength, determination, and will to survive will begin to emerge and spread. Maybe women and girls, after reading these stories of success, will feel encouraged and be determined to fight back should they ever be attacked. Certainly the interest is there: over two hundred women from all over the United States responded in writing to our call for stories.

Although these are subjective personal accounts, it is clear that women do succeed in influencing the behavior of their attackers. In fact, one of the most common and most satisfying endings for the stories we have heard is "and he turned around and ran away."

Acknowledgments

This book is a natural spin-off from a vast network of dedicated people and organizations: the feminist anti-rape movement that began in the early 1970s. Without our own participation in this ground swell of social change, we might never have even conceived of the possibility of *Her Wits About Her*. This powerful movement has grown over the past several years to encompass the battered women's shelter movement, child sexual abuse and assault prevention programs, and self-defense programs. This book represents the fruit of the labor of many people—the positive result of so much difficult work.

We would like to thank all the spirited and devoted people in that movement who helped spawn our vision of successful self-defense. Special thanks to Santa Cruz Women Against Rape, Men Against Rape, Women's Crisis Support and Shelter Services, the annual California Women's Martial Arts Camp, the Santa Cruz Commission for the Prevention of Violence Against Women, the California Statewide Coalition of Rape Crisis Centers, the Mid-Peninsula Self-Defense Collective of Palo Alto, and all the martial arts and self-defense teachers we've ever had, including: Sensei Keiko Fukuda for her pioneering efforts in women's judo, Kathy (Kaleghl) Quinn, Linda Hultgren, Lolma Olsen, and Katherine Eldridge.

Our work with the Santa Cruz Women's Self-Defense Teaching Cooperative convinced us that the success stories were there. We learned as much from the women who took our classes as we taught them. We thank all of our students and our fellow teachers: Rachel Harwood and Mary Gibino, the other founding members, as well as

Hecate Rosewood, Calle Haber, Bobbi Reyes, De Clarke, and Sigrid Hvolboll.

Every story sent to the Success Story Project was unique and wonderful. For space reasons, we weren't able to include all the stories, but each one bolstered our spirits and urged us on. Thanks to everyone who spent the time and the emotional energy to write a story or agree to an interview. We'd also like to thank everyone who wrote to us with encouraging words or offers of help.

The book is the richer for the supportive but hard-nosed editing help we received from Terri Frazier and Jennifer Meyer. Terri in particular put in many hours honing the fine points and deleting the extraneous. Our editor at Harper & Row, Janet Goldstein, brought her fresh insight to the organization of the book, long after we had become myopic. Bettina Aptheker shared her invaluable insights about racism and how it bears on the issue of self-defense. Emily Doskow and Kathleen Sodja, with their swift minds and fingers, took on the seemingly gargantuan task of tape transcription. Kathleen and Terri burned the midnight oil with us more than once, and proofread and typed their way through the endless versions of the manuscript. The self-defense programs section is the result of Kathleen's many hours on the telephone and poring over pages of listings. Rachel Harwood compiled the annotated bibliography. We should add that both the self-defense programs section and bibliography were far larger in their original forms, but, again, space requirements made it impossible for us to include everything.

We thank three foundations—Abelard, Vanguard, and Haigh-Scatena—for the seed money that enabled us to get the Success Story Project off the ground.

Finally, we want to acknowledge all our friends and associates who never wavered in their encouragement and who shared our excitement about this project. In particular, Gail would like to thank Dinah Phillips—for everything. Denise thanks Jane Brecha, Ann Creely, and Janet Ross Danforth for their consistent friendship and support over the miles and years. And both of us thank the women of *Matrix* newsmagazine for helping us hone our skills and develop our confidence as writers and editors.

A Note on Racism

Throughout U.S. history, black and brown men have been accused and convicted of rape in disproportionate numbers to the percentage they make up in the general population. Historically, this can be traced to the association of rape with lynching and the racist myth that white women are frequently raped by black men.

Despite the correlation of lynching and rape in the public mind, only twenty-three percent of the *known* victims of lynch mobs between 1882 and 1946 were even accused of rape or attempted rape. Study after study has shown that the vast majority of rapes are intraracial [within the same race]. In cases of interracial rape [different races] it was Black women who were victimized by an overwhelming number.*

During the same period, such sanctions as lynching hardly existed for white men, who were allowed and even encouraged to rape and degrade black slave women. Most of the men who go to prison today for rape are men of color. The classic image of a rapist as portrayed on television and in movies is that of a crazed black or brown man brutally raping a young, lily-white virgin.

However, according to the Los Angeles Commission on Assaults Against Women, over 98 percent of all rapes happen between people of the same race, generally between people with similar backgrounds.

*Aptheker, Bettina. *Woman's Legacy: Essays on Race, Sex, and Class in American History*. University of Massachusetts Press, 1987.

And over 75 percent of all rapes happen between people who know each other.

Because of the racism of the criminal justice system, it is mostly men of color who go to prison for rape. The public seems to believe the stereotype of the black and brown rapist. This same public rejects the testimony of a woman against her white male doctor, or father, or boss. This serves to protect white men with status and power from rape accusations and convictions.

In this anthology we have attempted to deal with racist assumptions about rape by deleting irrelevant references to race in the stories. Since most rapists, proportionately, are white, we ask that you not assume the attacker to be black or brown as you read the stories.

On the other hand, an opposite assumption, also racist, is made about the woman who fights back: that she is white, able-bodied, young, and highly trained in self-defense. The women who wrote the stories in this book, however, vary in race, background, occupation, age, sexual preference, and self-defense training.

If you want to imagine what the woman you are reading about is like, imagine someone like yourself, using her wits, and taking care of herself the best she can. And if you are white, allow yourself to see some of these women of courage as women of color.

Introduction: Women Who Resist

Denise Caignon

When I was four and five years old, I often woke in a snarl of sheets and blankets—on the floor, heart booming in my head, the smell of my own animal fear all around me. It was always the same confusing nightmare: a man made of shadows—an inarticulate sketch of a man—would sneak into our house and go to our laundry room, where he would steal clean clothes from the dryer. Then he would slink to my room and try to add me to his bag of laundry. A kind of reverse Santa Claus. In my struggle to get away, I would wind up on the floor. I was certain the dream was real. Something about him lingered in the empty room even after my eyes were open.

Later, the nightmares would change as my life experience became richer, and the texture of my fear more intricate: gangs of men chasing me, chasing me, threatening me with death or worse. Fleeing their leering faces, I make my way, alone, down the well-worn labyrinths, across those underground rivers polluted with women's fears. Not realizing, in the dream, that I am not alone at all, but running stride for stride with all the other dreaming women who explore that fear, and their response to it, while their bodies sleep. How many women around the world wake together on any given morning, exhale with relief at their escape into the waking world—the very world that spawned the dream?

This book is written by women who have faced the nightmare: women who resisted. It is the story of how they fought with the tools available to them: their hands, their feet, their eyes, their voices, their minds, certainly their wits, and, most of all, their will to survive.

Every part of me that is woman
is struck, shoved, grabbed, yelled at, violated, hated.
I am lost in unendurable loneliness.
Terror traps my spirit and
fills me with paralysis,
until the most primitive part of my brain,
survival,
pure survival, screams for life.

—Janice Angevine, from "Newark—August 17, 1981"

I believe this will for survival is something all of us are born with. But many of us, especially women, are systematically taught to discard or ignore the tools we have. We learn to cast our eyes down demurely, throttle our voices, flutter our hands ineffectually: sheathe our weapons.

I can still hear my mother's litany of don'ts. Don't open the door to strangers. Don't get into a stranger's car. Don't take candy from anyone you don't know. Since I was young and had to look to adults for my every need, this sense of the sinister my mother knew she had to instill in me was a troubling contradiction.

Without thinking about it, we slowly realize that there is something ominous about other human beings, the same beings we are taught to trust.

There was no one incident that prompted me to take my first self-defense class. But when I moved to California from provincial Kentucky in the mid-seventies, I knew I wanted something to ground me in my new community. And, too, I was told, like every Santa Cruz newcomer, that the town had been besieged by a rash of rapes and murders in the recent past.

There were two basic ideas that took root in me as a result of that first class, ideas that would later inspire my own work with survivors of violence. The first—the one that underlies any act of self-defense—is will. Will boils down to a joint decision made by the mind and the body. To articulate this decision, we practiced an exercise called the Unbendable Arm. First, a woman held her arm out and was told to do everything she could to keep it straight and inflexible. Her practice partner would then try to bend the arm. It wasn't difficult to make the rigid arm buckle, stiffened—even weakened—as it was with sheer muscular tension. After that part of the exercise, the woman held her arm not straight, but with just enough flex in the elbow to be supple.

At the same time, she was told to send one clear, vivid image down from her brain, out through the arm, and beyond—as far as her mind could think. The exact image was unimportant; what was important was that the mind and body together equaled a single meaning: calm, resilient strength, instead of brittle resistance.

Some of the arms in that class were thick fire hoses, pouring out a stream of molten steel. Others were heavy, green oak branches, solid with sap. When I focused my mind, my whole self, on the latter image, my feet took root in the scuffed floor, sent out tendrils deep into the earth beneath the building. I had never felt more prepared.

The point of the exercise was to show that an arm fortified with elastic strength would not buckle under brute force. Our practice partners would struggle and press, stand on chairs and bear down; the arms were not to be bent.

Later, when I took judo, I saw how that calm sense of resolve made effective fighting possible. It was only when I allowed the static to take over my mind—fears of being clumsy, of not doing it right—that I took a bad fall, or jerked my partner into a sloppy hip throw. My stiff resistance was the only thing that marred the smooth, easy roll-dance that judo can be.

The other idea I took from that first self-defense class is that the body is a collection of potentially lethal weapons and vulnerable targets. When police and other "authorities" warn women against resisting assault, they often talk about women's lack of bodily strength relative to men. In terms of brute muscle-for-muscle strength, men often are stronger than women. But every male human body has vulnerable areas—unprotected by Charles Atlas brawn— and every female body has powerful weapons to use against those targets.

For instance, women are not often told that they have especially strong legs, or that it takes only fifteen pounds of kicking pressure to break a kneecap. An elbow to the solar plexus, a foot smashing an instep, a knee to the face or the groin, a scream against an ear-drum—these acts are not beyond the scope of women. There are so many possible combinations of techniques, some more lethal than others, but all capable of, at the least, buying time, loosening a hold, or opening the way for another strategy.

And not all attacks call for a physical response; many attacks can be stopped before they become violent. As you will see, particularly in the section entitled "The Power of the Voice," many self-defense success stories involve an assault that is cut short by a verbal response.

The Success Story Project—as we called ourselves during the years we were collecting stories—seemed the next logical step after my work with battered women, rape survivors, and self-defense. Gail and I knew the stories were out there—we heard them in our classes and from our friends. Women are hungry for tales of successful self-defense. When I would mention to a woman that I was collecting stories about women who fight back, a common response was a delighted smile and "Oh, I've got one!" or "I have this friend who . . ." As if she had just been waiting for the chance to tell her story.

Even though I knew that women were fighting back, I was often astounded by the magnitude of the response to the project. It wasn't just a few women who told me their stories; nearly every woman I talked to had her tale to tell.

The Success Story Project fed my own hunger, too. More than once, the book provided an emotional point of reference during hard times in my life. And when fear cropped up—as it inevitably does for most women—I would remember success stories. Just knowing that other courageous women had defended themselves made it easier to walk down a dark street at night, or believe in myself when I was feeling uncertain.

To be a woman or girl in this society is to know what it means to be hunted, and to learn not only the ways of the hunted but also those of the hunter. It is this knowledge of the attacker that helped so many of the women in these stories to defend themselves. Since an attacker is so often an insecure, desperate person, uncertain of himself and his motives, there are openings where a woman can slip in a remark, a gesture—or a fist or a kick, if it comes to that.

Because women know the myths men believe about them so well, they can often use them against an attacker. Women Really Enjoy Rape is one such myth, and Jane Polansky uses it to her advantage in "A Woman of Common Sense and Courage." When she tells her attacker, who is pinning her in the front seat of her car, that she can help him get her pants off, he relaxes for a moment, thus releasing her for the crucial seconds she needs to get away.

Those precious seconds . . . again and again, the women in these stories show an exquisite sense of timing. Sometimes they watch and wait, then spring to action when the time is right. Other times, they lash out with an immediacy that startles even themselves. In "Fighting Back in the Park,'' Kitty Geneva feels time slow to a crawl as her assailant attempts to strangle her. Suddenly, in those distorted seconds, there is enough time to think clearly, to realize that she is intensely angry at this man—and to act effectively according to that anger.

And each of these women does think clearly. This sometimes means she can remember the smallest detail, as one author remembered the pair of dice tattoed on her attacker's arm, down to the number of dots on each die. Or it may mean she simply acts immediately and succinctly. It is that ability to keep her wits about her that makes each of these women a self-defense artist of the highest rank.

It's not that they are all self-assured and fearless. Many were terribly frightened. But the common denominator is their desire to live, to get through and beyond the experience. Because when an attacker tries to force a woman against her will, he is challenging her most fundamental instinct: survival.

One of the basic premises of the Success Story Project is that any woman who gets away alive has a success story to tell. Py Bateman writes of her battle to save her life in the painful and inspiring ''Coming Out Alive.'' She didn't emerge unscathed from this fight for her life—but she did emerge. Too often, women don't take credit for the things they did to survive. Some never tell anyone but their closest friends, others don't even realize they've fought back. ''Oh, but I didn't really do anything,'' women in our self-defense classes would demur—after telling how they had kicked, negotiated, screamed, or sprinted their way to freedom.

This is one of the main reasons we decided to put this book together—to help women reevaluate their assault experiences, help them feel proud of themselves for the things they did, instead of guilty about the things they didn't. Kim Rosa says she didn't think of ''Adrenalin: A Hitchhiking Story'' as a success story until recently. But when I read this harrowing story, I was stunned by Kim's presence of mind in the face of her assailant's obvious intent to kill her.

An assault is a serious matter, yet sometimes a woman's sense of humor is her best weapon. There's a famous story about a woman who was grabbed while riding a crowded subway. She plucked the hand off her body, raised it over her head, and announced loudly: ''Who does this belong to? I found it on my ass.'' Her assailant did his best to melt into the crowd.

After all, even an attacker can be offended—he's only human, right? In "I Just Want to Talk to You," Priscilla Prutzman fends off a nervous man with a knife by simply talking to him—one human being to another—about her life, his life, about what she is and isn't willing to do with him. When he asks her to do something they both agreed she wouldn't, she appeals to his sense of honor: "You're not going to go back on your word, are you?" An assault is an act of power over another person. To maintain that power, the assailant must effectively dehumanize the woman he is attacking. When the woman simply looks him in the eye and says exactly what she means, sometimes his whole rationale for attacking her begins to crumble.

But what if it doesn't? Everything a woman tries doesn't necessarily work. Self-defense is not a guaranteed formula; it is a fluid, ever-changing way of looking at the world and your rightful place in it. It's like a chess game: as your opponent makes moves, some of them anticipated, others totally unexpected, you must bend your strategy to fit the changing situation. Pat Deer tries a few techniques that don't work, then finally succeeds with an eye poke in "I Let Him Have It Right in the Eyes." In fact, most of the women in this book used more than one tactic to get themselves free of their attackers.

But women who fight back are not champion chess players; they are housewives, mothers, workers, senior citizens, disabled women, young girls—every sort of female person you can imagine. There is a myth about women who fight back, even in feminist circles: that you must be young, strong, and trained in a martial art to successfully defend yourself. But only a few women represented here are experienced martial arts practitioners; most have no martial arts or self-defense training at all, but are simply people who were going quietly about their lives when they were assaulted. When the moment came, they fought as though they'd known all along what to do.

I do not intend here to discourage women from taking either self-defense or martial arts classes. Having studied both, I know the strength and self-confidence they can bring. What I am saying is that self-defense skills are innate, and these stories, by mostly untrained women of all ages and physical abilities, are evidence of that inborn knowledge. A self-defense or martial arts class only serves to enhance those instincts, to refine them through practice.

As you read the stories, bear in mind that the women who told them are not "experts," but ordinary people who responded to our nationwide call for stories. They are people who happened to pick up a magazine or turn on the radio at the right time. This book is the stuff of kitchen table conversations, of neighbors talking over the back fence. Although the chapter introductions and concluding essays contain self-defense information and suggestions by the two editors, you'll find a wealth of practical information in the stories themselves.

What you'll learn from these stories is that there is no right or wrong way to defend oneself; it all depends on the situation. You'll also see that self-defense does not consist of sensational, daredevil deeds. The women talk about their feelings of what happened to them, about what they did. They express their fear, anger, sadness, relief, and exhilaration.

In these success stories, women defend themselves in the country, in the city, in foreign countries, in their homes. Chances are that you'll read about women fighting back in ways you've never thought of and in places that seem particularly dangerous to you. There are attacks/defenses in urban settings like elevators, subway tunnels, and parking garages. There are hitchhiking stories, self-defense in auto-mobiles and at campsites. Women defend themselves against strangers as well as acquaintances and family members.

If you have been attacked, you may or may not find a story here that speaks directly to your experience. Depending on where you live, the kinds of issues you face will be different. Also, there are cultural differences in how women look at self-defense. Stella Moreno and Dora Gonzalez, both Latinas, offer some fascinating insights in their stories about the Hispanic family and how it bears on a woman's ability to defend herself. Likewise, Cindy Nakazawa speaks about the stereotype of the quiet, submissive Asian woman—and her story illustrates how out of step that stereotype actually is.

We found it interesting that several verbal—and often humorous—stories were sent to us by black women (see Nancy Rawles and Kikanza Robins, for example). It's possible that black culture in general is less constricted by the taboos against speaking out (and up) that are so prevalent in U.S. Anglo-Saxon society. It's also pos-sible that a sense of humor is one of the many tools black people have had to use to defend their culture against racism.

When I traveled to Asia a few years ago, I taught a brief self-defense workshop in New Delhi, India. I found that some experiences and attitudes about self-defense were quite different from what I knew in my own country. Specifically, female bonding is very strong in India and Asia in general, so it was easy for the women to role-play about effective *group* defenses against assault.

There are also generational differences; see Marjorie French's "Hitchhiking in the Forties" for an interesting commentary on how the United States has changed in the past forty years. There are differences in physical ability, too. Sandi Collins, Suzette Garay, and Autumn are all women who are challenged by physical disabilities, yet claim their right to physically defend themselves. In every story, the way women defend themselves is influenced by the way they were brought up, their ethnic background, their unique life experiences.

Whatever past or potential self-defense situations you face, there are common threads that weave through all the stories: determination, a willingness to try more than one strategy, intuition. Certainly you will find something you can use in every one of these stories.

Dividing the book into the seven parts you see here was not an easy task. There are so many ways to look at these stories—in fact, we considered and discarded a number of different ways to organize this book. At various times, we thought of grouping stories by type of defense, type of attack, type of woman. . . . Finally, somewhat frustrated, we let the stories themselves suggest their categories, and settled on the mixed bag you see here.

Each section is prefaced by a detailed introduction. These introductions are full of tips and information about the aspect of self-defense that is highlighted. Also see the concluding essay, "So What Do I Do Now? Ways to Learn More About Self-Defense," as well as the compilation of Self-Defense Programs and the Selected Annotated Bibliography for further exploration.

The stories in Part I, "Loss of Innocence," are by women who were attacked during their childhood. Part II, "The Power of the Voice," contains stories in which women fight back with their vocal cords—using words, yells, or some other verbal techniques. In Part III, "Intuition and Willpower," women use these two fundamental tools to maneuver their way out of dangerous situations. The women in "Weapons at Hand" (Part IV) used objects—from a gun to a potted houseplant—to aid them in their self-protection.

Some of the most dangerous situations are dealt with in Part V, "Life-Threatening Assaults." Because of the seriousness of the attacks, some of these stories, although inspiring, are more difficult to read, so you might want to start with some of the other chapters first. "Teamwork" (Part VI) would be a good place to start; here women talk in encouraging ways about how they have worked with others in self-defense—both during and after an assault. Finally, "Life Strategies and Self-Defense Tips" (Part VII) contains a cornucopia of self-defense tactics and experiences, from tips for bicyclists to a philosophy of self-defense for an entire culture.

This book is made to be browsed through. Though its subject is serious, *Her Wits About Her* is, after all, a storybook. As with any good stories, we hope you'll read them aloud, discuss them with friends, study them in school classes, enjoy them. These success stories are meant to inspire you and make you feel strong. *Her Wits About Her* is a celebration.

Newark—August 17, 1981

Janice Angevine

Jan wrote the first draft of this poem during a ten-day period immediately following the rape attempt. It was previously published in the *Radical Reviewer* in Vancouver, British Columbia, in the fall of 1982. Now forty-one years old, Jan is a writer, artist, businesswoman, and single parent to a sixteen-year-old daughter.

"The poem is really about all kinds of survival. It is about the collective consciousness from which we women can draw, endlessly—from the past into the future. We are stronger than all the centuries of brutality. I know this now."

The city air is full of demolition
dust and sweat; dangerous with
Friday night.
Friday/payday
Friday night/violence
I forget this.
A fierce pacifist,
I exclude images of violence.
I am not violent, therefore
I will not be violated.

I know that life is more complex than this,
that brutal harm has come this year
to many of us, over and over,
that no one is safe.
I know this.
I know so much that
I can hardly stand it.
So I walk steadfast, sturdy.
I do not want to smell of fear.
Yet there is a weirdness in this air tonight.
There is no tenderness in the streets
and hope lies bruised and sleeping in doorways and
      gutters.
I quiet my senses, steel myself.
I enter the gaping mouth of the city garage,
walking rapidly down the stairwell
that stinks of urine and feces, into
the cement cave, the dark lethal bowels of the garage.
Fear wells up in my body.
I turn quickly to look it in the eye,
ward it off. No one.
Mentally, I exercise a defensive
karate kick Michael has taught me.
Walking, I think, could I do it?
"Remember, knee up first and
then kick."
I hear Michael's words, as we changed
the spark plugs in my car last summer.
My car, nose to the wall, waits
like a tank to hold me, hold
off the streets. It is only feet away now.
I see no one, except a moment earlier,
the sweaty man bounding up the stairs past me,
muscled and dirty.
He is returning for me.
He is full of drugs and violence.
But, worse, he is a man. So he is
filled with images that tell him
he is measured by what he can take.
Take money. Take sex.

He is returning to take me.

He cannot take legitimately.
His color and poverty
exclude him from killing
in the market place
busting balls
at the negotiating table
commanding
genocide
raping
the land.
These ruinous takings are not
among his options,
so he will take me
take sex
the male option,
marketed like junk food;
exercised when bereft of
manhood,
unsure of status,
displeased with life;
rape of a woman, any woman.

I open the car door.
My poetry, rich with life,
rests on the front seat.
I pause to think as I slide my thin smiling body
behind the wheel; Phyllis, Julia, Lorraine, Marilyn.
My collective family, plotting together to
put feelings on paper, stealing time
from our multiple responsibilities.
Voyagers in exploration, we are full of courage.
(These thoughts will sustain me.)
I hear his feet running toward the car.
I see the flash of him through the rear window.
I know what is about to happen.
The door is torn from my hand
as I try to close myself off from the
Mongol, the Turk, the Viking, the slave owner,
the Crusader, the G.I., the marauding hordes,

centuries of brutal men,
masculine force,
rapists,
monster-full.
Their creation, their true believer,
swings his arm and my lips,
smashed against my teeth, split open.
The car is invaded with violent colors.
A holocaust of black and blue fills the space.
I am breathing blood from my lips.
It is chaos. His body crashes full force
onto me. He is demented, hallucinating,
groaning. His tongue swollen with violence
comes for my mouth, now open with screaming.
Revolt and terror twist my body,
pinned to the seat.
My mind shrieking with death,
explodes with horror,
breaks into infinite pieces.
His knee shoved between my legs, is driven
with wild force to crush my soft helpless genitals,
again and again.
I am over the edge, head on the floor.
He is tearing at my clothes, throwing
blows to my stomach. He is enraged
at my khakis, which won't open,
won't yield to him.
One hand thrusts into my pants, the other
grabs the door, slams it shut.
Every part of me that is woman
is struck, shoved, grabbed, yelled at, violated, hated.
I am lost in unendurable loneliness.
Terror traps my spirit and
fills me with paralysis,
until the most primitive part of my brain,
survival,
pure survival, screams for life.

For an instant there is silence, so grave,
so stricken, a ring of silence surrounding me

like an aura
as the attack goes on.
I am filled with the images of strong
women, my daughter, my home. In this
moment I envision hundreds of women,
the powerful, the loving women,
running for me in mobs of silence,
inexhaustible spirits,
crying for me
pleading with me to
fight my non-being, to live
for all that is yet unlived, unsaid.
They lift my knees, free my feet,
free me from my fear
to kick like a newborn child for my
right to live, my lifetime.
The kick increases in force.
My legs are charged.
They are filled with the power of
a million women, centuries of women,
violated burned drowned
tortured raped impoverished.
We kick for life
and pin the monster,
his back to the door.
For a moment
he stops.
I stop.
No cell moves.
His head falls back against the window.
From deep inside, starting with a groan,
he slowly screams, "I'm so scared!"
Connecting, I tell him, "Run,
run for your life,
they are all coming for you!"
I keep my vision alive in my mind:
The women, the women of loving courage.
I see it.
I hold on to it.
I feed it to him

over and over.
"Run, run for your life,
they are all coming for you!"
Until, finally, he turns
throws open the door
bending its hinges
and runs
to no one
to nothing
leaving me
marked
forever
and spitting these bloody words,
". . . and you ask us to love you?"

Part I

Loss of Innocence

Introduction

As young children, we are taught that some adults—primarily strangers—are not to be trusted. Yet we are also taught to respect our elders and those with authority—teachers, policemen, anyone older. On the one hand, this early training instills a healthy sense of caution in a child. On the other, it makes her suspicious of other people— the very people she is also taught to rely on for her every need.

At some point in a child's growing-up process, she must integrate and learn to live with this contradiction. This point—sometimes a moment of painful insight brought about by an adult betrayal—is often experienced or remembered later as a loss of innocence.

Many adults are left with a tremendous (and often unconscious) sense of guilt and responsibility for bad things that happened to them when they were children. The women who have written the stories in this section have broken the vicious circle of guilt simply by believing they have the right to tell those stories.

Since so much of what happens in childhood sets the stage for our adult feelings and behavior, it's important to reflect on your own childhood and the messages you were told about your right to take care of yourself. Some admonitions are healthy and necessary: "Don't open the door to strangers." "Don't take candy from strange men." "Hold Mommy's hand while we cross the street." Others teach us not to trust ourselves and our own resources, teach us that not only is it a dangerous world, but we are helpless to protect ourselves against it. But try as they might, parents cannot completely shield their children from the perils of the world. Children go to school on their own, come into contact with strangers, see frightening images on television that they must cope with the best they can. Parents rarely instruct children about what to do if something bad does happen to them.

Were you taught that your only recourse was to lock yourself up tight with deadbolts and burglar alarms? Did your mother feel confident about taking care of herself and you, or was it made clear that only Daddy could keep the family from danger?

What situations are particularly frightening to you? Are there times when you feel utterly powerless to have any impact on your environment at all? Since children are generally denied any sense of power and control over their own lives, feelings of powerlessness can be directly traced to what we were taught as children. Understanding the source of fears and limitations is a first step toward moving beyond them.

Assaults on children by known adults are far more common than is usually believed. Many of the women in this section were molested or attacked by "friends" or family members. An assault by a close family member is particularly devastating. Because a child is often forbidden to rebuff any touch from an uncle or a grandfather, she may experience confusion when a touch doesn't feel right. Even those of us who were taught important skills about protecting ourselves from strangers were never told that those close to us might betray our trust.

Current statistics indicate that one in three girls and one in six boys are sexually abused by the time they are eighteen. Professionals in the child abuse field are coming to realize, however, that boys may suffer abuse in far greater numbers than the statistics reflect.

It is the child's own gut reaction that can help her recognize that something is wrong. In "It's Worse When They Don't Mean To," Jeni Schreiber loves her grandfather. She even knows that when he touches her in an inappropriate way, he doesn't really "mean to." But she is able to talk to her mother about it—with much trepidation—because it simply doesn't feel right.

Whether or not a child can actually talk about what has happened to her is based on her family environment. If family members both express and discuss feelings in a constructive, supportive way, it will be easier for a child to speak her mind. That ability to talk about feelings is grounded in trust, since we don't open our minds and hearts to people we think will betray us. If it's difficult for you to talk and express your feelings, think about your own childhood: Did the family really discuss things at the dinner table, or were real issues and feelings avoided? Did you eat in front of a blaring television set, or really talk with one another?

Do you trust your own children? There are many cases of child abuse that go untreated and undetected simply because the adults will not believe what the child is saying. It takes enormous courage for a child to speak up about being abused. She must fight through her own guilt and feeling of betraying someone she looks up to. There is a commonly held myth about children: that they enjoy making up stories about just about anything. If you believe that your child would lie just for the sake of lying, it will be hard to believe her when she comes to you with difficult news.

Alcohol can be a complicating factor in family abuse situations. Parents may drink to "unwind" at home, and their children often become the victims of the pent-up rage and frustration that have exploded. Because alcohol abuse tends to cause irrational behavior, a child may be doubly confused by the mistreatment she is receiving: not only is she being abused; she also sees her parent behaving in terrifying, unpredictable ways. Untangling the jumbled emotions that come from a childhood steeped in alcohol can take a lifetime; in "Crazymaking," twelve-year-old Andrea Sorenson stands up to her father and so begins her own long process of recovery.

It's important to give the child within you credit for the survival skills she learned as a child. Each of us has a unique repertoire of resources that are the result of our experiences. As an adult, Suzette Garay ("Deaf and Not Defeated") possesses a whole range of self-defense skills. She developed her resources in response to the abuse she has suffered since she was three years old, as well as the added trauma that comes from being deaf in a hearing world. Rachel Harwood, in "Journey to Confidence," grows from a shy and gawky child into a confident adult who teaches self-defense to others. Looking back on her experiences from an adult perspective, she can see how effective her self-defense strategies were—something she couldn't see at the time.

A wily child is a safe child—especially in a large city. "Streetwise" is an apt term for those who find their wisdom in the alleyways and avenues of urban America. Abby Bee's sophisticated delivery in "Going for the Throat" is a thin cover for an enraged, sensitive spirit learning to cope in a dangerous environment. Add the inherent dangers of being a teenage girl in teeming New York City to the racial tensions seething just below the surface, and you've got a recipe for street smarts. Jo Kenny ("The Shortcut Home") learns one of the hardest truths about urban attack situations: the level of violence in our cities is so acute that many people would prefer to turn their heads than come to the aid of someone in trouble.

There is a growing movement in the United States that concerns itself with empowering young people to take care of themselves. The child assault prevention movement challenges some of the most basic assumptions we all grow up with: that a child should not question an adult's authority, and that a child cannot and should not attempt to fight back against an attacker. One of the pioneer programs in this field, the Child Assault Prevention Project (CAPP), was started in Columbus, Ohio, and now has offshoots in all parts of the country. CAPP workers use role-playing and discussion to encourage *children themselves* to pay attention to their feelings when they receive unwanted advances from an adult—*any* adult—or another child. The program teaches children as young as kindergarten age new self-defense skills, and takes advantage of the natural exuberance and keen awareness most children possess.

For instance, yelling is a natural activity for most kids (and something that is often discouraged). The CAPP program provides an outlet for yelling, a positive way to release a child's boundless energy. Crying out "NO," or just making a loud noise, is one of the best ways for a child to defend herself and attract the attention of someone who may be able to help.

Child assault prevention is based on a fundamental belief: all human beings, including children, have the right to control what happens to their own bodies. If something doesn't feel good, it must stop. Whether it's Uncle Harry, the man in the toy store, or a stranger beckoning from a car, a child's right to say NO is as inalienable as the right to shelter, food, and love.

The CAPP training center in northern California has compiled a number of children's success stories in recent years. These stories come from follow-up data collected on children who have gone through the CAPP program. A sampler:

From Alameda County, California: A ten-year-old girl named Ginny had just finished going to the bathroom, when a strange man pushed open the door to the stall she was in and tried to grab her.

She immediately started her special self-defense yell and kicked him very hard in the shins. This stunned him long enough for her to be able to get past him and out into the hallway, where she called for help. The man fled the school with teachers in pursuit, but got away. Ginny, however, was safe.

Children trained in self-defense have a lot to teach adults. From Columbus, Ohio: Mrs. Green, an elementary-school teacher, was walking to her car when a man came up from behind and tried to steal her purse: "The first thing I did was the yell I had learned along with the children in the workshop. I didn't even think about it, it just came automatically. As I struggled to hold on to my purse, four children who had been playing four-square at the far side of the playground came running in my direction, all doing their yells together. You can imagine how surprised the thief was, and he got out of there as fast as he could."

From Shasta County, California: In the CAPP workshop, there is a role-play about an "Uncle Harry" who bribes his niece and makes her give him a kiss she doesn't want to give him. After a CAPP workshop, a sixth-grade girl came to the crisis counseling session and said to one of the staff, "I'm Uncle Harry." She was very upset and ashamed because she had been molesting her younger sister. The staff knew immediately that no child commits such abuse without learning it somewhere, without being a victim first. After a short discussion about getting help, this girl started crying and said that she had been molested by her uncle.

And from Alameda County, California, comes this letter from a kindergartner:

I used one of the Safe Strong and Free rules today. This boy he said are you in kindergarten or are you a baby. I said, I'm a human being, arnt I? He said yes, you're a human being. I said, I have rights, don't I? He said, Yes. He said, I beter not mess with you again.

I like you, CAPP.

Love, Becky R.
Kindergarten

Human Being

For more information, see Self-Defense Programs (page 263).

The Shortcut Home

Jo Kenny

Jo Kenny grew up in Brooklyn, New York. In 1974, she boarded a Grey-hound bus, got off in Santa Cruz, California, and has lived there ever since. She currently works for a nonprofit organization that provides chemical-dependency recovery programs and youth counseling services. In her spare time she does community-based political work.

"I deliberately left out my adult analysis of this attack. My purpose was to truthfully tell what happened, and how, as a kid, I felt about it. It had been a long time since I had consciously thought about this attack, and it was difficult for me to admit that I wasn't brave or tough but just a terrified young woman."

My father told me to be home before dark that night. It was a weekend and I was pissed that he wouldn't let me stay out later. After all—I was fourteen and bigger than my mom: five feet tall and a hundred pounds. Besides, I was a street-wise kid and already in high school. But arguing would only get me grounded, so I said okay.

When the streetlights went on, I knew I was asking for trouble with my dad, so I decided to take the shortcut home. My girlfriends walked me to the highway and from there it was only a five-minute walk across the back lots and up an alley to home.

I was walking up the alley when I heard running feet on the cob-blestones behind me. My first thought was that it was my brother. It sounded like his shoes and who else would be trying to catch up with me? I didn't have time for a second thought. A hand clamped over my mouth and I saw the streetlight shine on a serrated kitchen knife as it went to my throat. I froze. I couldn't believe what was happening.

He was pulling me back toward the empty lots. He kept repeating that he only wanted to know my name. I panicked and begged him to let me go, even though I knew he couldn't understand my muffled words. I tried to get myself to think of how to break away, but it was as if my brain had split in two and I was having an argument with myself. The loudest voice was saying, "You sure blew it this time, kid. So where's all that toughness you thought you had? He's not much bigger than you and he even sounds scared. Besides, how sharp can a stupid serrated knife be? Do something!" The other voice was saying, "Okay, okay. Stop bugging me and shut up. I can't think. I know I'm more scared than he is. It's so quiet back here. Where is everybody anyway? How come no one's walked by? Oh, shit, we're almost in the back lots. I'd better think of something."

My feet refused to move. Unconsciously, I started throwing my arms around and I hit him in the ribs with my elbow. I don't know how hard I hit, but he began to loosen his hold on me. I broke away and started running. About halfway up the alley I looked around and saw that he was right behind, grabbing out at me. I jumped to the side, then froze again and started to scream. I just stood there and screamed and screamed. He turned away and ran into the darkness. I felt my screams bouncing off the walls and coming back to me, wave after wave, growing louder and louder. I finally stopped when I realized no one was coming to help.

Silence. I was alone. No one had heard me? They must have, but why wasn't anyone there? I began to think I had made it all up. Maybe I had just stood there and screamed in my brain. Like in a nightmare when I try to scream and nothing comes out. That had to be it. I tried hard to make myself believe this, but my raw throat and shaking body told me that, yes, I had screamed, and, yes, people hadn't responded.

I didn't want to think anymore. I had to get out of there. It was over and I was okay. It was dumb standing there thinking that this was such a big deal. After all, I hadn't been raped or even stabbed, so everything was fine. Right?

I walked onto the street. Turning the corner, the first thing I saw was my father putting out the garbage. I stopped. This was too crazy to believe. I almost got raped and screamed my guts out and my own father didn't respond. I wondered if maybe he hadn't heard it. I couldn't be sure. It seemed a long time had gone by since I first walked up the alley, but by the light still visible in the sky, I knew only a few minutes had passed.

I was shocked, but at the same time my normal way of dealing with my parents took over: if he didn't hear or wouldn't acknowledge the sound of that scream, I didn't have to tell him that anything had happened. After all, the cops would never catch the guy and the only way my parents could protect me would be to keep me in at night. That was the last thing I wanted.

My decision made, I walked up the block, said hi to my dad and went right up to my room. I was thankful that neither of my sisters were there because I knew my calmness was a very thin front. I sat and stared. My mind kept going back and forth between "It's no big deal. Forget it," and "Figure it out. What does all this mean?"

About five minutes later, I got a phone call. I didn't want to go downstairs with everyone sitting around. But I went anyway; my mom would know something was wrong if I didn't want to talk on the phone. Luckily, no one was in the kitchen so I at least had a little privacy.

I was surprised when I heard Patty's voice. She was an eight-year-old who lived across the street. She told me she had just come from her friend Kathleen's house, which overlooked the alley. They'd both been looking out the window and had seen the whole thing. Patty thought that maybe I was in trouble, but Kathleen said not to say anything because she didn't want to get her grandmother upset. I started to get mad. First my father and now Patty. What was going on? My world seemed to be falling apart. I asked Patty if she knew what the word "rape" meant. She didn't, so I told her to ask her mother and then decide if it would have been worth upsetting Kathleen's grandmother.

Somehow I made it through the rest of that night. I waited for my sisters to fall asleep and then I cried and cried into my pillow.

I never went into the back lots after dark again. And for a while I wouldn't walk home alone. Even if I had only a half a block to go alone, I ran the whole way. But that didn't last too long, and as my recollection of that night faded, a lot of my old confidence came back. Yet many years passed before I again learned to trust that people would come through for me when I needed them.

A Stable Tale

Elisavietta Ritchie

Elisavietta Ritchie, a writer, translator, teacher, and editor, has published six books of poetry, and her work has appeared in a variety of magazines. She is of Russian-American descent, has three cats, "occasional black snakes, pet squirrels, and wounded creatures," and three grown children.

Here is an excerpt from one of her poems, which speaks of self-defense:

To kill a man when you have no
weapons: be tough, keep cool, maintain
surprise, pick up two sharp rocks and
like cymbals swing a wide curve at
his temples: he'll squash like a frog
You can also hug-break his ribs,
bite his neck, shark-kiss his throat, cut
his soft skin, drown him in the mud . . .

By age five, I was already nuts about horses. They had tried to keep me away from the barns—"Honey, you might git kicked!"— but when it was finally my birthday, I was permitted to sit on the gray Percheron. I did not fall off. Every day, I walked two miles from the house just to hang around. That July, I got to ride every horse in Seven Oaks Stable except the stallion, Big Prince.

"But I don't like to be called Honey."

The stablehands laughed, and hugged me, and tugged at my honey braids, and taught me to trot. In my dreams, they were cowboys and Cossacks, cavalry colonels, Arabian sheiks.

But they were only old men gone lame from the track, and boys with corn-tassel hair and the warm smell of manure who dreamed themselves jockeys and hot-rod champs.

Elmer or Joe or Hank would lift me high to the saddle, hold the reins, lead me once more round the ring, and often keep a hand on my thigh, so I wouldn't fall off, or so they said. I begged them to teach me to canter and jump.

"When you git bigger, Honey," Joe promised. "Not yet." Warned to stay out of the stalls, between rides I climbed the rickety wooden ladder up to the loft where swallows swooped from their nests in the eaves. I wasn't afraid of the spiders who tied up the beams, and though the black wasps terrified me, they left me alone. I tamed all the piebald kittens nested between bales of hay, and brought the mother cats food so they wouldn't eat up the mice.

When other riders returned from their rides, I would bring them an icy bottle of sarsaparilla, cream soda, or real root beer, and then climb on the fence to help the stablehands dry and curry the horses.

In the tack room, they let me rub soap on the saddles until the slippery flesh-colored stuff foamed like the cantering stallion. The radio crackled out hillbilly songs, and ladies with silly faces and glossy dresses simpered out from a decade of calendars nailed to the walls. I swore I would never wear lipstick nor grow any breasts.

"I'm going to be a jockey."

"Someday," argued Hank, "you'll git tired of only a horse between those nice li'l legs."

"Don't talk like that," Joe would cut in, and throw an empty tobacco packet into the cold iron stove.

On one August morning that was too rainy for riding, I walked from my house past the grove of pines and the huge willow tree and crossed the corrals to the barns. Since nobody hired a horse in the rain, no one was about. The horses ate the damp sugar cubes that crumbled in my slicker pocket, then I scrambled up to the loft.

"Here, kitty kitties, I've brought you breakfast!" I climbed the haystack and slid down the other side. "Mother Cat, Mother Cat, where have you hidden your babies today?"

"In here, Honey!" called Hank from somewhere below.

I climbed back down the ladder, my inner pockets bulging with kibbles for cats. I ran to the tack room that was fragrant with apples, tobacco, and saddle soap, and began to search among dusty horse blankets and saddle pads, as if on an Easter egg hunt.

"Here, kitty kitties! Where can you be?"

"Here, Honey," whispered Hank, "come kiss this nice pussy cat. . . . Here, down here, in my lap."

I stared, confused, at the strange unfurred thing.

"It's time for me to go home now for lunch."

"Ain't lunchtime yet," he answered. His hands reached for my braids and began to tug. "Jus' come here a moment . . . and later, if the paddock dries out, I'll teach you to canter. . . . I'll let you ride on Big Prince. Even—" His voice became hoarse and he was pulling hard on my braids. "I might even teach you to jump."

"Thank you," I answered politely, then jerked my braids free and backed toward the tack room and out into the rain.

I crossed the muddy corral studded with jumps, then out to the road, past the huge willow tree and the grove of pines, and though it was pouring, and though the car that stopped on the road carried only our next-door neighbor, I turned down the offer of a lift the rest of the long way home.

Going for the Throat

Abby Bee

Abby Bee is a poet and photographer living in northern California. She spent her first twenty-one years in New York City, where this story takes place, then moved to Gainesville, Florida, for ten years. Her first collection of poetry and photographs, *Nauseous in Paradise,* was published in 1986.

"Perhaps the motto of my personal self-defense experience is 'Disqualify Yourself as a Victim Today.' This is a true story that happened when I was eighteen. It became clear to me as a teenager in Brooklyn that when women refuse to take the role of the victim in a threatening situation, the lure of attack is lost.

"The second ingredient of defense is the correct expression of anger and personal outrage. My own experiences have taught me that if you act like an uppity burning bomb, they'll drop you like a hot potato."

I was forced to do it. By you placing your hand on my shoulder: you, a stranger to me, and I, wanting nothing but to walk home. You, a boy in a pack of punks on a city street, and I, after a long day at school with my books and a pen in my pocket. The autumn sun was slowly sinking behind square brick buildings.

At first, I tried to ignore those guys: four white kids smoking a joint, leaning on a car. I ignored the "Hey, baby, wanna get stoned?" remark. They didn't look like a serious bunch of greasers or ghetto escapees looking to jump a white girl. No problem. Ignore the assholes and they'll go away. It's just not worth getting mad at these guys. Better save your anger for someone who really deserves it. Just ignore them. Walk a little faster. Get your tired ass home.

But this was different. They began to follow behind me. Oh, Jesus. All the times men have whistled and muttered at this female body. Every time I ask myself: Is this real danger or a petty annoyance?

"Don't you want to hang out with us, chickee?"

"Get outta here."

"Whatsa matter, you don't like us or something?"

To my right was the flat wall of an apartment building next to a backyard alley. To my left was the street with two guys running herd, pushing me toward the apartment-house wall. There wasn't time to think. The guy in front of the pack placed his hand on my shoulder. I knew he intended to push me toward the wall.

There were times in high school when girls with incredible muscles threatened to cut me. Now, that scared me. And there were times when a drug-crazed born-again Muslim said he'd shoot me if I didn't stop disgracing his religion by wearing a fez.

But this was stupid. This made me mad. A bunch of assholes showing off to one another in the male pack syndrome. What the hell was I doing here? My chest was tight and electric.

"Hey, chickee."

The hand in my pocket connected with a ballpoint pen. With the point turned upward, I caught him with a swift uppercut in the soft spot between his neck and chin. He screamed with pain and blood ran down his neck. He looked glazed, but was still standing. The boys were shocked. They were scared and started to scatter. After one instant of frozen panic and seeing his blood, I ran. One boy shouted, "You didn't have to do that! We weren't going to hurt you!"

I ran and I ran until my breath was a sharp pain doubling through my body. I felt sick. I was disgusted. Why did I have to do that? Did I have to? That was awful. It felt degrading to be forced to strike like an animal in a corner. I hated myself as I walked slowly to my block, a busy street with cars at a stoplight. Waiting for the light to change, did anyone know I just stabbed someone?

I looked around. I was crazy, fuckin' crazy. Men pick on boys, who pick on women who pick on girls who pick on kids who pick on each other. What were they trying to prove? Why couldn't they just be people?

"Hey, mmmmmmm, mamacita." A car slowed down to my left

at the stoplight. Something snapped inside my head, my shaky nerves tightened. Goddamn it!

I approached that car with the winking man with my fist cocked.

"You motherfuckin' cocksucker prick," I screamed, pounding on his windshield, then kicking the passenger side of his car. My fist was at his face on the other side of the glass and I was screaming at the top of my lungs. Then the light changed. He stared at me in disbelief. No one on the street looked at me.

I don't remember walking up the stairs to my apartment. But I must have gotten there, because I do remember sitting at the kitchen table—and crying.

Deaf and Not Defeated

Suzette V. Garay

Suzette Garay has a 110-decibel hearing loss, indicating profound deafness, yet she has an unusual ability to speak. She is extremely perceptive, an excellent lip-reader, and wears a special hearing aid to modulate her speech. She has recently taught herself sign language.

She is currently at work on her autobiography and is studying psychology at the University of California.

"I was born completely deaf, but nobody knew, not even myself, until I was thirteen years old. I was taken away by the social service people when I was two and a half because my mother was not taking care of me properly. From there on, I was in and out of different shelters and institutions for orphans and foster homes."

As told to the editors in an interview: I was seventeen, a senior in high school waiting at a bus stop on my way home from school. Because I'm deaf, I didn't know that a man was approaching me from behind, so there was no way for me to set up my defense, even though I had taken self-defense. I'm almost a black belt in karate, so I'm pretty sure of myself.

It had never occurred to me that my deafness would get in the way of my defending myself. When the man approached me and put his hand on my shoulder, I thought maybe it was someone asking for the time. A lot of times people will ask me what time it is, and if I don't see them, they'll touch me and say, "What time is it?" When I turned around I recognized a man who had raped me three years before. The first thing that came to my mind was "I don't know what I'm going to do." I got really scared.

I remembered being raped by him three years before. Everything started rushing back.

He said, "Hi. It's been a long time since I've seen you." He was friendly because I had never allowed him to feel like what he did to me was wrong. At the time, I hadn't even realized it was wrong. Anyway, since I had never confronted him, I guess he didn't have a reason to be uneasy, and probably assumed he could get away with it again.

I knew I had to do something, something fast. I knew I couldn't run away fast enough. I didn't want to do anything to scare him, or make him feel a need to grip me really tight, because he still had his hand on my shoulder.

Then I got an idea. Another man was coming up on the other side of the street, and I figured, well, I could yell at this man and ask him for help, but I wanted to play it really cool. So I pretended that the man across the street was my dad. I said, "Hey, Dad. Hey, Dad, wait. Hey, Dad!" And the attacker started getting really shaky, and the other man turned around, and I just kept saying, "Hey, Dad, I forgot I have to tell you something, I'd like you to meet my friend." So the attacker let go his grip on my shoulder, and I was walking real fast across the street and saying, "Hey, Dad, I forgot, I forgot." I'm still talking to this total stranger I don't even know, and this man is looking at me really puzzled and I'm thinking, Keep still, don't move, just wait till I reach you. The next thing I know, the attacker split, and I got up to the other man and I said, "Oh, I'm sorry, I thought you were my dad."

I was really upset that the whole thing had happened, so I ran, and I couldn't call my parents, because I'm deaf, so the only thing I could do was take a bus to the other side of Santa Cruz. I felt that if I went to another bus stop across the street or in the area that he might get me again. So I took a bus across town and then rode the bus home from there.

I felt that what I did was really a good device to use in terms of my deafness. If there are other people around, I could perhaps use that device again. It has made me more aware of the fact that someone can approach from behind without me knowing, so I am more conscious about things that happen behind me. I don't tend to stay in one particular position very long, because I know that if I'm out on the street alone, especially at night, my vision is the only thing I have in terms of preparing myself for another incident.

At age nine, I knew some karate. I went into a two-year program in one of the best places in Chinatown in San Francisco. I've been in a variety of situations where I had to use my skills. I was not only concerned with physical defense, but also with *mind* defense. Sometimes I succeeded and sometimes I was defeated. I learned from each situation and I knew that the next situation could be like an earlier one. But nothing is ever guaranteed. You can't spend months practicing a certain defense because when you're actually in the situation, it's a totally different story.

Even though I have been raped, my body is not damaged and I'm alive. I call that being successful.

Another story: One summer my foster parents sent me to camp in Napa Valley. It was one of those places where there are lots of teenage counselors and they're all going after each other. All this sex stuff is happening and all the little kids are peeking on their counselors.

There was this one counselor, Joel, who was very dangerous. He had a reputation for being a pervert—he was always talking about sex and reading dirty magazines. I was about eight years old at that time, and because I was deaf, I never heard the stories about him. When I was eight, people didn't know I was deaf and neither did I. This was mainly because I talked so well, and I assumed that everybody was doing the same thing I was—lipreading—because you can't see hearing.

One day, he was supervising some of us kids at the lake. He was calling all the kids to come in, to go back to the cabins and prepare for dinner. I was fishing, and I figured, oh, it must be late, so I took my fishing pole, and this nice-size fish I had caught. I could hardly wait till I got back to camp to show I could actually fish.

I was walking back alongside the lake when I remembered that I had left some stones that I had found on top of the rock I had been fishing on. By this time, the kids had gone up to the cabins, and Joel went back to the lake to make sure he had everybody. He saw me, but I didn't think anything was wrong.

I was afraid to put my fishing pole on the ground because I was afraid the fish would take off, and so I had the thing wrapped around my hand. As I swam up to the rock to get my stones, the fish came off my fishing pole. It was floating on the water. And I was scared, I didn't want to touch it, I didn't want to pick it up, so I swam back to where I was supposed to be, and Joel said, "Now, you go back in that water and you get that fish, you go get that fish." And I was scared. He got really violent, he was grabbing me and shaking me and swearing and everything and saying, "You get that fucking fish right now or I'll kill you right out here."

I was amazed that this guy was threatening to kill me if I didn't go out and get that fish. At eight years old, that upset me, so I started crying. So I said, "Okay, okay," and I walked a little way into the water, up to my knees, and I knew I couldn't do it, I didn't want to touch that fish. So he came up to me and he started drowning me, and the first thing I realized was that he wasn't kidding, he was serious.

He was dunking my head in the water, and I thought I was going to die. I was physically trying to use my defenses, but this man was three times bigger than me and I was only eight years old, so there's just no way, physically, that I could've defended myself. So I started to stand up in the water, and I was saying anything I could possibly say to get him off me. I said, "I promise I'll do anything you want me to do, but just don't make me go get that fish, please." He said, "Meet me here tonight." And of course I knew from the past that when they say, meet me here, or meet me there, I knew what was going to happen. So I said, "Sure." And I'm thinking I'll go up to camp and tell one of the counselors that he was going to try to hurt me.

But I wasn't sure about doing that. Other times when I had told people about being molested, they sometimes hadn't believed me. I also knew this guy was really violent, and if I didn't do what he wanted me to do, chances were he could get me the next time. So I promised him I would be there and at seven that night I showed up at the lake and he was there.

Before I went, I told one of my favorite counselors what had happened and what was going to happen. We were really close—I had told her about being molested in the past and she had believed me. And she had been wanting to kick Joel out for a long time.

So I met him down there at seven o'clock sharp and I acted like nothing was happening. He said, "Come here, I want you to sit behind me.'' And he showed me disgusting books, with really violent pictures. I was scared. I was afraid the counselor might not believe me and people might not show up.

So we're looking through the books and I'm taking my time, just saying, "Yeah, that's interesting," and just stalling, just saying, "Well, I've never done it this way before, have you?" and just talking back and forth and trying to waste time. And he says, "Well, come here." He puts his arm around me and starts kissing me and I'm just going along with it, and he says, "Now take your clothes off," and I said, "Right now? It's cold out here. Why don't we do it during the day, it's better." But just when I'm starting to take my clothes off, the directors and the counselors came and he was kicked out of camp.

I never heard what happened after that, because I was also sent home, and I felt really bad because I enjoyed camp. I also felt like I was partly to blame for what happened. Now I'm starting to realize that most of the things that happened to me weren't my fault.

I was raised in many institutions and shelters. Lots of children are overlooked, and people don't pay attention to the kids that may have some kind of physical or mental problems. They're too busy with thousands of kids and big things and they don't take time to focus on each individual. For me, it was a really emotional time, those thirteen years of my life, because there were many, many times when they should have noticed I had a disability. But because those times didn't happen in a series, it always looked like I just wasn't paying attention—that I didn't care, or was being uncooperative.

One day, I was coming home from school and I was kicking a can out on the street. One of the neighbors happened to see me—she was driving behind me—and she honked the horn, and kept honking for a block or so. I was just kicking the can and she pulled off the road and she called my name, and she ran up and grabbed me. Later she talked to my foster parents and said I must have a hearing problem.

Back in those times, when you took a hearing test, it was in a bus, and all the little kids wore headphones. You're supposed to raise your hand every time you hear the sound. Now, remember I'm really perceptive and I'm thinking, this is a game—who can raise their hand fastest. So here I am raising my hand, playing around during this test. Crazy. So they think I'm being a jerk or a bad kid, not being cooperative, and I had to take the test every day for three months.

First I thought maybe I should count to ten, and raise my hand every time I get to ten, but that didn't work. Then I found another way to cheat. The only way they know if you're raising your hand is if they look at you, so I figured out that it was an eye-to-eye thing. When the tester looked at me, she gave a nod, so I knew that when she moved her head, she was turning the dial, and just before she could turn her head to look at me, I raised my hand. And I didn't have to take the test after that.

It wasn't until later that I went to a professional place for a hearing test. Here they put me alone in a room, and the window's dark so you can't see what the people are doing. And they were just shocked when they found out. They said, well, maybe she had perfect hearing when she was little and then she lost it when she became this age. But they did X rays and a brain scan and they found out that my nerves were never developed, so I was born completely deaf.

I have been through a lot. I have lots of friends who are just amazed at what I have gone through. I'm a fighter and I'm a survivor and I have a lot to show for it. I say to people, everybody has a different way of dealing with a situation, but I know that giving up and letting it ruin your life is not the solution. The more I deal with it, the stronger I become and the better I can help others who aren't able to do that yet.

Crazymaking

Andrea Sorenson

Andrea Sorenson (a pseudonym) is a free-lance editor and writer living in the San Francisco Bay Area. She currently is attending graduate school and plans to pursue a career in social work. She is also working with a therapist to unravel the issues she faces as an adult child of an alcoholic.

"I hope that people reading this story, especially someone with an alcoholic parent, will realize that there are places to get help: Al-Anon, Alateen, and ACOA (Adult Children of Alcoholics) groups, or a therapist experienced with the issues surrounding alcohol abuse. There's a great sense of relief in realizing that you're not alone, you're not crazy, and you will heal."

"You get in here right now, young lady!" My father roughly grabs my arm and pulls me into the house, kicking and hitting me along the way. He pulls me over to the sink and lets go of me. "You get all these dishes done and then go in your room!" I cry silently, my teardrops falling in the dishwater along with the Lux Liquid and dirty pots. Once again, I was doing something wrong. Once again, I was having fun. Once again, I was talking with the neighborhood boys, something my father couldn't handle.

This all-too-familiar scenario started when I entered puberty. My breasts, my interest in boys, their interest in me, my budding sexuality, all combined to produce a volatile mix that provoked a curious reaction in my father. His drinking increased, his interest in my activities increased, his verbal harassment increased. And the hitting began.

I mostly remember the confusion, the sense that it was my fault. My breasts *were* larger than my friends', and my figure more womanly. Maybe it *was* my fault. My father used to brag about the fact that I was a large child, saying, "The bigger they are, the smarter they are." Now my body was doing these traitorous things to me, making my father uncomfortable and uneasy.

I still find it hard to think of this without making excuses for my father. I wasn't hurt badly. No violent purple and yellow bruises or broken bones to justify my inner pain. Maybe it wasn't that big a deal. But then I think, why are you trembling as you type this? Because it *was* a big deal. Because the confused sense of sexuality and anger wasn't my "stuff," as they say in therapy. It was my father's. And it should never have been placed on me.

Before my father started hitting me, he harassed me verbally. He needled me about schoolwork or my friends. He thought up a never-ending list of chores for me to do. He particularly relished embarrassing me about my figure or my budding womanhood. He'd comment on the size of my breasts or "joke" about whether I'd got my period or not that month.

He generally made his comments when no one else was around, but sometimes my mother would be there. Instead of defending me or getting angry at him, she would sometimes join in, making the situation into a funny "joke" that I was just "too sensitive" to understand. One time, she even brought up the subject of my breasts to my father. She commented to my dad, "Andrea's breasts are starting to grow. Just look at how big they're getting. Show your dad your breasts." I was offended, and said no. But she insisted, and he again commented on my prudery, saying that breasts were natural and that I shouldn't be embarrassed. They cajoled me into unbuttoning my blouse and quickly showing my father my breasts. Later that night, I cried with shame and humiliation. I was ten.

As I became more interested in boys, and they in me, my father became really strange, almost jealous. When my neighborhood girlfriends would visit, he would leave us alone and only come out of his workroom to get an occasional drink. But when neighborhood boys visited, he went off the wall. He'd send them home with no explanation. He forbade me to visit my friend Steve, the first person I had found who really appreciated me and shared my interests. Steve and I innocently read and wrote poems together, listened to the Beatles and Ravi Shankar, and discussed politics. It was around this time that my father started hitting me. I was angry, bitter, and confused. I had growing doubts about his sanity, but that was too awful to think about. It was easier to think that I was to blame. It wasn't until I told my mother about my father's physical abuse of me that I thought maybe I wasn't wholly at fault.

The day I decided to tell my mother, my father began hitting me because, as he said, I was "washing the dishes too slow." So, I finished the dishes at a more pleasing speed for him and then started to dust and vacuum the living room. My mother saw me wiping away my tears and asked me what was wrong. I was so angry at the injustice of it that I told her. When she wondered why I had never told her before, I just mumbled, "I don't know." But I knew why. It was because I didn't think she would do anything about it. After all, she managed to ignore the fact that he was drunk and surly all the time. Why should she be any different about this?

But she was. She told me that she'd make sure it didn't happen again, and that if it did, I was to tell her immediately. She surprised me by asking me to please not run away. Me, run away? I was too shy to raise my hand in class—I was not going to run away.

Well, she apparently did talk to him, because for a while he left me alone. Until the last time. Again, it centered around washing the dishes. Such a banal, everyday thing, but it seemed to bring out all his hostilities. I was washing and my sister was drying. He was sitting at the kitchen table, reading the newspaper and keeping an eye on us, alert for misbehavior. Suddenly, he was angered by her pace— she wasn't drying the dishes fast enough. He got up out of his chair and started pulling her hair and hitting her. It was the first time I had seen him hit someone other than me.

I became enraged. I started hitting him and kicking him, and he turned from my sister with a wild look in his eye. Here was the fight he was looking for. He started to hit me harder than I had ever been hit, but my pain was counterbalanced by the satisfaction I got from knowing that I was hitting him hard, too. I liked hurting him for all the times he had hurt me. I don't know where I got the strength, but

I finally grabbed his head, turned his face so that he was looking directly at me, and yelled at him, "You are crazy. You are a crazy man. Why are you hitting us? You are just crazy!" Tears came to his eyes, and he left the room. My sister and I silently finished the dishes and went our separate ways; we didn't discuss what had happened. Emotions were not something we were used to dealing with in that house.

The next day, my father knocked on my door and entered my room. He said, "I have been treating you badly, and I'm sorry, and I'm not going to do it anymore." I started crying, and he got irritated. "Why are you crying?" he asked. "I was the one who did something wrong." But I couldn't answer, and he quickly left the room. He never touched me again.

Journey to Confidence

Rachel Harwood

Rachel Harwood teaches self-defense and is a founding member of the Santa Cruz Women's Self-Defense Teaching Cooperative. The series of self-defense episodes in her account illustrate the variety of imaginative ways—both physical and verbal—that a woman can defend herself. The stories also show how she grew from an awkward adolescent, unconscious of the skills she possessed, to a confident adult.

"Being a self-defense teacher is very complex. It's good because I have practice all the time in dealing with situations. I've done everybody's 'what-ifs.' It really keeps you on your toes. But the fact is that there are lots of ways in which I'm not nearly as assertive as I'd like to be, especially in social situations. I'm fine about defending myself against strangers, but when it's people I know, it's a little more difficult."

As told to the editors in an interview: When I was a little kid, I was a tomboy. I fought a lot, and I won a lot because I was really fierce. I often fought off groups of kids, and kids bigger than me. I never had any fear of being vanquished in those days. When I got older and went to high school, it was a totally different thing, because I was very socially intimidated. I was really withdrawn and very shy and couldn't even look at people—I wouldn't even breathe if somebody was looking at me. So I lost many of my natural weapons that I didn't even realize I had.

One day, when I was about sixteen, I was riding my bicycle home from school. This man started following me in his car along this long stretch of road. He was saying all kinds of disgusting sexual things that he bet I wanted him to do to me.

At first I couldn't hear what he was saying because I had a muffler wrapped around my ears and the wind was blowing. I asked him to talk louder and he did. I couldn't think of anything to do, so I kept doing that, asking him to talk louder over and over again. Pretty soon, it was obvious that I could hear him, but I didn't know what else to do, even though there were houses all along the road. I didn't even think of stopping and asking somebody for help, or making a scene, or doing anything that I would think of now. My main objective was to get rid of him and I couldn't do it.

I thought if he thought I couldn't hear him he would go away, but it wasn't really clear in my thinking at all, and it definitely didn't work. It was obviously a panicked-scared reaction, which is the kind of reaction men hope for. So he was driving along slower than the rest of the traffic, with his window open, talking to me. I tried going really slow, too, so there would be a traffic problem. That sort of worked, because eventually he did leave. He turned left, but he went around the block, which I didn't realize at first.

I was almost to my house, and I turned off onto my street. The street had big hedges between the road and the houses, and long driveways, and there was a ditch by the side of the road. It was much more isolated than the street I had just been on. And I knew there was no one home at my house. I didn't want to show him where I lived. So when he showed up right as I was making the turn onto my street, I was really scared.

As we went along the side of the road, he tried to nudge me into the ditch with his car. I was really scared at that point, and that's when I started really defending myself. I kind of freaked out, and sometimes that can be a good thing. I don't believe in auras and that sort of thing, but I told him there was a black cloud floating over his head, and I described it in rich detail, and I looked at it while I was talking to him.

I pointed at it and talked about the bad things that he had done and described what the cloud looked like. Everyone I knew at the time was into auras and so forth. My parents traveled in hippie circles, so I knew all the vocabulary.

Pretty soon, he started making little glances up toward "the cloud," and I could see that this was having an effect, and that was what I wanted. I sped up my bicycle again—I had slowed it down before to try to bog down traffic again, but it wasn't working because nobody was coming along—but he zoomed his car to catch up to me because I got a little ahead of him. The next time he looked up, I immediately stopped and turned and went zooming down one of those driveways and he didn't see where I went. I was able to escape, but it turned out there was nobody home at the end of that driveway.

He was driving back and forth out in front on the street, trying to figure out where I went, and then he started going in and out of the driveways. When he was in one driveway, I got out of the one I was in and went to the next neighbor's house, where people were usually home, but it was much more exposed. There was a hedge in front and one of those half circle driveways, and there was a big bed of marigolds right behind the hedge in the half circle. I drove my bicycle right into the marigolds—which for me was an extremely bold action at the time—to hide it behind the hedge, and then I went up and banged on the door. They weren't home. And they were always home—I didn't know them, but I had noticed that. So I was really freaked out. I ran back to my bicycle and just lay there behind the hedge, hoping he wouldn't bother to come in that driveway because it was one we had already passed. And he drove back and forth and back and forth and I just lay there looking through the hedge for what seemed like hours but was probably only twenty minutes.

He finally left. I just waited for a long time and then I went home. I was really scared when I got home, so I locked the doors. My brother didn't understand, so I told him what had happened. He didn't seem to think it was anything to worry about—he was only fifteen— and that made me really upset and angry. I felt like I hadn't defended myself at all and I felt really bad about it. I felt bad that I hadn't looked for his license plate. I didn't know what kind of a car it was, I only knew the color, and I couldn't describe the man either.

For years, I felt bad about all those things, like I hadn't defended myself, until I figured out that I had. Later, when I started to learn about self-defense and hear other people tell their stories and say that *they* hadn't defended themselves when it sounded to me like they had, I started to reevaluate my own story, and I realized that I did a number of things that were really brave for me, and they worked.

Just a few years ago, when I was working at a restaurant, I had the same experience of somebody following me in a car. This hadn't happened to me for years, certainly not in any kind of serious way.

I used to walk home late at night, because I worked from 3:00 to 11:00 P.M. This was a Saturday night, so it was even later. It was about eleven-thirty when I got out the door. I usually walked home along Pacific Avenue, which is a business area of town, and often encountered some kind of mild harassment. But on this particular night, I was on another, less well-lit street. There was a man following me in his car with his window rolled down, making remarks, trying to get me to come over to the car. I told him I wouldn't.

I was really tired that night, it was one of those nights where you just work your fingers to the bone and then you have a lot of messy cleaning to do at the end and you're just totally worn out. I was carrying an orange in my hand. I was planning to eat it when I got home. I was looking forward to that. So this orange was all I had with me. I didn't want to deal with this guy following me, and I was just sort of ignoring it, even though I know that doesn't work. I tell people in my classes that it's fine to ignore someone if it works, but most of the time it doesn't.

Well, it wasn't working. And he was bothering me more and I was starting to get worried about it because I was getting toward home and I didn't want to take him home. As I got to the corner, I realized I had to do something about this, rise out of my tiredness and do something. I decided that this was not a very dangerous situation. I could certainly go up to a house and knock on the door, or do any number of things, and it would be to my advantage for him to come out of his car anyway. I considered my options for a minute and decided maybe this was an occasion where I could have fun. I took my orange and I assumed a wide stance, and in slow motion did a big dramatized windup with that orange, and by the time that I was just about to throw it, he was already starting to speed up the car. Already he was getting the message, and that felt good. I aimed the orange at the window, hoping to hit him, but as he sped up, the car moved and the orange hit the car right on the round top—it was a VW bug—and it made a really loud boom. It was really fun. He went zooming around the corner and he didn't come back. It really made my evening. I went across the street later and collected my orange. It was a little bruised up but it was fine, and I took it home and ate it.

The nice thing about this incident was that it was really different from earlier experiences, even though it started off being the same: me not wanting to deal with it, having memories of the earlier times when that had happened to me, feeling down, feeling tired. I wasn't really liking myself at the time, but I was able to pull the thing together and deal with it. I had the anger from those past experiences in me and I could reach out and tap into it to help me with the situation. I was also aware of my power at the time, that I didn't have to be scared like I was before.

Not too long ago, I was walking along the main street downtown, and at an outdoor café there was a party of four, two men and two women in couples, probably about my parents' age.

"Hey, I haven't seen you since you were so high," one of the men called out to me. "How've you been, anyway?"

So I approached him, because a lot of people do recognize me from when I was a kid. I have a real distinctive face that hasn't changed a whole lot since then. And I don't necessarily recognize them.

"Hello," I said. "It's a nice day. Where do you know me from?"

"Oh, I'm an old friend of yours, don't you remember me?"

"Well, no, but maybe I would if you gave me some hint about where."

"Oh, I'm your old Uncle George!"

At that point, it was obvious to all concerned, the people at his table and to me, that he was just kind of having me on; that's how he was entertaining himself. The ladies were sort of laughing nervously at the table. I guess he was just partway drunk and that was his way of entertaining people and expressing himself. I knew he was kidding because I only have so many uncles and I know what they look like.

"Oh yeah, right, right," I said. "The last time we saw each other was at Cousin Sally's party, and you were acting really funny that night. I remember what you did, you were up on the table. When'd you get out of jail, anyway?"

And you know, halfway through all of that he started getting nervous and acting like he didn't really know me to the rest of his table, and he just kind of turned back and ignored me. I just kind of figured, hey, that'll do it, and I turned away and walked on. I figured if he could do that, I could do it, too.

As I learn more about self-defense, I realize how important it is to care about yourself and to draw on your caring about yourself when somebody else is attacking you in any way—whether it's just to have fun by making you the butt of a joke or to actually attack you.

In terms of how it makes me look at my past experiences, I realize that I was told that I should be polite, that I should not make a scene. I ingested all that information and tried to do what my parents said, because I've always been one to follow rules if they make sense, and they seemed to make sense in high school. It seemed to make sense to ignore people, to be quiet and as self-effacing as possible. Unfortunately, that also fed into a lot of self-dislike and other things that made me quite helpless.

When I look back at things that happened to me in high school, I can see that when I defended myself, I was doing a lot more than I thought at the time. Then, I thought the only way to defend yourself was either by hitting back or to seek legal recourse.

Now I see that it was really bold of me to use that fantasy stuff in an effective way. It amazes me now that it really worked, that he was really looking at that black cloud. It's not something I would necessarily specifically advise someone to say; it's a matter of intuition and it happened to be what worked with him.

I'm so much more aware of my options now. I can say with confidence that it would be a real mistake for somebody to climb in my window and try to rape me. It would be a mistake for somebody to jump me. It would be a mistake for somebody I knew to try to put the make on me in a forceful way. I can and I will defend myself.

It's Worse When They Don't Mean To

Jeni Schreiber

Jeni Schreiber (a pseudonym) is a thirty-three-year-old "woman-identified" woman, a mother of four, a professional writer and translator, a peace-loving person, a voracious reader since kindergarten, a resident of Israel for the last sixteen years, a veteran of the Israel Defense Forces, and proud of all of the above.

This story is about something that happened to Jeni Schreiber when she was a child. The first and last parts of the story are written in the third person, and are told from the perspective of Jeni's mother, Rachel Goldin. The rest of the story is written in the first person, from Jeni's perspective.

"Had this book been available twenty-five years ago, my story—and those of many other sexually abused women—might never have happened. I rejoice that this book will be available to my sisters, and to my daughters, who are my sisters."

"Mama? I need to talk to you." Jeni's voice slashes through the Sunday-morning quiet like a hot knife.

Rachel Goldin throws down the newspaper—her single, forty-five-minute luxury out of an inhumanly crowded week—and glares up at her daughter. Jeni, almost twelve, is already in the eighth grade of the city's school for the gifted. Even there, she heads her class. Surely she is smart enough to know what those few healing moments of quiet mean to Rachel—and what their interruption means.

Then, seconds after Rachel has heard the words, she understands them. "Need," Jen had said. "Need." To the best of Rachel's memory, Jen had never before expressed a desire other than as an offhand, casual remark.

Rachel smiles, pats the worn beige sofa next to her. "Sit down, sweetie." But Jen remains standing before her, elbows pressed close to sides; the girl's white cotton nightgown smells faintly of sweat, though it is only April and the heat isn't on. "Well, tell me about it, then."

Jen looks at the carpet, up at the wall above Rachel's head, with eyes squeezed into aching slits. Her knuckle steals to her mouth and she begins to nibble it. Rachel reaches up to move the hand away; Jen, anticipating her, whips it back to her side with a flinching gesture.

Something is seriously wrong.

A minute, a minute and a half, and Jen is still frozen in indecision. Rachel opens her mouth, prepares to ask—what? She does not know herself—but Jen has made up her mind now. For an instant, the girl's indrawn breath is loud in the sunlit living room. Then, softly: "Mama, when I slept over at Grandma and Grandpa Goldin's last week . . ." Even less audibly: ". . . something happened . . . he touched me, Mama.

"My breasts."

I had often stayed there before; but always with Matthew or David, and usually with both; always at my parents' convenience, rather than my own request. Mama had had three children in three years—and none of us was what you'd call a "good" child. Either we teamed up, like the time Matthew and I redecorated our freshly papered room with Crayolas, as high as we could reach; or the time David and I played "lost in the maze" behind the furnace, then smeared our sooty selves all over the house "so people would have clues to come and find us." Or we fought. After the time I pushed Matthew into the radiator and cut his head wide open, I gave up physical violence—but foul language and nasty practical jokes remained fair game far into our teens.

Looking back, I realize that after a grindingly hard day at the office, coming home to deal with the three of us must have taken superhuman effort. So, every few weeks, Mama simply needed to have an evening off from us. And since baby-sitters cost money, and her own father was a frail little man who used his fifteen-years-gone heart attack to keep from doing anything so energetic as riding herd on kids, the three of us nearly always spent those evenings off at Dad's parents' house.

This time, though, I'd asked to sleep there. For two reasons: Grandpa's hardware store, and Susan Ross.

Grandpa's store fascinated me. I loved the prickly feel of a loosely held fistful of tiny nails—and the way I could line up a dozen of them, head of one to point of the next, with one small magnet heading the procession. And I used to imagine that if I could only rub the filings from the key-grinding machine into all my skin on the same day, I would become invulnerable. But with Matthew and David constantly urging me outside to play tag or hide-and-go-seek, I never got enough of a chance to explore its wonders on my own.

And Susan. She lived around the corner from Grandma and Grandpa, had been in third grade when I was in first; I'd skipped two grades, caught up with her in fifth, and been her best friend for a term before they transferred me to a special school. Sue had been a wild child, who chewed gum openly in class and threw stones at the Safety Patrol. Now nearly fourteen, she was a tough adolescent, with thrilling, horrifying stories about cigarettes and boys. We'd moved out of the old neighborhood, and I saw Sue maybe once a month— always with my two shadows hanging around my neck. I was dying for a chance to talk to her alone . . . so, needless to say, when I pleaded with Mama to let me sleep over at Grandma and Grandpa's house, I didn't even breathe her name.

When I rang the Ross' doorbell that afternoon, Sue opened the door, gave a gleeful shriek, and bear-hugged me as if she hadn't seen me for a year. I'd promised Grandma to be back in an hour, but I spent nearly three closeted in Sue's room, listening to the latest sagas. They got a bit monotonous after a while, and I'd started counting the flowers on her wallpaper and figuring out the number of roses per square foot, when I realized she'd said something riveting: ". . . stuck his hand in my shirt.''

"In your SHIRT!'' I echoed. I'd learned "the facts of life"—the ways of human reproduction—from my own reading, at least three years before. And I knew that nobody but a doctor, or Mama, had any business seeing your panties. But the only people I knew who would possibly be interested in the impressive protuberances under Sue's shirt (and it was a shirt, even then, when most of us meek female adolescents still wore frilly blouses) were babies. Breasts, the books had all said, were for lactation.

Sue nodded. "Sure . . . to feel my tits. Don't you know boys do that?" Blushing, I shook my head. "Well, they do. And y'know what, Jen? It feels real nice. Shivery. Like . . . like wings inside you." For a moment, her usually hard face was soft and dreamy; then she sighed briefly and pulled herself together. "And then, shit and damn, Miss Perkins remembered she'd left the home ec room unlocked and came back and caught us."

"What did you do?" I whispered, enthralled.

"I started to cry, natch. Loud. And silly old Perkins let me go. Jimmy got suspended for three days, though. . . . Listen, Jen, I don't want to scare you, but it's almost seven. Your grandma's probably having cat fits by now."

I grabbed my coat, raced Sue downstairs, paused with one hand on the doorknob. "Sue? Do you love him?"

She shrugged. "I guess so. . . . I mean, if you let a boy feel your tits, I guess it means you love him. But—well, sometimes I wish it wasn't him feeling them."

"What do you mean?"

"Oh . . . forget it." She hugged me hard, kissed my cheek. "Get on home to your grandma before she sends the cops for you." Left hand in mine, she opened the front door; right hand on my fanny, she pushed me out.

Rachel reaches out, takes both Jen's hands—the child's fingers stiffen in hers, but she does not actually flinch again—pulls her down gently onto the worn beige sofa. "Tell me exactly what happened," she says, in a soft, yet intense voice Jen has never heard before.

Jen looks up, down, up again. "Well, I got to Grandma's house, and I fooled around in the store a little—"

"By yourself?" Rachel asks with the same strange intensity.

"Yes . . ." Jen has never told her mother about the tiny nails, like the claws of infinitesimal magic mice; never mentioned the in-vulnerability. Now, suddenly, she would like to, but does not know how. "And then I asked Grandma if I could go see Sue Ross . . . we talked some, and it was kinda late when I got back to Grandma and Grandpa's house.

"Then we had dinner, and I finished my homework and went upstairs and got ready for bed. And about fifteen minutes later, Grandpa came up to tuck me in, like he always does when we sleep over. But this time, it was different." She has found an almost perfectly round, half-dollar-sized worn place on the sofa arm, and runs her finger around and around it.

After a moment, Rachel prompts: "Different . . . how?"

Her eyes on the sofa arm, Jen answers: "Well . . . first he asked me if I wanted him to tell me a story. I mean, he stopped telling us stories years ago. But he sounded like he really wanted to tell me one, so I said okay; and he told me 'Beauty and the Beast.' But different . . . like he meant me to know it was me he was talking about. And then he pulled up the top sheet and kissed me good night, and he touched my cheek . . . and, well, I don't know why, but I felt kind of sorry for him, and I turned my head and kissed his hand.

"And then he took that same hand, and he put it on top of the top sheet, on top of my breasts. And he kind of moved it back and forth, real slowly and softly, a few times. And, well, he looked like he was going to cry.

"Then he said 'Good night, Beauty,' real quietly, and turned off the light and went out."

For the first time in many months, Rachel is at a loss for words. She wants to hold her daughter close, to shield her from this evil; but, twice now, she has seen Jen recoil from her touch. So she sits silently, trying to sort out her thoughts, while Jen's finger circles and recircles the bare patch on the sofa arm.

A noise from upstairs—Matthew has thrown a shoe at David—makes Rachel realize that she does not have much time.

"Jen, listen," she says urgently. "First of all, you were right to tell me, and I know how scared and confused you must be. And thank you for trusting me.

"Now, I'm going to talk to you like an adult, and if there's anything you don't understand, please say so. Because I want you to understand.

"Sometimes, men get . . . well, a kind of sickness. Almost . . . no, not almost. A kind of mental illness. It has to do with feeling unloved, which is something pretty scary in itself. It may be because they're getting old, or because someone's been unpleasant to them. And it makes them say, or do, unpleasant things to women, or sometimes to young girls.

"It happened to a man in my neighborhood, Jen, when I was about your age. I was coming home from school with my friend Lisbeth, and he exposed himself to us. Do you know what that means?" Jen nods. "And I told my mother, and she explained to me—just as I'm explaining to you—that men who get that way don't really mean to harm, or to frighten. I'm not talking about the real criminals, the violent ones. I'm talking about sad, scared, sick men, Jen. And I guess Grandpa Goldin is one of them."

Rachel takes a shaky breath, runs her hands across her face. "But we can't tell Grandma Goldin, because it would hurt her. And we can't tell Dad, because it would hurt him. So you let me handle it, Jen, and I'll make sure you're never alone with Grandpa again."

Jen shakes her head. "That's not enough. We have to tell Aunt Laura. Because Cousin Anne sleeps over there sometimes, too, and she's a year younger than I am."

Rachel, amazed at her child's sagacity, nods. "Okay. But let me tell Aunt Laura. And . . . well, you're still going to have to see Grandpa sometimes, at family gatherings and so forth. Please be nice to him when you see him . . . because he doesn't really mean to."

Part II

The Power of the Voice

Introduction

The voice is a powerful weapon, not only when words are spoken, but when the full force of the will and the intensity of sound combine to repel the attacker. The voice has an intelligence of its own, often surprising even the woman who possesses it. Many women dream of not being able to scream, yet when attacked, they find a voice they never knew they could muster. Some of the best advice given to women by the police is to make a lot of noise. Self-defense courses often include instruction and practice on yelling like a banshee.

Effective verbal self-defense consists of knowing what you want in a given situation and expressing that as clearly as possible, sometimes repeatedly, until either the message gets across or the attacker gets bored. In "Like a Broken Record," Stella Moreno gives us one of the best examples of the broken-record technique, an actual practice exercise often taught in assertiveness training courses.

Sometimes verbal self-defense can be confusing because the woman has conflicting desires. This is most problematic in situations with a known attacker, who may even be a current or past sexual partner, or someone the woman is attracted to. She may feel uncertain about whether she wants to be sexual, but quite sure that she doesn't want to be forced. These ambiguous situations may also cause a woman to feel especially guilty afterward. She may judge herself as contributing to the attack, simply because she had sexual feelings at the time of the attack. "She Means No," by Pamela Morgan, concentrates on these complex issues.

Other verbal strategies include acting crazy, being creative, or using humor. Although an attack is a serious situation, who says self-defense can't be fun? Humor can be one of the most effective tools a woman has, because it tends to disarm an attacker who expects a passive, fearful victim. If a woman can make a joke while being threatened, she has already rejected the victim role. Victims don't make quips—they are frozen with fear. By finding the humor in a potentially serious situation, a woman shows her attacker that she is an individual with wit, intelligence, and the gumption to stick up for herself. This too surprises many would-be rapists, since the woman is no longer a faceless receptacle for his fantasies, but a real-live adult woman who has something to say for herself.

In many verbal attacks, the attacker relies on a "script." "Don't I know you from somewhere?" or "Hey, baby!" are examples of opening lines. Making a joke or a witty remark can disrupt that script. Kikanza Nuri Robins demonstrates this well in "What Mama Taught Me," when she and her companion are being harassed at a bar.

An obscene telephone call is a common way that an attacker feeds his fantasies. The woman on the other end of the line is—if anything—a frightened voice, a hint of a human being. After continued harassment by an anonymous caller, Nancy Rawles in "Insult for Insult" finally decides to give him a dose of his own medicine—to his stunned surprise and her triumph.

As with many other self-defense techniques, a woman often uses her creativity in an unpremeditated way. Indeed, the essence of imagination is spontaneity.

Pretending to go along with the person is known as the "passive" defense, and can be used to buy time or to get to a better physical location. In "I Just Want to Talk to You," Priscilla Prutzman uses elements of this strategy in a dialogue with her attacker that lasts several hours, as she convinces him that he should not proceed with his plans to physically assault her. In "Singing in the Rain," Irene van der Zande talks with her attacker all afternoon while they drink tea—until he leaves.

The one verbal strategy that is often associated with being raped is pleading, which may be an expected, and therefore less effective, way to deter an attack. If the attacker wants to intimidate or scare the woman, her attempts to plead may play into his gratification. In fact, Dr. Pauline Bart, in her research on women avoiding rape, found that pleading was associated with being raped, not with avoidance.

One verbal strategy is saying "No!" when you mean no and sticking to it, not only in attack situations, but in general practice. Pamela Morgan also uses this strategy.

Ann Alberts, in "A Jog on the Beach," hears the voice of her self-defense instructor in her mind, advising her to "yell anything! Show him you're going to fight, that you're strong. That scares some men off." Nancy Miller verbally challenges an attacker who says he has a gun, and wins a struggle in the subway, in "Calling His Bluff."

The purpose of a yell is twofold: one, to frighten your attacker, and, two, to release yourself from the paralysis of fear by engaging your lungs in the physical act of expelling breath. In Japanese, the word for this is *kiai* (pronounced "key-eye"), literally meaning the release of spirit. This is also the word for the so-called judo or karate yell.

Yelling may also attract attention, and occasionally even some help. Many women have been told to shout "Fire!" rather than "Help!" This may be helpful in a building, where others will be more likely to get involved if they feel they are also in danger. Hollering "Fire!" may not be so useful in a field or on the street. Yelling outdoors requires persistence if you really want to attract help. At least three sustained bellows are needed to let others know something is going on, give them time to get outside, and help them figure out where you are. In "A Night Out Alone," Linda Forest uses vocal power to express how she feels about the attack and in the process attracts some reinforcements.

One last note: shrieking in a high-pitched voice may not sound like serious distress and may hurt your throat. Making the sound lower will release more breath and allow you to roar like a lion in a most uncivilized fashion. Few attackers are willing to mess with a woman who is making a lot of noise.

A Jog on the Beach

Ann Alberts

Ann Alberts (a pseudonym) was brought up in a small, affluent town near San Francisco. For most of her childhood she says she was sheltered from the crime, violence, racism, and starvation that can be seen in most urban areas.

> *"My father felt there was too much violence on television, so to add to my sheltered life, I grew up without TV until I was twelve. Then I really realized what violent crimes were. Being unused to seeing violence, I would have terrible nightmares about shootings and stabbings. It wasn't until high school that I saw a few of my rights violated."*

I had been jogging a lot that winter, so I knew it would be no problem to run the three miles from my house to the harbor. One, two, hold, three, four—that calf seemed stretched enough. A few slow toe touches, and I was ready.

I followed my usual route to the beach. As I approached the harbor, I found myself thinking about my dad, who had recently passed away, and decided to sit on the beach for a while to have some quiet time with him and the ocean.

As I got up to start my run home, I had to go to the bathroom. Running with a full bladder wasn't much fun, so I walked up the beach to the public rest rooms. Since it was a weekday afternoon, there weren't many people around. Besides a few distant dots, I saw only one older man, sitting on a bench about thirty feet from the rest rooms.

As I walked up the stairs to the women's rest room, passing the men's to the left, I was aware of a strange, uneasy feeling. I glanced over at the older man on the bench, but he wasn't paying any attention to me. So I rounded the corner to the open door on the women's side. Still uneasy, I checked all the stalls before choosing the middle one. As I might have expected, the lock mechanism that keeps the door closed had long been broken. I stepped inside and pulled the door closed.

While I was pulling down my pants, I peered through the crack in the door. I could see the door to the rest room, and the sun behind it. Just as I started to pee, I noticed the sun was blocked and a very tall blond man was in the doorway. Suddenly, he got on his hands and knees and started crawling toward my stall.

I had taken a one-hour rape-prevention course in college four years earlier, and I could hear the instructor's words in my mind: "Yell anything! Show him you're going to fight, that you're strong. That scares some men off."

I pulled up my pants, stood up, and kicked the unlatched door out toward the approaching man, hoping it would hit him in the face. At the same time, I yelled, "What the hell are you doing in here?" He got up, spun around, and ran into the men's room to hide. At that point, the word "Scream!" came into my mind, and unlike so many of my frustrating nightmares, a piercing scream came out of my mouth.

The old man on the bench slowly looked up and said, "Is anything wrong?" I started to explain, but realized that he really didn't care, and that the man was still hiding in the bathroom behind me.

In pee-wet shorts, I ran to a phone booth and called the police. Fifteen minutes later, the police arrived. The officer checked the bathroom but didn't find the man who fit my sketchy description. On my way home in the police car, the officer explained there wasn't anything he could have done even if he had found the man. Unless the man had touched me, he couldn't have cited him. I asked him if this kind of thing happened often. He said no.

When I got home, I had a good, long cry. I cried partly out of relief that I was safe, and partly to let go of the fear—to allow myself to think for the first time how scary it had been.

I still have a fear of public rest rooms, and don't use them unless

I am accompanied by a friend or unless there are lots of people around. I learned that I need to be aware at all times, not only at night.

I feel good that I had the strength to show this man that I was going to defend myself. And that I can trust my inner voice, my gut feelings.

Calling His Bluff

Nancy T. Miller

Nancy Miller was living in Chicago with her husband and working as an engineer at a television station when the incident in her story took place. Now they live on a farm in Minnesota, where she's a part-time student and a full-time mother. "I lock my doors when I'm home," she says, "a practice that astounds my rural neighbors. I guess I've lost the 'It can't happen to me' attitude that I used to have."

"Whenever I think of my own experiences with harassment, I remember Phyllis Schlafly's classic remark about the subject. She said something along the lines of 'If a woman is righteous, men will recognize it, and she will not be harassed.' Obviously, Mrs. Schlafly has never ridden a subway or walked anywhere by herself."

I remember that it was cold, an unusually cold day in April. I was still wearing my boots and my winter coat. I had been working the second shift for two, maybe three months. I guess I thought that I was invincible, that nothing could ever happen to me. It was just a few blocks from the subway station to my apartment, and I had told my husband it wasn't necessary for him to come meet me at the station to walk me home.

"Get some sleep," I had told him. "There's no sense in both of us keeping weird hours."

I was just two blocks away from the train station when I heard footsteps behind me, a steady walk that kept pace just a few feet in back of me. I quickened my own gait a little, and prayed that my instincts were wrong; I could feel trouble coming.

As I crossed the next intersection, he joined me. He wasn't a large man, not what you would call muscular or imposing. In fact, he was hardly taller than I. He tried to start a conversation, and I tried to avoid giving any straight answers. When he asked for the second time where I lived, I replied, "Oh, just up there," and waved my hand ahead of us. Maybe I could talk my way out of this; maybe I could get close enough to home to get help from my husband.

At the head of an alley, he turned toward me. "We're going down there," he said, as he motioned with his left hand, deep in his coat pocket. "I've got a gun."

I tried to reason with him. "Look, I've had a long day, and I'm not interested. Okay?" Then I prayed out loud. "Lord, you've got to help me." And then I said something that amazed me. "You've got a gun? Okay, let me see it. I don't think you even have a gun."

He pulled his hand out of his pocket. There was no gun. He held a heavy piece of twine in his hand, and whipped it around my throat. "I'm gonna lay with you," he said.

I tried kicking him in the groin. It didn't faze him. In fact, he seemed amused by it. "Didn't work, did it?" he gloated.

He was pulling me into the alley by the twine, choking me. I couldn't reach him, couldn't bite or scratch or hit him. I concentrated on the piece of twine that was biting into my neck. I forced my thumbs up underneath it and took a long, deep breath.

It was a loud, clear scream. It was something he hadn't counted on.

"Okay, lady, okay. Lighten up. I'm leaving."

I watched him walk away, until he had disappeared from sight. He really was gone. I ran home, bruised and scared, but I had won.

A Night Out Alone

Linda Forest

Linda Forest was born in Bristol, Pennsylvania, in 1955, the youngest of three daughters. She earned an M.S. in counseling and human relations and is now a supervisor at a social service agency in suburban Philadelphia.

"Yes, I am furious that we as women in our society must feel the vulnerability we do, but instead of letting my anger and frustration cause me to behave carelessly and stupidly, it has provided me with more constructive energy. Also, it has inspired me to share my story with other women in hopes that it provides them with strength, and courage."

On that wintry Saturday evening, the Penn State campus was buzzing with activity. Some students were walking from their dorms into town, where most of the entertainment took place on weekends. Another rather large group of students was heading to and from the campus buildings where, on any given night, there would be two movie showings. A third, smaller group was headed for the campus library for a more productive, if less enjoyable, evening.

I lived on the town's main thoroughfare, across the street from campus. Having nothing to do that evening, I decided to attend *A Night at the Opera,* one of the few Marx Brothers films I had yet to see. It was being shown in the dorm closest to my apartment. I decided to go to the 8:00 P.M. showing, so that when the film ended, there would still be plenty of students around.

Bill, the man I lived with, was a disc jockey for the campus radio station. Since he was working that night, I thought I would walk across campus after the film was over and stay with him until his progressive rock show ended. I never went to movies or anywhere else at night alone, but I wanted very much to do something.

Bill and I had discussed my going to the film and then walking alone to the building where he worked. He was very concerned. I stood my ground, explaining that the walk would be short, others would be milling around on campus, and I would stay in well-lit areas. He finally succumbed to my pressure and agreed there should be no problem.

Just to be on the safe side, he suggested that I carry the wooden stick, which looked a lot like a billy club, that his father had recently made for me for self-defense. I chuckled and told him that his suggestion was absurd. But he persisted, so I eventually agreed.

Once on campus that night, I tried to stick close to groups of students until I jogged into the building where the film was. Going somewhere alone at night was a very unusual experience for me, and yet I felt good about it. I was tired of being paranoid about others. I was sick to death of feeling vulnerable and limiting my activities because I was a woman. I felt truly oppressed. Having successfully gotten to the movie gave me a feeling of accomplishment.

The film was even better than I had anticipated. As I left the theater, I chuckled to myself, remembering my favorite scene, in which the entire ship's passengers crowded into one minuscule room. I was anxious to see Bill. We would, undoubtedly, spend the time between his song introductions repeating hilarious lines and imitating Harpo's mannerisms.

I quickened my pace in the bitter cold air. Luckily, I had worn my new long johns, my parka, my overalls, and my thickest flannel shirt. I put my hood up as the air stung my ears. A slight young man was walking on the sidewalk across the street from me, but I gave his presence very little thought. I crossed the street and turned the corner.

Finally, I reached the mall area. I loved this part of campus, with its tree-lined walkway. Looking up at the bare but still beautiful trees, I noticed that the sky was clear. The Little Dipper sparkled above. As I neared the building where Bill was working, I looked up and saw a lit window. He was in that room and I was glad to have arrived safely.

At that moment, I felt a body jump on my back and shove a hand into my mouth. I gagged and bit down on the fingers. The hand lowered to my neck. Before I could think, I let out a bloodcurdling scream. "GET THE FUCK OFF ME YOU SON OF A BITCH!" The volume of my voice surprised me. Bill was so close, and yet he did not come to my rescue. I screamed again. "HELP! HELP!" Why didn't Bill hear me?

After my second scream, the hand released my throat. I squeezed harder on the stick in my pocket, which I had been clutching throughout my walk. The body was still pressed against my back and I thrashed my elbows into its stomach. I screamed again and then saw two men running to help me. As the man on my back released me, I clobbered him with my stick.

The two men approached and I pointed toward the now running figure that had been pressed against my body. The thought made me shiver with disgust. I looked at the attacker as he fled. It was the same man who had been watching me from across the street when I left the movie.

The men chasing him were too far behind and finally gave up. In the meantime, two women ran over and I told them what had happened. They insisted on walking me to the building. I tried the front door; it was locked. I went to the side door and it too was locked. How could Bill do this to me? I started to cry harder. The women walked me to their apartment. Once there, I called Bill. He was there in five minutes.

As we walked back to the radio station together, my tears turned to anger. Why was I locked out of the building? Why hadn't he heard my cries for help? He answered that he had been in a soundproof booth. He made me telephone the campus police—something I was reluctant to do. They met us at the station and I told them what had happened. After they left, I saw my gentle, pacifist boyfriend turn into a wild man after revenge. "If you ever see that fucker," he said, "point him out to me and I'll kill him!"

We finally got home. I didn't sleep at all that night. I couldn't believe how close I had come to . . . to what? To being raped or hurt or killed? My imagination ran wild. Bill caressed my face and his touch made me shiver. Would I ever enjoy being touched again? And what if I had been raped? How could I ever be physically close to someone again?

I recuperated from this episode quickly, feeling fortunate, not only because I was not seriously damaged physically or emotionally, but because I saw how I reacted to an attack. Though the experience taught me to be extremely cautious, I know how I would react if this were to happen again. I would scream, louder than I ever would have thought possible. And I would, again, fight like a tiger.

I Just Want to Talk to You

Priscilla Prutzman

Priscilla Prutzman is the program coordinator for the Children's Creative Response to Conflict Program in Nyack, New York, the co-author of *The Friendly Classroom for a Small Planet*, and has written articles about nonviolence for several publications. At the time of the incident she describes here, she had led several workshops in personal nonviolence and had facilitated role-plays about creative responses to street hassles.

"I have thought about what happened many times and described the scenario to many people. Some have said it was luck or chance that I escaped a potentially fatal situation with no harm at all. I still believe that I was using whatever skills I had to try to transform the violence of the man. I tried to get to know him as a person and to humanize the situation. I think I projected nonviolent strength. I would try the same thing again."

One day, while bicycling north on an isolated viaduct in New York City, I was stopped by a tall, athletic-looking young man. The following dialogue took place during the next forty-five minutes.

MAN: Hey, can you tell me where Broadway and Amsterdam meet?
ME: As far as I know, they run parallel up here. *I continued riding my bike.*
MAN: Hey, give me a ride on the back of your bike.
ME: You're too big, and I'm in a hurry.

MAN: C'mon, give me a ride.

ME: It won't work.

MAN: Sure it will. Let me show you. I can ride you because I'm the man.

ME: But it's my bike.

MAN: But I'm the man.

ME: Hey, I've really got to go. *He ran alongside the bike for about twenty yards, holding on to my coat. Suddenly, he stopped the bike and pulled out a knife.*

MAN: (*Pointing the knife at me*) I've taken enough shit from you; now you're going to listen to me.

ME: I was listening to you before.

MAN: No you weren't. You gave me the brush-off. You were mean to me back there.

ME: I wasn't mean to you. I just wanted to go where I was going.

MAN: You were mean, and now you're going to do what I tell you.

ME: Okay, what are we going to do? You want to ride the bike?

MAN: I want to ride you on the bike.

ME: I'd feel funny doing that. You want me to ride you?

MAN: Look, I'm not taking any of your shit, you hear? You just do what I tell you or you're going to get cut up. My knife is right inside my pocket, see?

ME: Okay.

MAN: You don't believe me? I've been in jail for murder, robbery, you name it, I've done it, baby.

ME: I believe you. What do you want to do?

MAN: I want to talk to you, that's all. Just for about half an hour.

ME: All right, we'll talk. What do you want to talk about?

MAN: I want to talk alone, in a certain spot.

ME: Why can't we talk here? We're alone.

MAN: You think I'm stupid? We'll go where I say and I want to talk alone.

ME: Okay, but I have to put air in my tires and I'm supposed to meet my mother at three.

MAN: You can be a little late.

ME: She'll worry if I'm late.

MAN: Look, I'm not going to take any shit from you. You do what I tell you. And don't try anything foolish or I'll kill you.

ME: I won't do anything foolish.

MAN: I keep on the jacket so I can hide the knife. It's there. You saw it. So don't try to run or anything.

ME: I told you I wouldn't do anything foolish.

MAN: I know people all over this area, people with cars. I can move around fast and get you.

ME: I believe you.

MAN: Look, you don't know nothin' in this area. You make one false move and I'll slit your throat. *Silence.*

ME: Hey, man, I haven't done anything to you. Let's talk, okay? You know I've only got till three o'clock.

MAN: Let's make it ten after three.

ME: Okay, ten after.

MAN: All I want to do is talk.

ME: Well, let's go over there and sit down and talk. We'll have more time. We can start right away.

MAN: You think I'm stupid or something. I want you just to talk where I want to talk and you're going to do what I say. I'm tired of taking shit from people like you. If you do something crazy, I'm going to kill you. And if you happen to get away, the next time I see you I'll kill you.

ME: Are you warm in that jacket?

MAN: No, I always wear this jacket.

ME: You could take it off and carry it and still have your hand on your knife. You look awfully warm. Why don't you look at me when you're talking?

MAN: Because I'm mad. You were mean to me and now I'm mad. I never look at people I'm mad at.

ME: Why are you mad at me?

MAN: Because you ignored me back there.

ME: I'm sorry. I didn't mean to. I'd like to talk to you.

MAN: Okay. Well, don't do anything foolish. I have this favorite spot in the park. You'll like it there.

ME: Why don't you take your coat off?

MAN: Look, do you think I'm stupid? I wear this coat to hide my weapons. I have a gun in my pocket, too. One false move . . .

ME: What do you do? Do you have a job?

MAN: I'm a house painter. Look at my fingers. See, they're all full of paint. You get to see a lot of people's houses that way.

Some people are pretty strange, but I like it. Sometimes I paint black folks' places, but mostly white.

ME: Does that bother you?

MAN: Yeah, I've taken enough shit from white folks.

ME: I worked at a camp this past summer where it was totally integrated—a third black, a third Spanish, a third white. I really like the idea of that. You know, it gives a little hope to the world. Do you like that idea?

MAN: Yea, sort of. It doesn't work, though.

ME: It worked there. Everyone respected everyone else. It didn't matter what color they were or anything. The camp was set up by the Goddard-Riverside Community Center. Ever heard of it? It's not too far from here. You ought to go there sometime. They have classes and groups and stuff to do. It's nice.

MAN: Look. Let's get to the park, okay?

ME: Okay. Where's the nearest gas station? I really need air in my tires.

MAN: It's down that way, but we've got to talk.

ME: You said I could put air in my tires. You're not going to go back on your word, are you?

MAN: No, I wouldn't go back on my word.

ME: Could we go for coffee or something? I'm very thirsty.

MAN: No, we're going to the park.

ME: Well, I've got to get something to drink. *My mouth was so dry it was sticking to itself.*

MAN: There's the gas station. They have a soda machine. I'll get you a soda. *We walked the short way to the gas station.*

ME: Thanks. There's the tire pump.

He went for the soda, about twenty yards away. I leaned over and put air in the tires, nervous. I put too much air in one and the tire blew out. I was tempted to ditch the bike and run. I looked over to the soda machine. He was acting as if he didn't know me. I couldn't predict what he would do next. When we were talking, one person to another, he seemed nice enough. Did he really have a gun? Would he shoot? Did I have any control over what was happening? I thought I knew what I was doing. Time was passing quickly. I decided I wouldn't offer to pay him back for the Coke. That would put us in a negative male-female relationship instead of a black-white one.

I decided I would next ask to go to a bicycle repair shop. That was reasonable, although I doubted he would agree to it, since I had urged him to go to the gas station. But, to my surprise, he didn't seem to mind. He seemed to like being able to do normal things—like stopping and getting a drink. I was bewildered that he had bought me the Coke. Perhaps he was thinking that he had power over me.

He had held brute force over my life for the past thirty minutes, and his recognition of my powerlessness was working in my favor. I pushed my bike over to the soda machine and asked the attendant if he had a tube for my tire. He said no. I asked him where the bike place was. The attendant seemed surprised that we were together.

As we walked away from the gas station, he pushing the bike with a flat tire, me drinking my Coke, I wondered why I didn't just run or get on a bus. I realized that I had decided that I would learn as much about him as I could, and when the time was right, I would escape. We walked up the street to the park.

ME: Thanks for the Coke. That tasted good. I guess that bike had a pretty weak rear tire. It's flat.

MAN: I saw you trying to escape. I saw you looking around to see when you could get away.

ME: I wasn't trying to get away. I was busy putting air in my tires. I came right over when I finished. I wasn't trying to get away.

MAN: Well, you better not try anything foolish.

ME: I told you I'd talk to you until ten after three. That's your time.

MAN: That's right, it's my time, and you're going to do what I say.

ME: I'm not really sure what you want. We could talk here.

MAN: I want to talk to you alone, in my spot.

ME: Do you want sex?

MAN: Look, if I wanted sex, I'd tell you.

He paused. He almost sounded angry. I wondered if I'd insulted him in any indirect way by suggesting he wasn't involved with any woman, or that his way of becoming involved was to force women. Maybe he thought I was implying that he was impotent. But, at the same time, the question seemed to break the ice, and the conversation became more personal.

MAN: Are you married?

ME: No. I have a boyfriend, though.

MAN: Do you have any children?

ME: No. Are you married? Do you have children? *He mumbled something about being married once.*

MAN: You know, now that I think of it, it might not be a bad idea—
sex, I mean. Only if you want to, of course. When was the
last time you had any?

ME: Last night.

MAN: Man, it was a week ago for me. I didn't realize it was that
long.

It seemed he wasn't interested in sex if I wasn't. What else could
he want, then? To rob me? He could have done that many times
already. Maybe it was just loneliness—the need to talk to somebody.

MAN: I've been with a lot of women.

ME: I'll bet you have. You're real athletic-looking.

MAN: Tall, dark, and handsome, right?

ME: That's right.

MAN: I used to play basketball.

ME: You look like it. You're tall.

MAN: I'm a painter, you know, and when I go to people's houses
women are always after me. The last place I went, this white
woman was following me all around the apartment making me
tea and sandwiches and she kept talking. She asked me to stay.
One time she even climbed up on the ladder and was holding
on to my pants. I really wanted to get out of there, get the job
done. I really thought she was going to attack me.

ME: Sounds weird. I guess that happens to you a lot.

MAN: Yea, black *and* white women.

ME: Do you know of a bicycle repair shop near here?

MAN: No.

ME: Maybe we could ask someone.

He looked nervous, but didn't say anything. We walked in silence
for a while. When I stopped and asked someone about a bicycle shop,
he stepped back a little.

ME: There's one up that way. Could we take the bike there?

MAN: No. We don't have time for that.

More silence. We walked by four or five police in a line. I had
the feeling this was my last chance to get away. If I just ran behind
a policeman, I would be protected. But did I want to turn him in?
Did he have a gun? Would he go totally crazy and injure several
people in the process? I looked at the police, then looked at him. He
looked at the police and looked at me.

ME: How far is it to the park?

MAN: Not very, just up this street. *He was very nervous now, very confused.*

ME: I'm glad we're almost there. I'm going to have to leave pretty soon. Let's start talking right now, because it's almost ten after.

MAN: No. I want to go to my favorite spot.

ME: We're not going to have any time there. *We had arrived at the park entrance.*

MAN: This is where we go in. My spot is right down there next to that rock. C'mon, let's go.

ME: Look, it's ten after. We agreed I would leave at ten after.

MAN: But we haven't talked yet.

ME: It's ten after. We could have talked at any place along the way. Besides, we have been talking. I don't know what you really want to talk about. You never told me.

MAN: That's because I want to talk in my spot. Look, I kept my word on getting the bike fixed. Now you should keep your word on talking to me.

ME: But we agreed I'd be through at ten after. Now it's ten after, and I've got to go see my mother. I'm already late.

MAN: Don't yell or anything.

ME: Well, I've got to go.

MAN: You want to go. All right, just walk over here and get your bike and go.

ME: Okay.

MAN: But I'm going to kill you.

ME: Well, there's nothing I can do about that. If you're going to kill me, you're going to kill me. Right now, I've got to go and see my mother.

MAN: The next time I see you, I'm going to kill you.

ME: Why?

MAN: Because you wouldn't talk to me.

ME: I've talked to you for forty-five minutes, and now I've got to go and see my mother.

MAN: The next time I see you, I'm going to kill you.

ME: Like I said before, there's not much I can do about that. I'm taking the bike and going now.

I walked away at a leisurely pace, not looking back, knowing both of us were stunned. I wondered again if he had a gun. I forced myself not to look back, thinking that I would lose control and show fear. I had to appear strong, or everything I had done so far would be lost. I walked briskly up to a black woman and told her I had been held at knife-point for forty-five minutes by the man following me. I asked her if she could help me. She walked me very quickly to a group of construction workers, who turned the man around. I didn't see where he went.

The woman walked me three more blocks. I thanked her, got into a cab with my bicycle, and headed toward my mother's house.

Like a Broken Record

Stella Moreno

Stella Moreno is a Latina, the second of five daughters from Fresno, California. She is a kindergarten teacher who has been in education for ten years.

"I grew up in a family where the mother had more control. In my family, the daughters—including myself—have followed the independent part of my mom: that stubborn, strong part.

"In Hispanic families, it may look like Dad has the last say, but it's Mom who's doing it under wraps. But when I look at my male cousins, the machismo *ethic is definitely there. When it comes to conversation within the family, they get listened to more than women in our family.*

"It's hard for us to defend ourselves at all. We grow up learning to be caretakers, to take care of everybody but ourselves."

As told to the editors in an interview: I was a member of a group that was giving a retreat. Seven of us had gone ahead to open up the facility and get it ready for the high school girls who were coming for the retreat. It was twilight, and I had just finished sweeping and doing some things in the cabins where the girls were going to be sleeping. One of the priests from the church that ran this facility came out to give us the keys and he brought a helper with him.

I went into the bathrooms, which were behind the main part of the facility. I was in a middle stall and I heard somebody come in, and I thought, Oh, somebody's come in to go to the bathroom. Then the footsteps stopped, and the person didn't go into any of the bathroom stalls.

I heard breathing, but nobody moved, nobody said anything and finally I said, "Who's there? Is somebody in here?" Nobody answered, and I thought, Well, there's somebody there.

"I know you're there," I said. "I hear you." The person took a step and was just standing there breathing, and I thought, Well, somebody's here, and they're not talking, and I'm in here and they're out there, and what do I want to do about that?

A male voice said, "Are you scared?"

I thought a second and said, "Should I be?"

"Are you?" the voice said.

"Well, not unless—I don't know, do I have reason to be?"

By this time, I'm deciding that I just have to get out of here, and I'm just going to flush the toilet and walk out of the stall, and I don't know what I'm going to see or who it is going to be or what is going to happen. Yeah—I was scared. I thought he was there to rape, it was my first thought, rape, here we go, this is it. Nobody around, it was dark, I knew I was the only one in that part of the retreat center and I thought, I guess I'm going to fight.

I couldn't anticipate what was coming next. All these things were running through my head: violence, how am I going to protect myself, how big a person could I get away from, how fast do I run, could I beat him up?—you know, that stuff.

So I flushed the toilet and just walked out of the stall and the guy looks at me. It was the "helper" the priest brought.

"Well? Are you scared?"

"No, I've got some things to do and you don't belong in here. This is a women's bathroom."

He just looked at me and started laughing.

"So you need to get out of here, this is a women's bathroom." By this time, I'm just washing my hands, being very cool, like I'm not scared. I'm dying inside, but I'm acting cool. I go wash my hands, and he walks toward me.

I looked him in the eye. "You don't belong in here, this is a women's bathroom and you need to get out."

I kept repeating the same thing, like a broken record. It was a monotone, *I* was a monotone. It was a clear, direct message that had no emotion attached to it. I meant what I said. I know it works with children, especially kids who are really out of line and really playing the game. You just stand firm and be a broken record, be unaffected, don't have any emotion. The tone of voice is really important. And I just pushed him to the side, stepped past him, and walked out. He was laughing, and then he took off. I went directly to my friends and then to the priest and said, "Look, this guy you brought, this is what happened and get him out of here, because I don't want him around here with high school girls and I don't want him around us. Get him out of here!" And they took him out.

There was a point during the confrontation with the man when there was a standoff, a point when I felt, this is the moment and either it's going to happen or it's not. It was when I was washing my hands, standing there looking at him and he was looking at me. I felt like he was deciding, too, and I just thought I should be fearless and act like I belonged there and was in total control. I walked out and he split.

This experience made me more careful about people knowing where I am, especially in places I'm not familiar with. At the retreat, nobody knew where I was. I never thought of saying, "I'm going over there, there isn't anybody over there, I'm the only one that's going to be there, somebody come and check in on me at such-and-such a time." Now I think it's important to make some agreements about a checking-in time, so there's some built-in way of looking out for each other when you're in a remote place.

I now have a reasonable fear, and that makes me more self-protective. Making sure people know what, when, and where. I still go places alone, I don't stay out of adventure as a result of fear, but I'm just more careful and cautious.

She Means No

Pamela Morgan

Pamela Morgan (a pseudonym) began attending Incest Survivors Anonymous meetings last year. She says she has "made amends to my inner child who trusted the wrong people."

"I want people to know, however embarrassed I feel, that no man has the right to jump a woman, no matter what she says to him. My sister was raped and beaten by two men, and afterwards felt bad because she had smiled at them. She did not call the police. I want the public to know that this silence kills women. We can speak out. We can air our guilty feelings."

This is hard to write. At first, right after it happened, I wanted to tell people, let them know that a woman can win against an attacker. But since then, I've doubted myself: "If I hadn't been such an idiot, it wouldn't have happened. I could have prevented it." It's sad that I, or any woman, should feel guilty when a man oversteps his boundaries and acts with intent to harm.

What follows is a diary entry from four days after it happened.

A man tried to rape me. I was reading Nancy Friday's *My Secret Garden*, playing with myself, trying to get aroused. I heard a noise on the porch, thought it was my housemate, Joe. So what if he sees me? Everyone masturbates and it's natural. Then I reached to turn my light out, exposing my naked body, and snuggled in bed.

A few minutes later, I heard someone picking at my window.

"Who's there?" I asked.

"Does Lee live here?"

"No, try next door. There's no Lee here."

"Are you Lee's girlfriend? I want to buy a joint."

"No. Lee doesn't live here."

I watched him from behind my curtain. My bed was next to the low window by the front porch. He took a few steps away and stopped. My heart pounded as I waited for him to leave. If I had had clothes on, perhaps I would have shut the window or left the room or done something else.

Then he started to turn back.

"Go away," I said. "Your friend Lee isn't here."

"I want to fuck you," he said.

Well, I laughed to myself. Is this what reading about rape fantasies creates? Unbelievable. For some reason, I wasn't scared anymore.

"C'mon, I saw you playing with yourself. Now let me fuck you."

"No, I don't want to fuck you."

"Please."

"Hey, there's a dog around the corner."

"What you want me to fuck a dog for? Don't you care I haven't had sex? I'm going crazy."

"I don't care. That's your problem. Now go away or I'll call my roommates." I said this firmly and he started to leave, then said, "I've got an eleven-inch dick. It's better than a finger."

"Playing with myself is enough. I don't have to fuck you. I'm not gonna change my mind. I say no."

I wanted to teach this guy something. I thought I could talk him into respecting my "no," and he'd leave.

But he was begging. "C'mon, it's not love, just sex, and then I'll leave."

So I considered it for a moment. Maybe I did want this. But I quickly felt a strong inner "no."

"Don't you like sex?" he persisted.

"No. Now go away."

Next thing I knew, the window opened and he was on top of me, covering my mouth with his hand.

"Hey! Get out of here. That hurts. I can't breathe."

He was trying to shove his finger in my vagina. I yanked his hand off my mouth.

"I'm really not into this. Get out, get out." He had gotten the covers off and was touching my crotch roughly. I squirmed and shouted, thinking, If I keep shouting, I'll be okay. Then I realized that my housemate didn't hear me. Okay, I thought, I can deal with this myself. What is Joe gonna do that I can't?

"Stop shouting," he said.

Why didn't he hit me? I started kicking and kept kicking and suddenly he was off me, off the bed, and out the window, walking away.

"Get the fuck out of here," I screamed, enraged. And I slammed my window shut.

Whew. I was trembling but safe. Bathrobe on, I called the cops and woke Joe.

As I type this now, three months later, I still feel guilty. How could I have talked to him so long? Why wasn't I more concerned for my safety?

I believe that my sexual history contributed to my vulnerability in this situation. I was sexually abused by my father. I was not taught to say no, or to respect my body. I believed that if a man wanted to sleep with me, that meant he liked me and wanted to be nice to me.

The man who tried to rape me was arrested two hours later, prowling around someone else's house. His charge was reduced from a rape attempt to sexual battery; he received three years in prison. Fingerprints, my description of him, and my diary entry were evidence against him. He pled guilty.

In Defense of a Child

Adyson Peyton

Adyson Peyton (a pseudonym) is a school counselor who works with children in grades six, seven, and eight. The community she works in is a working class industrial town. The majority of families are single parents, and drug and alcohol abuse are rampant.

"I was amazed at my strength in not panicking. It made clear to me that the reserves I always thought I had were there but had never really been tested before. If I were in that situation again, I would do the same thing."

As told to the editors in an interview: I was working with a girl who was being sexually abused by her father. She was the second youngest daughter of six children, and she told me her father was molesting all six children. I reported to Social Services, and all six were removed from the home. Eventually, though, because they didn't have enough evidence, the kids all wound up back at home. One of the reasons that happened is that the girl I was counseling decided to say she had lied about the incest. I visited her while she was in shelter care, and she told me, "They don't believe me. They're going to send me back home anyway."

When she came back to school, her instructions were that she was not to see me. Her father had told the principal to keep her away from me. The child still wanted to see me, though, so I closed the curtains in my office so she could see me and no one would know.

I kept them drawn all day long so there would be no suspicion that I was just doing that with this kid.

One day, I was sitting at my desk thinking. As I often do, I had turned my chair around to face the window, to look out and contemplate a conversation I had just had with a parent. My windows were open and when I turned around, the father of this child was standing in my window with a .38 pointed at my face.

I panicked inside. I didn't know exactly what to do, so I thought, Well, I'll just sit here a minute. He said to me, "If you ever turn me in again, I'll blow your brains out." I just looked at him and said, "Well, if you ever abuse your kids again, I'll turn you in." I thought to myself, If he's going to shoot me, he's going to shoot me. I had no thought of trying to get out of my chair or trying to call for help or do anything like that. He just looked at me and put the gun down and walked off.

He didn't even look surprised. He looked at me the same way, putting the gun down as he did, telling me he was going to shoot my brains out. That, to me, in and of itself is frightening. There was obviously a volcano of violence underneath the surface.

Afterward, I went and worked out on weights and, as I recall, I lifted more than I'd ever lifted before. One of the thoughts I had was How dare you come and point a gun in my face? And then I thought that was rather ludicrous and I started to laugh because I thought, Well, how dare you turn yourself on your own kids? Of course, you're going to stick a gun in my face. You sexually and physically abuse your own children and who am I? I think he was angry with more than just the fact that I turned him in; he was angry with himself, with all the social service agencies that were supposed to provide help for himself and his family. And I just happened to be the closest person for him to get to.

I've been exposed to so much disaster among children and families, it's almost as though I'm not affected by anything anymore. There's nothing that could happen, there's nothing anyone could tell me, there's nothing I could see, that I haven't seen, felt, or heard.

When I think back on it now, him pointing that gun at me was insignificant compared to what I've seen happen to children. In essence, I guess I felt that kid's life was more important than my own.

An interesting aftermath to this story is that later on, the father actually requested that I be the counselor for one of his other kids!

He came in and talked to the assistant principal. At first, I was reluctant to do it. I thought, *This is all I need—to get involved with this kid and to find out the same thing's going on and knowing that I would turn him in again.* But I did it anyway. It doesn't appear that this other girl is being abused right now.

I've seen this guy on a couple of occasions since then and he's always said hello and been really nice to me. He's never threatened me again. It's obvious that this incident had a profound impact on him.

Insult for Insult

Nancy Rawles

Nancy Rawles, born in 1958, grew up in Los Angeles and currently lives in Chicago, where her favorite thing to do is ride the "el" trains on Sundays with her Supertransfer. Mostly, she writes plays.

"When I remembered my words later, it occurred to me that had this man stopped to think, for even a second, the situation would have struck him as absurd—me threatening him—and I might not be available to comment on it today."

The incident was not entirely humorous. He *did* threaten to rape me, and there was nothing even remotely funny about that. He *did* know my name, and that scared me to death. But a few days after I hung up the receiver from my first obscene phone call, a smile began to creep across my lips. And when I relayed the story to my friend, the foolish grin deteriorated into a giggle and then into a laugh. A peaceful, painful, proud laugh.

He has not called back and I hope he never will. I don't think *I* would.

I threatened him with every gruesome, awful crime I could think of—not the least of which was death. Then, I made like I was crazy. After that I made like I was cruel. Then, I tried to convince him that I wasn't the person he wanted in the first place. He ended up calling *me* sick.

"A pervert calls you and tells you you're sick!" I say to my friend, and we both chuckle.

But the day it happened, I was shaking. I cried a little and lay perfectly still for a long time, my brain waves trying to outstrip my heartbeat. My mother came over that day, but I couldn't make myself tell her what had happened. I was too afraid she would say, "Why do you give your phone number to strange people?" And I didn't think I could take that. For days after, I answered the phone *"Bueno"* or I didn't answer it at all.

Was someone writing my number on bathroom stalls? I don't give my phone number to strange people, only people I think I can trust. I felt betrayed, bewildered. Who would want to do that to me?

I have a hunch. Someone who works where I used to work and who I run into occasionally. A nice man, or so I thought. A talented man with whom I'd exchanged numbers in the hope that we could later exchange artistic ideas. A strong man, and capable, I'm sure, of all the terrible disgraces with which I was threatened. A lonely man.

He'd called me to chat the day before, and we'd had a brief, friendly conversation. "See you around" was our closing line, but to this he added a postscript. "Yeah. Until I see you, I guess I'll just have to fantasize about you." I hung up. Strange, I thought. He hardly knows me.

I was typing when the phone rang the next morning.

"Hi, Nancy. How you doing?"

"Pretty good. How are you?"

"Oh, I'm fine. What's going on?"

"Not a whole lot."

"Oh, no? That's too bad."

"Who's this?"

"You don't know who this is?"

"No. Who is it?"

"It's your lover."

I flush. No lover of mine. Can it be a friend, playing a joke?

"Come on. Who is this?"

"It's your lover. Don't you know me?"

I panic. No friend of mine.

"Your lover," he says.

"Which one?" I ask.

"The one with the seven inches."

I pause. What to do? Hang up? But it is someone who knows me, and I want to know who he is. I want to be as sure as I can be that it is who I think it is. I want to let his voice sting my ears; if I ever hear it again—on the phone, at the door, on the sidewalk behind me—I want to recognize it immediately and be prepared to escape its chilling call.

And I want him to know that he cannot do with me as he pleases, that I will fight. As I've fought before.

While living in Chicago, I had the unhappy experience of being the only woman on the elevated train. My job in the city sometimes kept me late, and the ride north to Evanston carried a few business-men, a few bums, and me. On such occasions, I'd try to look as unattractive and as unstable as possible.

Nevertheless, on one of these trips, a handsome man approached me and asked if he could sit next to me. I did not want him to sit next to me, but I was afraid to reject him so late in the day when I was feeling so weary. And who knows, perhaps he would look out for me if I should need a sudden ally. He talked and talked and I listened and said very little. Somewhere, in the course of his mon-ologue, he mentioned a destination, and I was able to determine the stop where he needed to get off. It was not anywhere near my stop, and for this I was thankful.

The doors slid open and I stepped out into a smooth, sweet night, punctuated only by the shimmering of a few dim bulbs and the scat-tering of some mice. I stole down the stairs into the silent street. Not a car, not a body in sight. Just the sound behind me of a man's stern footsteps.

My eyes darted wildly for someone to help me, somewhere to hide me. No one anywhere. I could run but, with the extra weight of my backpack, he was sure to overcome me in short order. If I dropped my pack and fled, he would still catch me soon enough, and if he stopped to retrieve my package, he would learn from its contents my name, address, and phone number.

I couldn't go home because he might follow me there. And how could I know if, once I arrived, there would be anyone around to come to my aid? Clearly, he had me. I could think of only one thing to do.

I stopped walking, turned around, and waited for him.

He approached me smiling. I met his greedy grin with the glassiest glare I could muster.

"You turn around and get right back on that train," I told him. "I know this isn't your stop, so you'd better leave me alone."

When I remembered these words later, it occurred to me that had this man stopped to think, for even a second, the situation would have struck him as absurd—me threatening him underneath the deserted train tracks—and I might not be available to comment on it today.

But he didn't stop to think. He backed away, contending that he'd only wanted to walk me home. I didn't stop glaring until he reached the top of the stairs. Then I took off.

I was so chicken I acted tough. And four years later, I want my telephone tormentor to know just whose number he's reached.

As his words become more outrageous, the insults more hostile and vulgar, my own outrage builds until I am matching him insult for insult. Each verbal blow he delivers I equal and surpass in venom. I am so angry and have been feeling so afraid lately that I sic all of my rancor on this menacing voice.

Halfway through my diatribe, I realize that my aggressiveness is having the desired effect. He is beginning to retreat.

"The police will put you in jail if you do those things," he says.

I laugh loudly. "Are you kidding? Do you think the police care about you?"

Silence. He calls me a few more names. I don't respond. Finally, he hangs up.

He hung up on *me*. That must count for something. I took the fun out of his funky phone call, and he hung up on me.

Says my friend, "You should have taken his number, so you could call him back."

Next time.

What Mama Taught Me

Kikanza Nuri Robins

Kikanza Nuri Robins lives in Southern California, where she runs her own business.

"If you are going to live and grow in this world, you will always find yourself struggling to win battles. Being black and female has caused me to struggle against racism and sexism. Being a feminist has caused me to wage battles to assert my new self in the presence of my old self's fears, prejudices, and values. For me that makes the difference between surviving a battle and winning one. When I respond to a crisis with my best self, I feel I have won the battle.

"If, however, I don't win by this standard, but I modify my behavior for a future, stronger response, then I have survived. I am proud that I fought back, and feel lucky and relieved that I survived. When I win, sometimes I'm a little surprised, but I definitely feel victorious."

Going out for a drink was a relatively new activity for me, so I gave little thought to selecting the place. Victoria and I had just finished taping a television talk show. The topic was "To Have or Have Not"; the issue was children. We made up the black and brown contingent of child-free women. Having just met on the show, we decided to talk over a drink at one of my favorite restaurants. I learned a lesson about restaurants and bars that night.

The restaurant was cozy, had good food and good service. I assumed the lounge would have the same atmosphere. Was I wrong! The bar was a "meet market"—jam-packed with people out to meet people while trying very hard to look cool and available at the same time. As we arrived, it began to rain. Since Victoria had a date later that evening and we couldn't think of another place nearby, we decided to stay.

A few moments after we had settled in our booth, one of the lounge regulars came over to greet us. Now one of the greatest problems I have in social interactions of this kind is that my mother has ingrained in me the need to be a lady at all times. Ladies are polite. They speak when they are spoken to. And they raise neither their arms nor their voices in public. On the other hand, the lesson Victoria learned from her mother is not to speak to strangers. As Victoria and I talked, the intruder extended his hand to her. She looked at him as if he were offering a social disease. When he asked her name, she replied coolly, "Lisa."

Don't know why I have to be so polite. Probably because I just assume that people are going to act right, especially in public. That was the second lesson I learned that night. Everyone who is in public doesn't know how to act. I shook the hand that was extended to me, but drew back from the kiss that was offered with the handshake.

"We just met. You don't know me well enough to kiss me," was my explanation. Third lesson: You don't owe explanations to fools.

"I was just trying to be a gentleman."

"Then be one—and leave."

"What kind of way is that to talk, sister?" Why is it, the only time I'm called "sister" is when I'm being insulted?

"It's the way I talk when I'm trying to have a private conversation."

At this point, Victoria and I decided to try the you-are-invisible strategy. Ignoring him, we plunged back into our discussion about interracial relationships.

Still standing by our table, Mr. Invisible was undaunted. "My mama lets me kiss her," he announced as he reached across us to bring the ashtray on our table closer to him.

"Well, ahm not yo momma." My tone of voice and my switch to ethnic dialect indicated that if I were standing, both hands would be on my hips. This change of tactics put the man on the defensive. He knew he had better shoot his best shot at that point, because he couldn't predict what was coming.

The dude put his finger in my face. And shook it. That was tantamount to saying, "What's wrong with you, bitch?" He opened his mouth to begin a tirade, but I jumped in.

Pounding the table with my fist, I rose as well as one can in a booth, aligned my nose with his, and screamed in my best Standard English, "Muthafucker, will you get out of my face?"

You know the commercial where everyone stops to listen to E. F. Hutton? People really do that. The bar was silenced by my outburst. Everyone turned to see who this mutha was. Moreover, the manager, three hostesses, and two bartenders were at my side before I could catch my breath.

I really didn't know I had it in me, but when pushed to the wall, I had fought back. And I had won. But I did not forget my mother's admonition to always be a lady. As the man was escorted out into the rain, I sat back in my seat, returned my attention to Victoria, and said, "Excuse me for interrupting . . . ."

In the War Zone

Linda Weltner

Linda Weltner's column "Ever So Humble" appears every Friday in the At Home section of the *Boston Globe*. She is the author of two books for young adults, and in 1985 was named Best Columnist by the New England Women's Press Association. The mother of two grown daughters, she lives in Marblehead, Massachusetts, with her husband, a psychiatrist.

The first thing I see as the subway car pulls out of the Kendall Station is the patch on the soldier's arm.

"Vietcong Hunters Club" is embroidered around the outside of the circle. Inside, framed in the cross hairs of a soldier's rifle, is the face of an Oriental in a yellow coolie's hat. The narrow black lines meet right between his eyes.

The patch is sewn onto a khaki sleeve that extends into the aisle in front of me. My eyes trace their way down to the cuff. Emerging from the sleeve is a powerful black hand.

I close my eyes.

Good Lord. This is the seventies. I thought the war was over.

I feel helpless, sick to my stomach. The racism of that damn war rides my subway on a Wednesday afternoon, floating like bacteria through the bloodstream of this country, but it is my blood that begins to pump faster with fear and anger. I wish I had the nerve to say something. I'd like to talk sense into him, but he is very big and I know better than to go looking for trouble.

We hit Harvard Square and the subway car empties. I am eager to flee, to suck fresh air into my lungs. I head down the long passage that parallels the subway tracks before veering left to the stairway up to Mass. Ave.

It is crazy to even think of accosting a stranger in a subway, but inside my head I begin a furious conversation with this man whose face I never saw. I feel a need to convince him in absentia, to quiet the agitation he has stirred up in me by putting my feelings into words.

Halfway up the stairs, I feel something brush against the back of my legs. It takes a moment to come back to reality. My first response is annoyance. Then I think to reach for my shoulder bag hanging behind my elbow, fully accessible to the person behind me. As I swing my arm to bring it forward, the man behind me on the stairs lunges forward.

One hand snakes between my legs, throwing me slightly off balance. The other hand presses one shoulder to the wall. Ahead of me, all the commuters have exited to the street. Below, the platform is silent. This is an exit. I know instantly that no new riders will be coming this way.

My eyes travel from the hand at my shoulder to the patch, now sitting with almost deliberate cruelty in front of me. I cannot look away. Those silent black-thread coolie eyes stare sightlessly into the ugliness of this deserted gray concrete hole underground.

"I want to talk to you." It is my voice, halfway between a cry and a snarl. With my free hand I grab the patch and crumple it in my fist as if mutilating it will erase it from my mind. "Why the hell are you wearing this? If you were white, would you join the Ku Klux Klan? Would you wear a patch that said 'Nigger Hunting Club'?"

I am beside myself, unconcerned for the moment about my personal safety. I barely feel his hands on me. This is not a ploy, but a release of all my pent-up anger and frustration. I feel as if his patch is a symbol of all I have been fighting against for years.

"Look, lady, I'm just back from Nam," he says, flip, with an exaggerated grin. He hesitates a moment, puzzled. He must have been expecting some particular response from me. Now he is confused, distracted from his original purpose. I can see him shifting his attention to what I've said. "Those guys were trying to kill me, you know."

"I'm not talking about war. I'm not even talking about murder."

All the rehearsed words come pouring out in a torrent. "I'm talking about treating it like some kind of sporting event. They hunted the Indians up in Gloucester like animals, tracking them through the woods and shooting them for fun. Goddammit. How can you be part of that?"

He backs away, both hands up in a gesture of surrender.

"You're not takin' it the right way," he begins. He tried to defend himself and ends up describing his plight: lost girlfriend, housing problems, his feelings of isolation. Listening, I hear another train pull into the station. I seize the opportunity to escape from this hidden curve at the bottom of the stairs.

"I can't hear you," I say, not needing to fake irritation. "Let's move out of here." I take him by the arm and lead him upstairs, keeping the conversation going until we stand together on the sidewalk at street level. People pass purposefully by. I am no longer alone with him.

"Look," I begin again. Strange as it seems, I am involved in this conversation. It feels vitally important to me that he understand the point I'm trying to make. "I'm sure it was hell over there, and the VC were trying to kill you, but if you look at some people as sub-human, you're no better than the whites who feel that way about blacks. You're degrading yourself."

"I see what you're getting at," he says. He does not seem to be mocking me now. "I do."

This time I think I really have his attention. I try to make out the expression in his eyes, but his wire-rimmed glasses with dark tinted lenses defy my efforts to read him. I have no clue to what he is thinking.

"How long have you been back from Vietnam?"

"Just a few weeks."

"You got a job?"

"Yeah, I got a job as a carpenter's assistant. Matter of fact, I start tomorrow."

"Is that something you want to do?"

He pauses. Both of us are confused about what we are really talking about. That we are talking. I don't know how to break off the conversation. Neither, it seems, does he.

"No, no, I'm glad about it. I might go back to school, but I'm not ready yet. I need time to get my shit together and this will give me the chance."

"Then I'm glad for you." I am. I reach out and touch his arm.
He looks away, then back.

"Look, I'll probably take this thing off tonight," he says from behind black lenses.

"I'm supposed to be meeting somebody," I explain, turning and heading down the street toward Lamont Library. My legs are unsteady. I remember that in the five minutes we stood in the stairwell, not one person passed us by. I am safe because I refused to think of myself as his victim. But now I can.

I ease into a sling chair in my psychiatrist's waiting room, grateful that no other patients are there. The *New Yorker* magazine that I am blindly leafing through shakes in my hand as it suddenly occurs to me that the enlisted men have been back from Vietnam for years. How much else of his story was a lie? Should I have screamed or tried to locate a policeman? I could blame myself for falling into the trap of feeling sympathy for him.

At the same time, I feel victorious. Not bad to talk myself out of a tense situation. I coped. I took charge. I could even get excited about how well I handled this. Actually, I am very proud of my quick response.

"Public transportation is no joke, but I'm still in one piece," I say, rising as my psychiatrist appears at the door to his office. "I think I'm fine."

Two weeks later. It is mid-afternoon in Cambridge, sunny and warm. The elevator in my psychiatrist's office building has a bright orange door. There's a dark glass wall beside it where you can watch your reflection, posing and grimacing while the elevator drops down to ground floor.

When the door slides open, a well-dressed black man in his fifties looks out, as surprised to be in the lobby as I am to find someone in the usually empty machine.

Warnings flash through my mind. They are reflected on my face and in my hesitation. The woman in the mirror does not move. Shall I be polite and lock myself in with a stranger? Or shall I protect myself, be cautious if not rude, and decline to enter?

I am caught in uncertainty. He takes the initiative.

"Going down?" he asks.

"No, up." With relief.

It is a solution which does violence to neither of us. I can wait. I can catch the elevator when it returns from his destination. But racism defies rational solution. He is already leaving the elevator with an accommodating nod.

"I'll walk it, then," he says, deferring to my right to take the elevator without waiting, legitimizing the fact that I am afraid to enter an elevator in which he is riding. I feel reassured. Now it all seems so hurtful and unnecessary. As I watch his back disappear through the stairwell door, I wish there were some way I could apologize.

Brooding, I push the button for the fifth floor. As the elevator responds by heading down, I pull back from the doors, huddling against a back corner. I am wary, but I have no plan. I anticipate that he will be waiting for me in the basement. In my head, there is only the cynical conviction that his deference, the act that gained my sympathy, has been the cover for some sinister plot.

The doors open into a hallway, gray and chilly and empty. The elevator has merely been responding to his original directive, I realize, as the doors close and the metal container quietly whirs its way up.

Singing in the Rain

Irene van der Zande

Irene's story describes an experience she had in 1971, when she was a VISTA volunteer living on the Omaha Indian reservation. She has been involved in the development and funding of community service programs ever since. Recently, she became a board member of a nonprofit agency set up to support the self-defense organization Model Mugging.

After VISTA, Irene hitchhiked through several Western European countries. On the way, she met a Dutchman whose last name means "from the sand." They now have an eight-year-old daughter and a five-year-old son.

One of the nice things about singing in the pouring rain is that nobody can hear you. Especially if you have a voice like mine. So I sang loudly, without a care in the world, and washed about a week's worth of dishes. The rain beat a deafening accompaniment on the metal roof of my trailer. The warm, sudsy water splashed all over the place. And the clean dishes piled up.

I don't know how long it took for me to notice that someone was pounding on the door of my trailer. Hands still wet, I looked out the window. A man stood by the steps that led up to the door. His black hair was soaked. Water ran in streams down his face. Behind him, the trailers and shacks of the Omaha Indian reservation looked like they were drowning in a sea of mud.

He stared at me through the window and said, "Let me in."

I thought about how alone I was. My roommate was away for the weekend. All the people in the trailer compound had gone to a powwow. "I'm busy," I said, raising my voice so that he could hear me.

He looked at me pleadingly as the rain beat down on him. "I need help," he shouted. "You're a VISTA volunteer. You're supposed to help people."

Well, I thought, if I'm not here when people need help, then I have no business being here at all. I opened the door.

He came in quickly and slammed the door shut. "Give me your smack!" he said. "I've got to have it."

"What are you talking about? There are no drugs here!" I couldn't take my eyes off his hands, resting on the knives I had laid out to dry on the kitchen table.

He towered above me in my tiny trailer.

"You're a hippie, aren't you? All hippies do dope."

"Really, you've made a mistake." I tried to sound calm, bottling up an enormous desire to scream. I told myself there was no one to hear, and if I acted like he'd hurt me, he was sure to hurt me. Some piece of my mind thought abstractly about how mad my parents would be after all the times they'd warned me never, never, never to let a strange man into my home. I hoped I wasn't about to find out that being carved into little pieces was just as awful as they'd always said.

The man glared at me. The pupils of his eyes contracted into tiny slits. "I'm not kidding. You've got to get your stuff and get it now!"

"Look," I said firmly, "there are no drugs here."

His fingers started to tighten around one of the knives. From somewhere I conjured up a warm smile and a cheerful voice. "But I do have tea. You look cold and wet and you said you were in trouble. Why don't you sit down. I'll make you a cup of tea and you can tell me about it."

"You have some, too," he said. When he sat, he was still taller than I was standing up. I made hot water and started to clear the table.

"What are you doing!" he snapped, grabbing the knife again.

"We need room for our teacups," I pointed out. I tried to pretend this was just a young man who wanted to talk to me, and to ignore the knife. "So," I asked, trying to sound sympathetic instead of scared, "what happened?"

He gulped his tea, burning his mouth a little. His eyes filled with tears. "I was going to be a writer," he said. "My high school teacher said I had real promise."

Suddenly my sympathy was real. "I like to write, too."

"Really?" he said, and seemed to see me clearly for the first time. Then his eyes clouded over. He rested his hand on the knife and asked, "Where's the bedroom in this place?"

"Have another cup of tea," I said quickly. "And tell me what you like to write about."

"You drink, too," he said.

"I'm kind of full." My bladder was bursting, but no way was I going down the hall to the bathroom. The bathroom was right by the bedroom.

"You must drink with me!" He was upset. I remembered that the Omaha Indians that I knew didn't like to drink or eat alone.

"All right." I poured us both a cup of tea. "Now tell me what happened."

"I got sent to Vietnam." He sighed.

He talked and drank tea for three hours. I had to drink with him, cup after cup. He'd relax and talk for a while. Then his eyes would change and he would grab the knife. I'd ask another question. And he'd talk again. Once he thought I was his sergeant, and stood waving the knife and yelling at me. "I'll get you now!" he shouted. "You fucker!"

I stood and shouted back, "I'm not him! It's over! It was awful, but it's over!" He shook his head, his eyes cleared, and he came back from Vietnam.

"You have quite a story to tell," I said. "Why don't you write about it?"

We had another cup of tea and we talked some more.

The afternoon was almost over. I was worn out. My bladder ached. But I kept him talking, my mind working hard to think of the next question. Then the telephone rang. "They'll be worried if I don't answer," I told him, and picked up the telephone.

It was the VISTA volunteer in the next town. "Ann, you're late for our meeting," I said.

She knew there was no meeting. "Are you in some kind of trouble?" she asked.

"Yes," I said.

"Is someone there?"

"Yes."

"I'm on my way."

I smiled at the man. "It's been interesting talking with you, but we'll have to finish up soon. A bunch of people are on their way over for a meeting."

When Ann drove up, he left. The rain had stopped. "I hope you'll start writing again," I told him.

"Maybe," he said. He sloshed off through the mud. I never saw him again.

Years later, I told my self-defense class this story.

"Who knows?" said one of the teachers. "You might have changed this guy's whole life by making him talk instead of letting him attack you."

I kind of doubt it. I do hope so.

But it was too many years before I sang in the rain like that again.

Part III

Intuition and Willpower

Introduction

Women's intuition—it is joked about, trusted in, scoffed at. Men are supposed to be logical, rational, straightforward, and linear, while women are said to operate through their emotions and vague hunches. The stories in this chapter show what a practical tool intuition—fueled by willpower—can be for a woman under attack.

Intuition is not a mysterious power unrelated to everyday reality. In fact, it is just the opposite: intuition has its roots in what is happening from minute to minute. It is pure *awareness,* when the senses are finely tuned to every sound and sight and movement. A woman who is using, who is *listening to,* her intuition is like an animal in the forest, mindful of its surroundings, and ready to act when the time is right.

It is this combination of awareness—intuition—and the ability to act at just the right moment—willpower—that is at the heart of any successful self-defense effort. No matter what strategies a woman tries when she fights back, she can't really do without these fundamental resources. What is exciting is that we *all* possess these tools. Although they can be sharpened and exercised through self-defense or other kinds of training, they are available to us at any time. Intuition and willpower are what literally keep us alive from day to day. They allow us to understand and to act intelligently in every area of life.

But it isn't always easy to listen to the voice of intuition. We often talk ourselves out of our perceptions when we have no solid proof that they are real. In American society, "making a scene" is a social offense, so many of us want to be absolutely sure something is really going on before we act. But we are often reluctant to verify our feelings about a scary situation. Have you ever walked down the street, aware that someone is walking behind you, yet not turned to face the person because then it would be obvious that you were concerned? Yet, in many instances, simply turning and directly facing a potential attacker is enough to deter him. By literally standing your ground and looking someone straight in the eye, you are saying, "I am here. I have a right to this piece of sidewalk. I know you are following me. Stay away."

Intuition and willpower sometimes come into play without a woman's conscious awareness. A woman will sometimes literally "find herself" acting in self-protective ways, without consciously knowing what she's doing. In "Southern Intuition," Denise Caignon finds herself acting a role she hadn't planned as she tries to outwit her taxi driver. It is as if some wise, instinctual part of her, deeper than her conscious mind, has taken over the controls.

Although we didn't plan it that way, this section contains a number of stories about attacks in automobiles. Many of us think of our cars as extensions of ourselves, like little secondary homes on wheels. When a woman is attacked in her own car, it may be easier for her to summon her will and sense of outrage, since there is no question that her personal space is being violated. Any car is a small, enclosed space. A woman under attack in a car is likely to feel cornered, and that sense of being trapped seems to bring out an intuitive, highly focused escape strategy.

An intuitive response is also a flexible one, since (like everything in life) an attack/defense situation can shift course from moment to moment. The attacker may change strategies any number of times. To fight back, a woman must be adaptable enough to change her own tactics as many times as it takes to get away.

The way some of these stories were remembered and written is the most obvious testament to the power of awareness. Subtle shifts in the attacker's behavior, a sudden opening, an escape route—all the details of the situation are taken into account. Jane Polansky, in "A Woman of Common Sense and Courage," remembers the dice tattooed on her attacker's arm—down to the number of dots on each die. Some women carry on a running internal dialogue that helps them determine when to act. "Uh-oh, what's happening now? He let go of my arm, so now I can move away." These internal conversations often take place in split seconds.

Intuition often points the way to an opening. When Pat Deer ("I Let Him Have It Right in the Eyes") is accosted by a stranger on the beach, she removes his glasses "without any conscious plan." When he demands them back, she hands them to him, and seeing that his hands are both engaged, decides it is now her "move," and she makes it. Kathleen Zundell in "The Lesson of Three Billy Goats Gruff" recognizes an "instinct for self-preservation—a feeling centered around my navel" that enables her to escape two assailants.

Sheer willpower can see a woman through a situation even when she is up against incredible odds. In "The Spirit Fights Back," Hallie Iglehart is faced with an armed attacker who says he will kill her if she moves. Instead of fear, what she feels is fury and defiance—a raw will to get away. Jerilyn Munyon ("The Will to Survive") is moved by a "strength beyond the physical"—the same legendary strength mothers have used to pull impossibly heavy objects off their children.

There is a natural sense of outrage that arises when we are attacked. This sense of outrage is something a woman can use to fuel her defense of herself, to bring her will to the surface. The feeling of being violated sometimes expresses itself as a sudden, explosive response that may surprise the attacker. Surprise is one of the most effective self-defense techniques. When a woman suddenly screams, as Kitty Geneva does in "Fighting Back in the Park," "I hate you! Get away from me!" or pulls away at the right moment, the attacker may be so dumbfounded that he simply turns and walks (or runs) away.

It is our hope that the next time you "just have the feeling" or "get a hunch out of nowhere," you pay close attention. Those hunches and feelings—and how you act on them—are some of the best self-defense tools you have.

A Woman of Common Sense and Courage

Jane Polansky

Jane Polansky (a pseudonym), now thirty-one, was born in the suburbs of
New York, and moved to Philadelphia in 1981. Unmarried at the time of
the attack, she is now married to the man she was living with then. She is
a banker, and has a baby son.

*"I always thought things like this didn't happen to people like me—young,
strong, well-educated, and dressed in 'preppy' clothes, on a beautiful clear
afternoon, on a street corner with people nearby who were willing to get
involved. After my attack, when I talked about it with my women friends, I
found that the national statistics were borne out in my small sampling of
friends. Out of fifteen women, six had been attacked, one more than once.*
"This all must end."

My story begins late in the afternoon on the Fourth of July, 1982.
My fiancé and I were going to his parents' house. While he waited
for me in front of our apartment building, I went to get my car.

The car was parked around the corner from our home, on a street
that had very little foot or auto traffic. Across the street was a small
playground, which on that day was filled with children.

As I approached the car, I remember being in a very happy and
satisfied mood. I stopped on the way to play with a little dog that

was tied up across the street from the car. As I got up to cross the street, I was hailed by a man standing at the corner. He asked for directions to a location that was quite far away. I was a little uncertain about how to get there, but after some thought, I gave him the correct directions. The directions I gave him required him to pass by my car, so I didn't really think about it when he came closer.

He seemed very confused and uncertain. I remember feeling threatened by the fact that he didn't seem to be "all there." I dismissed the feeling of unease I had, since I knew that my fiancé was waiting for me and that there were a lot of people at the playground. Besides, it was 5:30 on a beautiful, clear, hot holiday, and these things just didn't happen to affluent young women like myself. I was strong, capable, and in charge, and I wasn't about to let this worry me.

Also (and this is to my shame, since it is racist), the questioner was white, and I therefore feared him less for it. My neighborhood is "borderline," meaning that there is a large, poor black population living one block away; middle-class blacks and whites have moved into the area and are "gentrifying" the neighborhood. If my attacker had been black, I believe I might have been more suspicious. But this is all hindsight, and only serves to show why I was willing to explain away my uneasy feelings.

I unlocked and opened the door to my car. What happened next is a bit unclear, but I think I got into the car and was closing the door when it was wrenched open and this guy got in and pushed me across to the other seat. That sounds simple, but it wasn't. In the first place, the car had bucket seats, with a gear shift and an emergency brake between them. Also, I was screaming and kicking and fighting. I actually left some large dents in the door of our car, which helped me to realize later that it all hadn't been a bad dream.

A neighbor heard me scream the first time, and came out on his second-story sundeck to see what was happening. He remained there for the duration of the attack, trying to figure out what was happening. By the time he came out, however, my attacker and I were already inside the car, parked directly below this neighbor's deck, so that he couldn't see us. Also, the car windows were shut, so he couldn't hear me screaming again.

So there I was. My attacker told me to shut up or he'd "really hurt me." I found myself sitting on the passenger side of the car, with my legs across his lap. He was sitting in the driver's seat, pinning my legs with his arms. I said okay, I wouldn't scream if he wouldn't hurt me. I looked for a weapon, but I didn't see one, so I knew that the worst he could do was punch me around. He was, however, much bigger than I, and I knew that I could get hurt.

I told him that I was very frightened, that nothing like this had ever happened to me before. He said, "Oh, come on, you've been fucked before," and I said, "Only by my husband." I was really stalling for time, and trying to figure out what to do. I knew I couldn't outbrute the guy, so I thought I would have to outwit him. I also knew that my fiancé would eventually miss me and come to see what happened to me. So I felt that I needed to get as much control of the situation as possible.

He turned the key in the ignition, but my faithful old car refused to turn over. Then he told me to put my seat back, but I knew if I did, I would lose any physical advantage I had. So I pointed out that the car was quite old, as witnessed by its failure to start, and that my seat was broken and wouldn't go back. I told him, however, that his did go back, thereby giving *me* the physical advantage. He put his seat back, but kept his hold on my legs.

I pointed out how hot it was inside the car and tried to open my window, figuring I could then scream and be heard. He threatened me then, so I didn't do that. He then bent over me and proceeded to pull down my top and fondle and suck on my breasts. I said to him that the children could see and that it would be bad for them. He told me to shut up; it would only be a few minutes.

I asked his name, figuring that I would need it later for the prosecution (because I was damned if he was going to get away with this), and he murmured "Bill." I noticed then that he had two tattoos on his left arm: one said "Mike and Lisa" and the other showed a pair of dice. So I knew that his real name was Mike, and that those tattoos were something he couldn't alter. I engraved them on my mind so deeply that I recalled on the witness stand how many dots were showing and which die they were on.

At this point he began to undo my pants. I thought, oh God, this can't be happening, I can't let this happen to me. I realized that my only way out was to get my legs away from him. I couldn't let this happen. So I told him this would be a lot easier if he let me help.

He let me swing my legs around but kept a firm grip on my arm. I showed him how I could take off the right sandal, to make it easier to remove my pants, but that I couldn't get to my left sandal, because he held my arm. He let go for a minute and watched me remove my right sandal. And then suddenly, as my hands went toward my waist to pull the pants off, he lay back in the driver's seat. I don't remember seeing him do that, but I knew he was away from me. The next part happened very quickly.

I realized that if I were to make a move, now was the time. I sprang for the door, which was locked. Somehow, although that lock was normally a little difficult, in one motion I got that door unlocked and open, and I hit the ground running.

Oddly enough, considering the relatively clear thinking I was doing in the car, I did a stupid thing. I ran *away* from the crowded playground and down the deserted street. I think it was because I expected my fiancé to be coming from that direction. Anyway, I ran. To all of you who ever wondered how you could run in a threatening situation, without the proper footwear, as I had often wondered, I'll tell you—it's a cinch. I ran barefoot about forty feet and never noticed that my feet were barefoot and cut and bleeding slightly until much later when it was pointed out to me. As I ran, I screamed for help, not the popular "fire" that we are taught, and immediately people came to my aid. The attacker jumped out of the driver's side and ran in the other direction, watched by my neighbor on the balcony.

I didn't see him go, except peripherally. A woman ran out of her house and asked me what happened. I said I was attacked, and she asked if I wanted her to call the police. I said yes, and she sent her husband in to call while she came to me. Meanwhile, the playground children came over, and some of them even pursued my attacker!

I sat on the sidewalk, with my pants open, my feet bleeding, and tried to control my onrushing tears, because I didn't want to scare the children. I kept telling one little girl, who stood by me and stroked my hair, that I was all right, all right.

It turned out that my attacker had dropped his wallet in my car, making it very easy to find him. He was brought to trial, after the usual runaround, and convicted of three counts, including attempted rape. It turned out that he was on parole for burglary, and was in a rehabilitation group for addicts.

At the trial, the prosecutor, who was "my" attorney, called me a woman of common sense and courage. I have derived a lot of comfort from those words over the last two years. They, and therapy, and the love of my husband and family and friends, have helped make the memory of this incident somewhat tolerable.

Yet my life has been changed in ways I would never have thought possible, including problems with sex, walking alone, trying to decide if the clothes I wear will stand up in court if I'm attacked again and have to testify to my good faith. And yet I know that women can resist, not be raped, and live. That means a lot to me.

In September of 1985 my attacker (convicted of attempted rape in May 1983) won his appeal on a technicality. The case came to trial again in January 1986, when I was four months pregnant. The old strategy was that I was a prostitute, or he thought I was, and that he ran away when I screamed. The new strategy was consent—that the guy had thought I agreed to sex and that he ran away as soon as I screamed. Bullshit!

The cross-examination was brutal, with no gentleness because of my evident condition. But we won anyway, with a super assistant District Attorney named Amanda Kaufman, part of Philadelphia's Rape Unit. He was convicted in a jury trial on all counts. The attacker was sentenced to 5–10 years, mandatory sentence with no chance of parole. Let's hear it for fighting back—both on the street and in the court!

The Will to Survive

Jerilyn Munyon

Jerilyn Munyon, born in 1947, lives in the Santa Cruz mountains with her teenage son, three cats, and a dog. She owns a small business, teaches Model Mugging, a women's self-defense and empowerment course, and has practiced aikido, a Japanese nonviolent martial art, for the past seven years. She has a second-degree black belt.

"As a survivor of childhood sexual abuse and two attacks on the street as an adult, I have spent a lot of time thinking about what it is to be a victim and how I can learn not to be one. As I move from victim to survivor to peaceful warrior, I want to share my experiences and participate in the empowerment of women."

Twelve years later: I am walking around my therapist's room. She is following me very close. She keeps getting closer and closer. I am getting very uptight. She comes even closer. Suddenly, I fall to the floor and scream in terror. Terror is coming out of every pore of my body, every muscle, my entire being. I scream for forty-five minutes.

Later, she takes my hand and says, "What happened?"

"I was attacked by a man with a knife when I was eighteen," I answer. "I got away."

"Do you know how courageous you are? You are a survivor."

I was coming back from the store around 9:00 P.M. As I turned the corner of my street, a car behind me bumped lightly into the back of my car. I was only a block from my house, so I continued until I reached the parking lot in front. As soon as I stopped, a man came over to my car and knocked on the window. I rolled it down and asked what he wanted. It was so dark that I couldn't see him. He said he was sorry for running into me and that he wanted to give me the name of his insurance company. I got out of the car as he stayed out of view behind me. As I walked around the back of my car to see what had happened, he grabbed me from behind and stuck a knife in my side. His gloved hand was across my mouth so I couldn't scream.

"If you try to get away, I'll kill you," he said. "I have a knife in your side."

He started to drag me to his car. At first, I was frozen with fear. I couldn't believe this was happening to me. But then I realized that if I submitted to him, I would be raped and possibly murdered. At that moment, I made the decision that I would rather be murdered while trying to get away than to find out what awaited me once in that car.

My will to live filled me with an incredible energy. It was a kind of strength that was beyond the physical. Effortlessly, I pulled away from my attacker and ran to my house screaming. He must have been very shocked. Later, the police didn't believe me. "How do you know it was a knife?" they asked. My parents felt my pain and their own helplessness.

For six months, I woke up every night screaming. I couldn't drive my car. I couldn't be alone. I realized I was becoming paralyzed just as I had when my attacker first grabbed me. I told myself that if I didn't force myself to overcome my fear, I would be paralyzed for the rest of my life. Slowly, I made myself get into my car and drive alone—only in the day at first, and then, later, at night. I began to stay alone for short periods and then longer ones. There was never a time when I drove in my car alone at night for the next twelve years that I did not look into my rearview mirror and remember that terrible night.

Many years, and many more therapy sessions, have led me back to the whole person I was before I was attacked. It has taken me twenty years to travel from victim to survivor.

It is important to bring the issue of self-defense inside myself, to look for understanding. What is my role in the cycle of violence?

How do I step out of the victim role without moving into the role of aggressor? How can I actively define my boundaries both spiritually and physically without having to use ''power over'' others? How do I carry the ''victim within'' into the rest of my life and how do I change that concept for myself?

I don't think that nonviolence comes by separating ourselves from or denying violence. It comes through understanding how we all participate in the cycle of violence. With self-defense, we have an extraordinary opportunity to create a whole new language for women, a language that benefits all people. We take responsibility for protecting ourselves and take ourselves out of the victim role. When we say NO to an attack we are really saying YES to ourselves and our right to live in safety. We can define power as integrity, equality, self-knowledge, inner strength—not domination, aggression, or escalation. My dream is to someday live in a world where there are no victims, to speak a language in which violence does not exist.

The Lesson of Three Billy Goats Gruff

Kathleen Zundell

Kathleen Zundell is a storyteller who specializes in Chumash Indian tales, children's stories, and stories of heroines and strong women. She does workshops for women entitled "In Search of the Wise Women," "Finding the Goddess Within," and "The Real Cinderella Story" and has co-organized several Women's Storytelling Festivals in Los Angeles. One of her favorite stories is "Little Golden Hood," a seldom-told version of "Little Red Riding Hood," wherein the grandmother, who is a wise woman, protects and rescues her granddaughter.

"Stories work deeply on the unconscious mind; they prepare us for life, for difficult situations. It's essential to our growth and healing as women to read and hear stories about women who are active and heroic. We are constantly bombarded by images and stories of women as helpless victims. I want to hear the old stories about the wise women and the goddesses and I want to read new stories about other strong women who have won."

As a professional storyteller, I have told the story of "The Three Billy Goats Gruff" many times. Although my child audiences have always responded with enthusiasm, I've secretly worried about the true meaning of the story. The little Billy Goat Gruff and the middle-sized Billy Goat Gruff, when confronted by the Troll who wants to eat them, say, "Please don't eat me . . . you don't want me, I'm too small. . . . Eat my brother instead.'' Isn't that betrayal? And when the big Billy Goat Gruff butts the Troll off the bridge, isn't that too violent for young children?

Psychologist Bruno Bettelheim, in his book *The Uses of Enchantment,* helped quell my worries. He says that a young child, when confronted by a big bully, should not try to take on the bully directly, but should get out of the situation by some more subtle means, just like the two smaller Billy Goats Gruff. He believes that children will model themselves after the Billy Goats and that they understand that the evil Troll will get the punishment he deserves.

Late one night, I sat in my car with a male friend. Since I was dropping him off at his car, the engine was still running. Suddenly, a strange man swung my car door open, indicated that he had a gun, and ordered us out of the car. Frozen, I got out and wondered how I'd gotten myself into this situation. My stomach twisted and my brain scrambled to find a rational reason for what was happening. I prayed fast. The car engine was still running and I expected the man to jump in and drive off in my 1966 Mustang, but he backed us into the darkness of the street. I sensed that my friend, an ex-Marine, was in a state of shock and could not be counted on for any kind of action.

Another man appeared and mumbled something about taking me into the alley. Suddenly, my instinct for self-preservation—a feeling centered around my navel—said, ''Get out of here fast. These men mean to do you harm. They won't touch your friend; they're after you.''

As this realization flashed before me, I found myself handing my purse to the attackers, saying, ''Here, take this.'' Then I ran to my car, jumped inside, and stepped on the gas.

The surprised attackers jumped on top of the car to try to stop me, but my determination was too strong . . . and my car fast. I drove around the block with a racing heart and gathered my sense of self. Driving back to see if my friend needed help, I saw that the two attackers had left and my friend was okay. He was just stunned and confused, but glad I had gotten away.

I think of the notion that had been ingrained in me, that a man would protect me in case of attack. But I learned that the only person I can depend on is me. My clever thinking and quick action saved me. I rescued myself. I said, ''You don't want me . . . take my purse instead.'' By doing that, I had found a means of escape—just like those three Billy Goats Gruff.

Fighting Back in the Park

Kitty Geneva

Kitty Geneva (a pseudonym) was born and raised in northern California. She is a junior high school bilingual teacher who has been active in nonviolent social-change organizations for several years.

"There's no guarantee that any particular self-defense technique will work. It may be better to defuse the situation, to put it on a different plane, than to retaliate with violence. There are many very active self-defense techniques, which are still nonviolent, and don't involve hurting someone else and escalating the situation."

It never occurred to me to go along with it. It never occurred to me to submit. What went through my mind were all those conversations about nonviolent resistance, about what-would-you-do-if-attacked, and all the unsure answers I'd rattled off.

I was eighteen, and it was the summer of 1968. The day I was attacked, I was walking alone in San Francisco's Golden Gate Park. The young man was one I had passed earlier as he walked with some others. He came up behind me on the path near the museums, grabbed my arm, and said something about where was I staying and c'mon baby we don't have much time, as he tried to pull me into the rhododendrons. A strange mixture of force and attempted seduction, which made it hard to believe his intent. I think he wasn't sure what he was about, either.

"Talk, talk him out of it," I remembered. Treat him as if he had some sense. Unfortunately, I hadn't had any real training or discussion about the kinds of things one could say. What I said was "No" and "Leave me alone" and "Why are you doing this?" I told him, "This isn't right. Go away. Don't be silly." Now I think that "silly" was an insult and not so wise to say. He became angry and really pulled on my arm. No one had ever grabbed me like that in my life. I had had no real experience with force of that kind, and I was not strong. I kept trying to pull away. I struggled. I realized how frightened I was, how my heart was pounding and I wanted to pee. For some reason I didn't think of yelling. I tried to trip him but that didn't work either.

Then he grasped my neck tightly with both hands and dragged me into the bushes. He was strangling me. Time slowed. I could not get my hands to pry off his hands. My balance was lost. I think I was starting to black out. I could feel my eyes getting bulgy. Odd—I had lost fear, and only felt great sorrow, seeing an image of myself probably dead under green leaves and sad people standing around me. I could hear my voice making a gurgling, rattling noise, and I wonder still whether I was at the point of death or whether my body was finally remembering how to yell.

The man suddenly threw me down and started to kick me. He could have killed me, I think, but he didn't. Apparently, too, he had given up on the idea of rape, which had been his original intention. Again I remembered conversations with peace activists, talking about how people protect themselves when attacked by police in demonstrations. This was well before nonviolent trainings were as common as they are now. I remembered to protect my head and face, to curl up and keep my back away from those hurtful feet. I began to take deep breaths and to scream and yell. It was difficult to protect my body—he kept moving around me so fast, kicking me hard. I tried to get up, to run, but he knocked me down.

I began to realize that I was being somewhat successful at shielding myself. Somehow I began to feel familiar with what was going on, not so panicked. And I was damn tired of it. It was a bad nightmare that had gone on long enough. Suddenly, I was really mad at this guy. He was down at my feet and I felt a great surge of anger and glared at him, at his face, and tried to kick him back—unsuccessfully, since I'd misjudged the distance and was in an awkward position there on my back—and screeched at him, "Leave me alone! I hate you!'' He looked at me strangely and then turned and ran off through the shrubbery. That was the last I saw of him.

I got up and ran, which was hard because I was shaking so. I stumbled up over a little hill and there were some park police, one with a horse. I wondered if they'd heard me yelling. Weeks later, I went through a time of thinking they had and was very upset that they hadn't come to help me. They looked at me as if they were just waking up, as I told them that I'd been beat up and yes I was more or less okay and would one of them please come back with me so I could get my glasses, because I was afraid to go alone, and my glasses had been knocked off me. Right then, it was very important to me to go get my glasses, not only so I could see better, but as a step back to normalcy. You get kicked in the head, the guy leaves, you pick up your scattered belongings and go on with your life. The policeman on the horse wanted to call a car, ask questions. I wanted my glasses. They said I needed first aid, I was cut. I wanted my glasses! The young policeman came with me and we found my glasses. The earth was scuffed up where I had struggled.

We went to the basement of the California Academy of Sciences and I washed up. The young policeman was shaken; he was sympathetic. His eyes were brown and gentle and sad. His hands shook as he picked sticks and leaves out of my hair. He kept asking, ''Did he touch you?,'' which I took to mean ''Did he rape you?,'' since it was obvious that I had been touched. This phraseology made me laugh inside. Calming this policeman down helped me to calm down. I told him no, the man didn't rape me, he beat me up.

Then there were questions by other police, and I related the events. They didn't think much of what I'd said when trying to talk the man out of hassling me, and I felt foolish and embarrassed. One of them took me in a patrol car—in the backseat, no handles inside, I felt trapped, hard to breathe in there—around to where a plainclothes cop was casually talking to a suspect. Too tall, wrong shirt.

There was an increasing conflict in me about what to do. I wanted to do something about it, but none of the options seemed right. Supposing the man was found and I was sure it was him, what good would come of sending him to jail? It would be more ill treatment and more cause for anger and would not prevent him from attacking more people when he got out. I tried to explain this to the police. The young one said, ''Yes, you're right, but at least we should try to get him off the streets for a while.'' I was in a quandary. There were no groups then to help, no women's crisis counselors, no community groups to help me seek and confront him personally. So the rest of my day and month and year were spent in this muddle.

They took me to the emergency station at the end of the park near the Haight. The doctor was distant, cleaned my cut nose, told me I'd have a black eye, dug the broken ring out of my little finger and wrapped up the swollen, cut place, looked at the hand-shaped bruises on my neck, adjusted my glasses and sent me on my way. He seemed to think it pretty dumb of me to walk in the park alone. I resented that. I had liked walking there alone in that refuge from smog and noise. Now that was spoiled and I resented that, too, still resent it.

The police took me to the place where I was visiting and left me there. Then I cried a lot. I couldn't stop crying for a while. My lover told me that every woman in that house had been attacked during that summer. His friends were all very gentle and supportive and quiet that evening.

A few weeks later, the San Francisco Police Department called; they had a suspect and wanted me to see the lineup.

I went with a woman friend to the lineup. While we waited, I heard some police belittling things that were important to me—the peace movement, counterculture, alternative communities. It confirmed my feeling that while I didn't know the "right" thing to do about the man who'd attacked me, turning him over to these prejudiced, hard-nosed cops was not it. It just wouldn't help anyone. I was spared having to really decide because the suspect in the lineup, while resembling the attacker enough to give me a start and turn me pale, was too tall and thick and somehow not quite right.

I have been dealing with the memory for a long time. My body remembers. It was two or three years before I stopped feeling afraid. It was eleven years before I could stand to have anyone touch me along the front of my neck. My voice still rises when I speak of what happened. I am very watchful when I walk alone at night or in uneasy places, and find myself radiating a jagged energy akin to flight and ferocity.

I had never thought of this as a successful resistance. I was beaten up. It hurt and I was afraid. But now I think of how I wasn't raped. I wasn't killed. I didn't give up. Even so, it's still hard to feel this as a success story. Only now and then does the feeling come, in brief moments. A strong feeling.

I Just Got Mad

Rosetta Smith

The Success Story Project first heard of Mrs. Smith through a newspaper
wire story about an amazing sixty-nine-year-old woman in Louisville, Kentucky, a double amputee who defended herself successfully. Although her
attacker was in his twenties, and took off her two artificial legs, she fought
him off, leaving him naked and unconscious on the floor of her home.

As told to the editors in an interview: I was sitting in my bedroom
watching the TV, and somebody came in my door—I had left the
side door open because it was a very hot night. Every time I hollered
he put his hands over my mouth, and then he started choking on me,
and I said, "Lord, please don't let anybody come in here and kill
me for no reason." I said, "Why are you coming in here and bothering me anyway, sitting here in my own home, I'm not bothering
nobody." He come in here taking off his clothes, when he came after
me. Come in here trying to make me get my dress off and I said,
"I'm not taking nothing off!" And I did not take it off, but he just
took my legs off and I just couldn't help it. He called me all kinds
of dirty names and told me to shut up.

I had my hair all rolled up, in curlers, and he pulled every curler
out and throwed them on the floor. He just took my head and just
pushed it up and down on the floor, and it was just like somebody
had poured a bucket of water on me.

Then he jumped up and he was running into the bathroom and I got behind the door, and he said, "Get me some money, I need some money," and then I just got mad, and I said, "I ain't got no money, I need money, too. We all need money." So he checked my drawers, he checked everything, but he didn't find no money, he didn't find nary a penny. I had just came from the doctor's and I had my purse sitting by the bed and I hadn't put my change away. I happened to have fifty dollars in there, and I took that and eased it up under the bed before he could see it, because if he had seen it, he would've took it.

But he didn't see that, he was just looking through the drawers; I didn't have no money in the drawers. Then he went in the bedroom, and he come back and jumped on me again. When he jumped on me again, I just grabbed him by his privates, and told him to leave me alone, and then he vomited all over my place and fell asleep on top of me.

I prayed, I asked the Lord, I said, "Lord, I got the faith but I just ain't got the strength." And the minute I said that, the good Lord put the strength in my hand. Then I wasn't scared no more.

So I made my way from under him—I couldn't walk because he had taken my legs off—I crawled to my telephone and then I called the police, my Sunday-school teacher and her husband, and they all came.

I was so scared he was going to get up and go away before the policemen got here, but just as he woke up, the policeman came in and put handcuffs on his hands.

I think that guy who attacked me saw me at church on Sunday and noticed I didn't have no legs on and so at night he decided to come in here after me.

They haven't tried him yet. He pretended like he is crazy, but they finally got him locked up, and told me he would never hit the ground again, and the polices all told me not to worry about it. I told them, he not crazy, he wasn't crazy when he came in here after me. He's just playing that just to get out of here. That's all. But they said they weren't going to let him out. His family is scared of him too because they wanted to lock him up a long time ago. He's only twenty-two years old.

I think I can handle it, if he comes back after me, but I hope he don't come back no more 'cause I ain't never had something like this happen to me before, I really haven't.

I've told my pastor about it and he says I was a very strong woman.

He said he'd never heard talk of such. So I just prayed, and the good Lord give me strength to take care of myself, he wouldn't let him mess with me no way.

That's the first time it ever happened to me. I hope it'll be the last time.

Hitchhiking in the Forties

Marjorie French

At the time of this incident, Marjorie French (a pseudonym) was a labor union organizer and civil rights activist in the South.

"As a child, I was warned that you had to be on guard all the time and that's what men wanted, period. My mother was horrified at the thought that I would hitchhike. My argument used to be that if you were going to get raped, it could happen anywhere and hitching was no more dangerous than anywhere else.

"Women have a lot of weapons they don't think they have, and if they struggle, it's going to make it a lot less worthwhile for the attacker."

As told to the editors in an interview: This all happened in 1942, during the Second World War. I was hitchhiking to Missouri to visit my family. My father was in the army and my husband was in the navy. I had been a hitchhiker for a long time. I used to love to hitchhike because it gave me a sense of freedom, being out on the open road, and it was a kick. I didn't ever feel it was particularly dangerous.

Back then, a lot of people hitched because they couldn't afford other transportation, although it wasn't that common for a woman to hitch alone. In the forties, though, with all the women in the service, it wasn't quite as unusual for a woman to hitchhike alone. People would often make the assumption that if you were hitchhiking, you might be interested in sex, but if you said no, they'd leave you alone. If a guy put his hand on my leg, I just took it off and said, "Look, I'll get out of the car now." Ninety-nine percent of the time that was fine. But I'm not sure that I would give my daughter that kind of advice. Overall, I had very little trouble, and I liked the fact that you would see people once, they'd tell you their life history, and then you'd never see them again.

I was in my early twenties, finding out about life in a way you couldn't otherwise. I really loved it. It used to drive my family crazy, so I usually didn't even tell them. I often started out with bus tickets and I would just jump off the bus and start hitchhiking because I loved to do it.

So I was somewhere in Missouri, headed for Myosha, where there was a big army base where my father was stationed, and a truck driver picked me up. Without any warning, he simply pulled off the road at some deserted stretch of highway and stopped the truck. I said, "What are you doing?" He didn't say what he was doing, but it was clear.

I refused to get out, so this big, burly guy lifted me bodily out of the truck and took me off fifty feet into the bushes. We were in a light woods, and he took a blanket with him that he had in the truck. He put the blanket down and put me down on the ground. This was a long time ago, but I have a vivid picture of the place in my mind.

I was screaming and hollering even though there was nobody to hear. I knew he was going to rape me, that was perfectly apparent. He got his pants down and tried to take my clothes off. I yelled, "Get your hands off me and leave me alone!" I resisted in every possible way I knew how. I kicked and screamed and hollered. By that point I was crying as well, but I was also doing everything I knew physically to ward him off. He finally just said it wasn't worth it, and decided to hell with it. He was utterly disgusted and nasty. He walked out to the truck, threw my suitcase out, and drove off.

I didn't talk to my mother because I knew it would just set her off. I told friends later. I don't know what I would have done if he'd pulled out a gun. A lot of guys used to make passes at me and men have said things like "If you don't want it, get out!" And I'd get out. I had not anticipated this situation. I hadn't thought about what to do; I just did what came naturally.

I think the tears were pretty effective. A lot of men freak out when they see a woman cry, although I don't think crying is a very forceful thing to do.

I had some other problems when I was hitching. There was one other situation when I was about fourteen, when a bunch of young guys picked me up once. I would never do that anymore, I wouldn't get into a car with a bunch of young men. They said they were going to rape me. I told them I was menstruating and it scared them off. So then I developed this great idea of what to tell everyone. I think nowadays it wouldn't be that big a deal, but in the South in the forties it was a big deal. People were more inhibited. You just didn't tell people you were menstruating.

There weren't the same kind of advertisements that there are now, there wasn't the same kind of sexuality then, there wasn't any TV. I'm sure there was porn on the street then, but it was not what it is now and it wasn't visible. I've read that there's a lot of violence against older women now, but I haven't run into any for years.

Now I'd say, fight back in any way you know how, whatever comes naturally to you; just make your position unmistakably clear and have the determination to resist.

The Spirit Fights Back

Hallie Austen Iglehart

Hallie Austen Iglehart is the author of *Womanspirit: A Guide to Women's Wisdom,* and the co-founder of Women in Spiritual Education.

"I've passed many long evenings in women's consciousness-raising groups, learning to express sorrow and rage at being continually attacked. In subsequent years, at women's spiritual gatherings, I developed my intuition and discovered ways to release my healing power.

"This synthesis of politics and spirituality, which I call womanspirit, has not only saved my life, but has helped me reclaim my sanity, develop my own power, find a strong and supportive community, and continually become a more loving and effective person. Most of all, it has taught me to trust myself and other women."

It is close to midnight. I am driving my Volkswagen bus across the San Francisco Bay Bridge. For some reason, I start to feel unusually quiet. Although I normally listen to music when I drive, I turn off the radio for the rest of the trip home as I go into a spontaneous meditation. Years spent studying different forms of meditation in the United States, India, and Europe have taught me to move easily into a deep, focused state of consciousness, even while doing something as mundane as driving a car.

I park in front of my home in quiet Noe Valley and open the car door. Suddenly, a man is standing there, holding a gun six inches from my heart.

"Don't make any noise, or I'll kill you."

I am furious at this invasion, this violation. I look at the gun and thoughts flash through my head in a split second. Guessing that he wants to rape me, I remember reading that rapists often kill their victims. I don't want to wait to find out. If he's going to kill me, I think, it'll have to be now.

I kick out sideways at him. "Get out of here, you stupid bastard!" I yell.

He pushes me, and we start to wrestle. Fighting with all my strength and cunning, I realize I'll have to yell louder to be heard outside the bus.

"Help! H-elllll-pp!" Those words I've heard in so many movies and stories but never had to use in my own life.

He pushes me down between the two front seats. I am screaming with all my strength now, hitting and kicking the best I can. He hits me on the head with the gun and runs away. I scramble up off the floor and am out on the street in an instant, just in time to see him running around the corner of my house. I put my hand on my head. When I take it away, it is covered with blood. I am alive. I am standing. I am still furious.

"Jeanne, Jeanne!" I scream to my roommate. "Call the police!" It feels good to be able, for once, to scream as loudly as I want in the middle of the street.

In the weeks and months I spent dealing with the shock and repercussions of this encounter, I realized that the synthesis of spirituality and feminism saved my life. Working with deep meditation helped heal me of the profound psychic damage. Some premonition had told me to prepare myself that night by meditating in the car. My intuition had told me that, in this particular situation, I could fight back physically and win.

I Let Him Have It Right in the Eyes

Pat Deer

Pat Deer (a pseudonym), now middle-aged, works at a blue-collar crafts job, where she is the only woman. Her story took place when she was in her late teens. She still likes to sunbathe in the nude.

"I hope this story can be used in self-defense classes. That's why I left all the dumb moves in as well as the smart ones. Too often a rape is reported with no details about mistakes the woman made, so that women reading the account can't learn from the mistakes."

I walked around a big outcropping into a little low-tide cover, thinking I might find some good shells there. Everything looked more desolate than usual. I almost didn't go into the cove, then decided to look around for shells for a short time. I went slowly around the rock, lost in thought and not paying attention to what was around me. I turned and saw a big, hard, stocky, middle-aged man following fast. He said, "Hey." I said, "What?" and saw his fly open and his penis, shockingly enormous, not even half up and propped up with his hand as it was. The thought went through my head that, still being a virgin, I'd split wide open if he got it in, so I was going to have to do something about it.

The man got my upper arm in a viselike grip and said, "Let me suck you off. All you gotta do is pull down your pants." He reeked of stale booze.

"Why don't you go bother other girls," I said.

"I don't want other girls. I want you!" And then a moment later, "I don't want you. I'm just pissing around." I felt what I faced was not human, but some force of nature, like a large freak wave to the inexperienced surfer. What I remember most vividly so many years later is the emptiness of a patch of winter-afternoon sunlight. My thoughts were all small, cool, remote, floating on a balloon five feet above our heads, as if filled with helium.

My uncle used to hold me by the upper arm when I was a little girl, so I'd listen, and tell me that if a man ever gave me trouble, I must "let him have it right in the eyes." Then he would demonstrate an eye jab with stiff fingertips. Without any conscious plan, I took off the man's dark-lensed shades. The eyes I stared into were blue, icy cold, with surprisingly tiny pupils.

"Gimme muh glasses," said the man. I felt a nauseous inability or unwillingness to knee him in the crotch, though I did jab once at his Adam's apple, but the blow glanced off in a rubbery manner, and the man looked disgusted. He cocked his head to the side in what I guess he thought was a cunning pose, and said, "I'll get you down, if you don't gimme muh glasses."

"Here's your glasses," I said rapidly, and as he took them with his free hand, I wound up and jabbed him in the eyes with stiff fingertips, still with no conscious plan and with all my weight in back of it. I felt the blow land true, not as impact alone, but as a shock from my fingers all up my arm. I thought of the man's senses crashing back in from pain. As he fell back with a grunt and released my arm, I ran into the surf.

Since I was experienced and at ease in the ocean, I thought I'd dive under the breakers and swim around to the main beach while the surf hampered him. From a five to six foot depth, I checked back, but saw him, surprisingly, not following at all, but merely walking dejectedly back toward the other beach, hand over his eyes. He stopped only once to zip up his pants. I probably waited around to give the man a head start; my memory is unclear.

There was no sign of him on the beach and parking lot. The shakes began at the bottom of the parking lot stairs. I was annoyed with myself for that. At the time, I was reading a lot of James Bond, so I told myself that what I'd just done, staying cool, was a James Bond thing, and now this trembling and queasy feeling was weak and fool-ish.

I sat down in the car for a while before starting it. Suddenly, I felt a tingling in one instep, and, looking down, saw foot and floor mat gobbed with blood. I must have cut my foot on a broken bottle, without being aware of it. The inch-long slice over a small vein was clean, nearly painless, never became infected, and healed with a small scar. I told my parents I cut my foot on broken glass and they weren't too happy with that. For a long time after, I felt that what I had done had saved some other woman's life by stopping the man's winning streak—though there was and is no proof of that.

Southern Intuition

Denise Caignon

Denise Caignon, who co-edited this anthology, has studied judo and karate, and helped found the Santa Cruz Women's Self-Defense Teaching Cooperative. She currently manages the publications department of a computer software company, but most of the time, she'd rather be traveling.

"As much as I've thought about self-defense, I can still fall into that self-defeating trap we women know how to set for ourselves: if "nothing really happened," then I question whether I needed to do anything to defend myself. But if something had really happened, would I blame myself for not taking care of it sooner?"

I step off the Greyhound bus into the languid, dingy station. It is a lazy autumn Sunday afternoon, and the bus station is not crowded, but stuffy with cigarette smoke and noisy with video games clanging. Little Rock, Arkansas, is the town where I was born, and though I haven't been back here since childhood, somehow this gives me confidence: like I have a right to be here, this town is somehow mine.

I have just spent Thanksgiving with my grandmother, and now I am on my way north to visit friends. The first order of business is getting a cab to the small airport a few miles away. I am thoroughly settled into my traveling mode—the way I like myself best: moving through cities and feelings in my own space-time capsule. Proving to the child in me that I am an adult, since only an adult can handle all the nitty-gritty of a journey: money, hotels, buses, planes, trains. And I love the chance meetings, the easy intimacy of strangers who have nothing to lose by self-revelation. I can be fluid, my personality no longer hemmed in by what my friends and acquaintances think I am.

I step out into the gray Arkansas afternoon and the unfamiliar scent of autumn. The air always smells different in a foreign place, and Arkansas is foreign to me now, accustomed as I am to the placid seasonlessness of California. There are two or three old cabs standing at the curb like worn-out buggy horses. The driver of the first cab in line nods, I nod back, and I put my bags into the trunk he wordlessly opens. I bounce onto the old black leather seat, landing with a thud because of the broken-down springs beneath. I glance automatically at the door to make sure it has a handle—one of the cardinal rules for women hitchhikers—and slam the door.

"Where to?" He glances back at me as he grinds into first gear.

"The airport. I've got a three-o'clock flight." I hear and like the slight Southern-girl lilt in my voice, the old, childhood accent that has been slipping back into my speech by osmosis these past few days.

I settle back, watching downtown slide by. I wonder about fate: the combination of circumstances that led my parents to meet, marry, to give birth to me in this place . . . all the influences that have sent my own life drifting to different cities, new people. . . .

The driver has made a few turns and we are now on what look to me like back streets—quiet, deserted streets. I don't know Little Rock, but I assume we need to get on a freeway, somewhere.

"How far is the airport?" I ask, still feeling easy.

"Couple of miles."

"Is this the quickest way to get there?" I don't want to be swindled out of a huge cab fare.

"Hey, baby, I'm taking the shortcut. Whatsa matter, you paranoid?"

It is said with a leer, and as if he has caught me, somehow. Caught me in a trap I set for myself and he's gloating over it. Enjoying it. I am wide awake now, out of my reverie. My mind starts itself up like a clean, well-oiled motor. I wasn't paranoid, and I'm not now—just alert.

"No. I'm just wondering," I answer smoothly.

"Sure you're not paranoid, baby?" he wheedles insinuatingly.

"No. Why should I be?"

Now I am beginning to be afraid. He laughs. Is he playing with me, or is this for real? I can't afford to give him the benefit of the doubt.

"Been a cabdriver long?" I say casually, leaning forward amicably. The Southern lilt has gone thicker still, automatically. I am keenly aware that if he does mean me harm, he will be able to smell my fear. I must act naturally.

"Nah. Got outta the army not too long ago."

"You from Little Rock?"

"Yeah, where else? Where you from?"

"California. Came back to visit my family—I was born here."

As if listening to a stranger's voice, I hear the molasses words flowing out of my mouth. A strange feeling: as if my mouth is on autopilot, saying what needs to be said. Smooth.

"You nervous, huh? Whatsa matter—scared I'm gonna do something to you?"

Not smooth enough, apparently. My mouth keeps talking, while, in the background, a part of my mind that seems to have been reserved for this very moment clicks into gear, in perfect step with the easy-talking Southern girl. It assesses the situation quickly and logically: these streets are still back streets, still deserted. I can open the door and roll out, or I can play it cool. Play it cool, that's it. Don't let him sense your fear.

But I have a very strong impulse to get out of this car. I don't feel safe, and I've learned to trust that feeling. I decide to tell him I am getting out, here, now—even if that means he knows I'm afraid. I hate to give him that satisfaction, but I must get out of here.

"You know what?" my mouth says.

"What . . . you leave something at the station?"

"Yeah. Goddamn it." Suddenly, he has provided me with a new opportunity, a new way to do this, and I slip smoothly into it without a hitch, without the slightest sign that I hadn't meant that at all. My mind machine-stitches the old and new strategies together seamlessly.

I search roughly through my belongings, releasing anxiety through this show of mock frustration. "Shit."

"You want me to go back?"

"Yeah. Damn it, how could I do that?"

He is wheeling the car around. We're going back.

"You can go see if you left it on the bus, and I'll wait for you."

"Shit. If it's not there, I'm going to have to call over to Camden and see if I left it with my folks there. It's got my plane ticket in it. How could I be so stupid?" The lies are simply rolling off my tongue. It's working and I'm actually beginning to enjoy this. I feel I'm in a secret race that I must win. Will win.

We pull up in front of the station and I jump out. Free. I could disappear now, not come back to the car. But I still need to get out of here, to the airport, and all the cabs are parked companionably together. They're buddies, and I have no allies here.

I go to the pay phone, drop in a coin, listen to the dial tone become a recording become a blank become a beeping. I try to collect my thoughts, which, now that I am free, have come strangely unstrung. I see him walking toward me, and my thoughts snap back together like magnets and steel.

"It's not in Camden," I lilt drearily. "So I've gotta call some friends in Little Rock to come pick me up. I can't go anywhere without my ticket." I know no one in Little Rock, and my ticket is burning a hole in my pants pocket.

"Well, you try them and I'll wait for you." Mercifully, he wanders off to a video game. Why am I still caught up in this charade?

I make my fake call. I go and tell him someone is picking me up. I sit on my suitcase outside the station, waiting impatiently for my fantasy ride. Meanwhile, he has gone mysteriously off-duty, and is loitering around the front of the station as though waiting for someone himself. I wait endless minutes for him to go away, then I slip to a cab driven by what looks like an innocuous, elderly man, who takes me to the airport by the same back-street route. I feel like I'm riding with my grandfather, and even enjoy the pungent Camel smoke that fills the car.

As we glide down the same deserted streets, I ask myself: was I just being paranoid? Nothing really happened, did it? Then I think of his eyes leering at me coldly, his relentless baiting—and I simply feel relieved to be out of his presence. Why should I question my instincts just because I wasn't brutally assaulted?

Later, in my hotel room in Memphis, I realize why I continued the game instead of telling him, simply and loudly, to get lost. I wanted to win. I didn't want him to enjoy my fear—whatever his motives. I couldn't drop my Southern-girl-home-for-Thanksgiving demeanor to reveal a woman who had been swayed in any way by his taunts. I had to play that scene to the end.

Part IV

Weapons at Hand

Introduction

The idea of using weapons at hand has long been advocated by self-defense educators. Indeed, many women use objects they happen to have with them to defend themselves.

Some self-defense instructors also teach women to carry and use intentional weapons, such as tear-gas canisters, key rings with sharp points, or even knives or guns.

One problem with any intentional weapon is that no one plans when they are going to be attacked, and most women are attacked by known people or family members, in their own homes. As a friend flippantly remarks, "How often do you carry your Mace canister into your own bathroom?"

In self-defense success stories, weapons at hand are most often grasped intuitively, when the attack begins, although, as you will see, some women have learned to include intentional weapons in their personal strategy also.

The weapons in this chapter vary widely. One woman thinks about using a comb with a sharp edge, another uses a rock she stumbles over. One woman carries a knife tucked into her boot for just such an occasion. One woman grabs a potted plant and beats her attacker with the pot. Another woman uses a wet paintbrush. Two women in this chapter use a gun as an integral part of their personal self-defense strategy.

All these women use their wits in reaching for the nearest helpful object to stave off an attack. Their focus, even if they were feeling fear, was on what they could do to stop the other person from continuing the attack.

"Found" weapons can be very helpful, as you will see, but rummaging in your purse or backpack and attempting to use objects that are not easy to reach or get out has its limitations.

Tear gas, Mace, or other sprays have been hailed by some as perfect weapons, and instructors who teach how to use sprays have made great amounts of money doing it. But members of the Los Angeles Commission on Assaults Against Women ran some tests, spraying each other full on in the face with the tear-gas preparation legal in California. They were still able to advance and continue to attack. They predicted that if the attacker's adrenaline was stimulated, the gas might have even less effect.

Weapons such as these can give their owners a false sense of security. A woman carrying a tear-gas canister might think she needn't bother to learn effective physical or verbal self-defense techniques. If a gas canister makes you feel safer, by all means carry it. But don't rely on it—learn some basic self-defense as well.

If you are going to carry a weapon, make sure you know how to use it. Dangerous weapons like guns and knives also have their limitations. Although guns have great scare value, they may limit your response to only two options: shooting or not shooting. Many situations are not so serious that you would have to shoot, and a loaded weapon can be dangerous to you.

Many gun owners don't know how to use their weapons properly. Most shootings in this country happen by accident—someone is not observing gun safety rules, or is just fooling around. If you are going to have a gun around, know how to load and unload it, and practice aiming and shooting it regularly at a firing range.

And by all means learn and follow the gun safety rules listed below. Use them at all times to protect yourself and your family and friends.

- Store gun and ammunition separately, in locked containers.
- Never assume a gun is unloaded, even if it was not loaded when you had it in your hands a few minutes ago. If you pick up or get handed a gun, open the gun and check to see if it's loaded before you do anything else.
- Never point a gun at someone, unless you are considering shooting him. Never point a gun in fun.
- Know how to operate the safety latch—how to lock and unlock the gun.

- Clean and oil the gun regularly so it will work well when you need it.
- Never let children handle a gun, unless you are in the process of teaching them how to use it properly, under close supervision.
- If someone is not handling a gun safely, attempt to get it away, or leave the area as soon as possible.
- Practice aiming and shooting regularly, to keep your accuracy high.

Keeping a gun (particularly a loaded gun) in a drawer and not knowing how it works could endanger your life, especially if your attacker also happens to be a burglar. He could find the gun before you do.

However, a gun in the hand of an experienced woman can prevent violence, as Ellen Jean Zoltak illustrates in her story, "Have Gun, Will Travel." Ellen carries a firearm as part of her overall self-defense strategy, but has never needed to fire it. Although this is not a choice many women will make, Ellen handles gun use with intelligence and caution. She also points out that there are times when having a gun and thinking about it all the time is definitely a burden.

Whatever choices you make about intentional weapons as part of your self-defense plan, be aware of the general rationale behind self-defense laws, which could be applied if you use a weapon or otherwise injure your attacker.

Laws of self-defense vary from state to state. You can read the law for your state in the Penal Code, available in most libraries. But, in general, you have the right to defend yourself, and this is defined as doing what a "reasonable" person would do in similar circumstances.

What "reasonable" means here is that you are allowed to use as much, but not more, force as the other person has used, or as you believe him *capable* of using. This may be tricky to prove in situations where you have a weapon and your attacker does not.

Retaliation is also taboo. If your attacker walks away, you generally are not allowed to injure him then. Once he stops attacking, you cannot attack him.

If you injure your attacker, if at all possible get legal advice from a lawyer or rape crisis center before you contact the police. You may need to report the attack made on you to police, to establish that you needed to defend yourself. It may be advisable to report what happened even if you don't follow through, just in case your attacker tries to take you to court on assault, battery, assault with a deadly weapon, or attempted murder charges, as has happened to some women who fought back. To report, you need to call your local police or sheriff's office. Since the "reasonable person" defense is based on the idea of two people with equal bodies, training, and experience, it may not always apply to women, who may have radically different bodies, and often have little experience fighting. Such inequities are being taken into account in some court cases in which it is argued that if a woman in an attack situation uses a weapon, she is compensating only for her lack of training or lack of physical strength.

In any case, get legal advice if you injure your attacker. And if you are going to carry a weapon, know how to use it well. Otherwise, grab what you can, and make it a "weapon at hand."

The Comb in My Purse

Lynda Steele

Lynda Steele manages residential care facilities for the retarded in Kent, England, and lives with her husband, an American.

"Writing [this story] was helpful to me—a kind of exorcism. That might be the greatest achievement of the Success Story Project: that women recall and face those situations on the page in front of them."

Until I was twenty-two years old, I believed I was a pacifist, and that I could never hurt or kill another human being. That all changed the night I was assaulted.

I had just left a group of friends and was walking the last three hundred yards to my home alone. It was a dark street with bushes and trees on both sides. I had walked home that way many times and I had never been afraid.

Suddenly, a man grabbed me from behind. He was shorter than me, but a lot stronger. He pulled me off my feet and down to the ground, into the bushes. He was so strong that I was unable to move; his weight on top of me was suffocating. I remember thinking that there were houses nearby and that I should scream. I opened my mouth to scream and no sound came out. My mouth was empty and dry and my jaws locked.

As he pinned my body and legs into the ground and began to tear my jacket, I tried to move, wriggle, slide away—anything—but my limbs felt like lead. Heavy lead legs that would not do, could not do, what my mind was telling them to. Something instinctive made me go limp, motionless. In that one second of lifelessness, my left arm came free. It rebounded elastically above my head and came down on my purse.

As I opened my mouth, my mind was shouting. Get the steel comb from your purse, get the comb, it's got a sharp-pointed end like a knife. Get the comb! It was as if all of my body was frozen in cement, except one flailing left arm and the left hand that clutched the comb.

I held the comb ready to stab him. All I could think of was plunging it into the black jacket on top of me again and again and again. I did not think it was a person on top of me. I did not think about injuring someone. I just thought of piercing the jacket so that I would be able to breathe again.

As I clutched the comb, the scream finally came out of my mouth. The sound of fear and rage filled the darkness. Distantly, I heard a voice say, "What was that? Someone is over there."

Suddenly, he was no longer tearing at my clothes. He was running through the bushes and I was lying there ready to kill. I looked at the comb, at my hand, at my clothes, and as the distant voices came closer, I began to shake with anger and relief and tears. Tears for him, tears for me, and tears because I could have killed, would have killed. Above all, tears of grief for an ideal that had just been destroyed.

I would kill in self-defense.

A Stone in the Sand

Marla J. Calico

Marla Calico was raised on a large farm in southwest Missouri. Her life revolved around the animals and the farm work. She could throw a bale of hay or sack of feed with the best of the guys, and she thinks this, more than anything, made her feel she could fight back when attacked. Today, she is operations manager for one of the top one hundred fairs in the United States.

"When I was attacked, I had no thoughts other than to fight back. For me, there was no other choice. Had I given in to my attackers, my life would have been lost. It is my sincere desire that this book convey to our sisters that there are those of us who have fought, and fought successfully—that to fight back is an option."

I'll never forget the date—Friday, October 13, 1978. I was visiting my lover on an extended vacation in his home country, Ecuador. We had taken a long, hot, and dusty bus ride to the beach to camp overnight. By the time we had the tent set up, it was nearly dark, and he decided to walk into town to find something for us for dinner. No problem, I thought, I'll have a nice fire going in no time and we'll have a cozy little dinner. It would be a prelude to the night I was anxiously awaiting. Who could miss with a night of love on a moonlit beach in South America?

After I had gathered sufficient firewood, I returned to a small wall near the end of the beach to urinate. As I was in that ridiculous position, shorts around my ankles, five men jumped from behind the wall and grabbed me.

My initial reaction was to scream—I knew there was a group just down the beach partying beside a bonfire—but the scream only reverberated in my ears. The wind was from the wrong direction, the surf was too loud.

In the next seconds, it became clear that there was a ringleader in the group, two strong followers, and two younger ones, only boys, that lagged behind the others. Struggling with the three in the sand was futile—I kicked my shorts free of my ankles, and found myself backed into the corner of the wall. To silence my screams, the leader tried to choke me—I carried the bruises from his fingers for several days.

The wall probably saved my life. With something to brace myself against, I could now push and make a few kicks. The ringleader kept shouting, *"Cuchillo, cuchillo!"* I knew enough Spanish to realize he wanted the younger one to get him a knife. Luckily, none appeared.

The struggle lasted only minutes, but it seemed an eternity. My legs gave way in the sand. They were dragging me up the steps by the wall. As my head bumped against the stairs, and my bare hips and legs were scraped by the sand and stones, I managed to grab a baseball-sized stone beneath me. I used that to hit blindly behind me, catching my captor in the head. In the next few seconds of confusion, I made a desperate kick and caught one of them in the groin. This gave me the time to jump and run.

Once back at the tent, I spent the next hour in utter terror, sitting in the dark, clutching my pocketknife. I soon realized they wouldn't bother me any more that night, and was able to start a small fire. When my boyfriend at last returned, I poured out the story to him—and saw his frustration and feeling of helplessness. He is an understanding man, and did all the right things to comfort me through the night and the next few weeks of fear.

The experience left definite scars—a certain fear that had never been present before. The one positive thing that came out of it was knowing I had used my head, and had successfully defended myself. Most of it, though, was luck: lucky to have been brought up on a farm and be a bit stronger than most women; lucky to have had that wall to my back; lucky to have been dragged across that small stone.

With the Help of a Houseplant

Marie Steinmetz, M.D.

Marie Steinmetz is a physician in private family practice in a Maryland suburb of Washington, D.C. The incident she describes occurred while she was doing her residency training in Asheville, North Carolina. Her work interests include wellness promotion and working with battered women.

It was a rainy May night in the mountains of North Carolina. I had been asleep about an hour when I heard a scratching sound. I thought it was my cat and got up to quiet her down. I took two steps into the living room and was stopped short by the reality of someone climbing into my window. A shadowy figure was outlined by the streetlight outside. I felt a cold wave of terror rise from my toes to my head. My mouth opened and I was surprised to hear a scream come out.

I walked closer to the window, still not sure the figure was real. It was. He was in the window up to his waist. The sound I heard was the window sticking. He couldn't get his body completely inside.

He said, "I have a knife. Be quiet!" Every ounce of my being wanted that knife away from me. My hands reached for anything and grabbed the stem of a potted plant in front of the window. I began beating him with the pot and screaming. I soon realized no one was coming to help me.

I turned into a madwoman. I hit him with everything my hands could grab. He finally pulled himself from the window and started to run away. I stuck my head out of the window and screamed at him until I couldn't see him anymore. I remember yelling, "You motherfucker, don't you ever come back to my place again!"

Since this episode, I have taken up Nautilus training (weight lifting). I was encouraged by many people to buy a gun. But I elected to adopt a large black German shepherd. He is my house protector and running companion, and I take him when traveling long distances alone.

On to Firenze!

Cheryl Byrne Walsh

Cheryl Walsh was twenty when her story took place. She had left the comforts of her "middle-class home" at sixteen to make a living and go to college. She arrived in Brussels, Belgium, with one hundred dollars cash, and began working in the tulip bulb harvest in Amsterdam.

"I was hitching alone through Europe. This in itself was rather brave, yet I hold the belief that most people are basically good and most men aren't rapists, that the rapist is a sick person. This story describes the only bad incident in one and a half years of hitchhiking all over Western Europe."

It was early in the day when I reached the France/Switzerland border. The border guard was very helpful. Even though he didn't speak English, nor I French, we managed to communicate that I was going to Milan, Italy, and that he would try to get me a ride from some kind soul.

After a few minutes, the border guard found a German truck driver who was going to Milan, and bullied him into giving me a ride. Now, I can sympathize with the truck driver not wanting to give me a lift, but being at the mercy of the border guard, he felt forced to take me. So I tried to be good company and dragged out my American-German phrase book. I tried to tell him animated stories in phrases about my travels. He wasn't at all impressed. As a matter of fact, he was sour about the whole deal and let me know it.

At 10:00 P.M., we arrived on the outer ring road of Milan. It was raining. There were twenty kilometers between us and shelter. He stopped his truck and motioned me to get out. Frantically, on the verge of hysteria, I looked through the phrase book for the sentence that read, "Please, PLEASE, don't leave me twenty kilometers from the center of Milan at 10:00 P.M. in the rain. PLEASE take me to the youth hostel!" But there was no such sentence, only the niceties of "please," "thank you," the time, the weather, and directions.

I am sure he understood the message without words because this time, a bit more forcefully, he motioned me to get out! So I did, but not before cursing and throwing my German phrase book at him just as I slammed the door as hard as I could. He drove away.

At this point, awful feelings and thoughts rushed through me—my fears of not making it through the night alive and anxieties about where I would go and what I would do until morning, all mixed with the drenching rain.

I shook my head, took a few deep breaths, and let go of what had happened, then looked around to figure out where I was going to spend the night. Ahead was an overpass bridge. Aha, I thought, I can sleep under it till morning, then hitch to the center of Milan, where I can check into a hostel, get cleaned up and peacefully rested.

Just then a truck stopped, the passenger door flew open, and a very sympathetic Italian man motioned me to get in. Within a split second, I knew I had two choices: to sleep under the bridge or to go with this guy, who was shouting "Firenze! Firenze!," which translates into "Florence." I got in.

Although there was no common language between us, we rode along merrily for three or four hours, chatting as best we could. Then he motioned toward the two bunks behind us and communicated that we were to stop and sleep until dawn, when he had to deliver what he had in the back of the truck. We would then drive on to Firenze. What else had I to do but agree or once more face the downpour? He seemed like an amicable family man.

Once stopped, he indicated that I was to sleep on the bottom bunk and he on the top. He asked me to remove my cowboy boots because the heels would tear the mattress, which I did. Sleeping on that little shelf with him on the shelf above me was like sleeping in a coffin closed in on three sides.

No fool in her right mind would hitchhike as much as I have without taking precautions before getting into each vehicle, or at times refusing to get in. However, in cases such as this one, one needs a little extra protection, like five years of martial arts or five inches of steel blade.

I had the latter—a hunting knife I bought in Amsterdam for the purpose of cutting bread and cheese and any potential attackers. It was in a sheath strapped to my leg with half-inch sewing elastic. So when this guy asked me to remove my boots, I knew full well what he wanted. But I could have outsmarted him with my eyes closed.

Two hours later, he climbed into the bunk with me. I was awake with my eyes closed, my back against the wall of the truck. My senses followed his hand from my shoulder to breast to waist to hip to knee. He felt he was home free, then he felt the knife. Then he felt both my hands and feet kicking out at his chest and at his stomach. I whipped out my knife and started swinging it wildly, screaming and kicking, until he got in the driver's seat and had the engine running.

He drove a few hours and reached his delivery point at dawn. Then he drove into a small Italian town, apologizing all the while and fearful of the knife I had out within easy reach. I hopped out at the first red light, shook my head, took a few deep breaths, and looked about, to decide where I was going next.

Have Gun, Will Travel

Ellen Jean Zoltak

Ellen is thirty-eight years old and lives with her dog, Murphy. She is "a typical overeducated (ex-nun with a master's in counseling), underemployed Child of the Sixties / Woman of the Eighties who has yet to compromise my integrity or sense of humor for financial security."

"Being humanitarian, being kind and loving, does not include entrusting my life or well-being to anyone whose intention or unconscious direction is to cause me harm. I am here to enjoy the life that Mother Earth gave me."

As told to the editors in an interview: My feeling about guns is that they have their place, like everything else in the world. There have been times when I've had a gun with me and was grateful that I did just for the psychological edge. I don't advocate that everyone run around with guns all the time. There are negative aspects to having one on your person. I'm not a person who loses her cool under pressure; the more pressure I'm under, the better I get. I wouldn't recommend a gun to someone who gets hysterical or feels bad about having one. That would knock you off center and you might make a poor judgment in using one.

For instance, when I lived in the inner city and I wanted to drive somewhere (to a party or a meeting) and had to return late at night, I felt safer if I had my gun along for protection. However, I usually decided it was not safe or necessary to bring the gun into the party, where it could be found and used by an irresponsible person or playing children. If I did decide to take my gun on the trip, I locked it in my car upon arrival.

A little bit of history. My father was in the navy and he taught self-defense and karate. He believed that anyone would be safer with a weapon if they were taught proper use and precautions. So my introduction to weapons and guns was not through just anyone on the street who carries them. It was from an intelligent man who I think had a lot of discernment around the issue. So I didn't have the kind of fear of guns that a lot of people have when they're not raised around them. I recall my father showing the guns to me when I was about eight, and teaching me the steps of using one.

He taught me the difference between handguns and rifles, and the difference between single shot, revolvers, and automatics; he told me the purposes and limitations of each. I learned about the size and power of different bullets, how far they traveled, and what they did upon impact. He also taught me the correct way to shoot, carry, and clean a weapon, and he carefully explained how easy it was for guns to go off accidentally. Especially, he taught me never to keep a loaded gun around people or to point it at a person unless you intend to use it. And that was that. My feeling was, Okay, that's the whole lecture on guns and you can relax now.

I went to a Catholic college and I used to drive back and forth between Chicago and Milwaukee. That was the first time I think I felt the need to have a gun, in case my car broke down or something.

Then, when I got married, we moved out to Idaho, where the farmers all carry shotguns in the back of the cars and revolvers in their pickups in the side panels of the doors. At the time, I thought that was rather extreme because I was a pacifist. My husband and I were against the Vietnam War. And yet, we lived in a farmhouse four miles from the nearest neighbor and ten miles up the canyon road from the bottom of the Snake River Canyon. Occasionally, someone would drive up at two in the morning, lost. They'd have been lost for five or six hours and we were the first sign of humanity they ran into. And I felt it was too great a risk to be in that farmhouse, that isolated, without weapons. My husband was not a physical type like my father was; he was more of an intellectual. Because he was tall and large, people never confronted him very much. But in a tight situation, I knew that he would lose his cool and I would have to be the one to pull it together.

So we got a .32 revolver. I was at that farmhouse alone a lot when he was at school—we had different schedules. And I felt safer, and that was the end of the issue. Throughout that period of living in that farmhouse (we lived there two years), there were maybe eight people that showed up at the door and each one looked stranger than the next. I never went to the door with a gun, but I knew where it was. And we kept it loaded because we didn't have children, we didn't have to be careful. When people came over with children, we unloaded the gun and locked it away. Just knowing the gun was there was helpful to me.

After I was divorced, I often went traveling or camping alone. I went for two weeks at a time and took a gun with me. There were a few times when I used that weapon. I never actually shot anyone, but just having it and exposing it was enough to deter a couple of men, and so it served its purpose.

For example, in the summer of '79 I had gone camping in the mountains of Oregon. I was driving along the road with a .32 revolver in a holster in the back of the truck. I pulled into what looked like a dam or a reservoir. I always pay attention to who's around me in situations where I'm alone and out in the open like that. I take a look at my surroundings. So before I just blithely got out of my truck, I took a look at how many people there were in the parking lot. There were three or four cars, one of which was an older man in an orange and white Pinto. I remembered all the cars and I thought to myself, Well, I'm a woman alone, it's obvious to all of them. Is anybody going to follow me when I leave this parking lot? I took off down the highway a short distance. In my rearview mirror, I saw the man in the Pinto pull out right behind me. There was a sign indicating that there was a lake ten miles up this gravel road. That was really more isolated than I wanted to be, but since I wanted to go swimming, I took a right onto the gravel road. I don't remember if I saw him follow me on that road, I don't remember if I took that road partly as a diversion to see if he would follow me.

When I got to the end of the road, there was a path that led up to the lake. I got out of my truck and I thought about the gun. I stood at the back of the truck and I thought, Well, do I want to take a gun to the lake or not? No one is parked here, so there's probably no one at the lake. But that's not always true in the woods; people backpack. So I tried to intuit. I sat down and took time to center and feel out the situation. I decided it would be safe at the lake and felt that if I wore the gun, I would feel overprotected and a bit too edgy. So I chose not to wear it.

I hiked to the lake and after about fifteen minutes, I got the urge to go back to my truck. Even though it was beautiful and serene, there was a voice that said, Just go back, so I said, Okay, I suppose I'm being paranoid, but I'm going to go back. So I went back to the truck, opened the tailgate, and this guy in the orange and white Pinto shows up. He did a U-turn right there, and pulled over right next to me and stopped. Just as he was pulling up, I decided to take the gun and holster and put it on my belt on my left side—I'm left-handed and that was the side facing him. As he drove around, he could very plainly see this .32 revolver with a four-inch barrel. That's a big gun, it's not the kind you carry in your purse. So he looked at that and I looked at him and there was a shotgun in the backseat of his car and I thought, Well, I don't mind having a gun right now. I'm very glad I have it. And he looked at me and said something like "Well, hi, how are ya, nice day," and took off.

Two weeks later, I was up in Seattle, visiting a friend of mine. He said, "What have you been doing?" "Oh, I've been camping." And he said, "Oh, did you hear about the man in the orange and white Pinto who was blowing people away with a shotgun out in the woods?" And I thought, I'm damn glad I had the gun on my hip because what would he have done? I'm sure it was the same man— how many older men are riding around in orange and white Pintos with shotguns in the backseat? And without the gun, he would have seen me as being at a disadvantage, since I was there alone. He was shooting people, from what I heard, with no cause, just isolated people in the woods. I'm very glad I believed in the philosophy of carrying a weapon.

Paintbrush in Hand

Louisa W. Peat O'Neil

Called "Peaty," Ms. O'Neil lives in the Maryland suburbs of Washington, D.C. The area was rural when she was a child but is now dense with townhouses and apartments. The eldest of five, she and her siblings were encouraged to practice yelling. "Scream bloody murder!" her mother said often.

Peaty's successful defense against a convicted rapist in Florida was surely due to her powerful lungs and uninhibited screaming reflex.

"Any woman can fight back. Start with mental strength, move those muscles, and show your power in your stride. And learn to scream without a moment's hesitation. You can laugh about it later if you make a mistake, but better not to take that chance."

I was whitewashing the interior walls of my garage on the day I was attacked. The garage was behind the bungalow I shared with two friends in St. Petersburg, Florida.

By early afternoon, I had been working four or five hours and the walls were nearly done. During the morning, my thoughts had traveled to my great-aunt and grandmother. I thought of their struggles and successes and wondered what they would have said to their energetic descendant.

I was painting the corner behind the door, which was ajar. Suddenly, I sensed something, looked down, and saw a sneakered foot just behind me. It was an unfamiliar sneaker, light blue and not the sort my pals wear. Screaming like a banshee, I flung back my freshly dipped paintbrush, a good wide industrial-size one. Arms gripped me. I flailed and kicked, striking out with the paintbrush still in hand. I never quit screaming. He flung me down against the wall and took off in a flash.

People came over from nearby houses; down the block, they stepped out to see what caused the racket. One neighbor had a shotgun in his hands. My housemates were at my side within seconds.

My right hand was bleeding from three nasty gashes. My housemates ran back inside the house to call an ambulance and the police. They gave me orange juice and a towel to wrap my cut fingers. My throat was sore from screaming.

Lying in the hospital emergency room, I waited for medical attention while police photographers took pictures of my wounds. A detective entered the curtained cubicle to question me in greater detail about the assailant. Police officers, who had arrived at the house before the ambulance, had already gone over the events once or twice. The wounds were cleaned but lay open for the better part of an hour; I wondered if they thought it best to let the wounds ripen before sewing them up.

I remembered, as the detective asked me to run over the details of the attack again, that I had painted white whoever had attacked me. This excited the detective immensely, who said it was a great clue and ran off, presumably to catch the attacker.

The doctor finally came to my cubicle and stitched up my fingers and hand. He mentioned the possibility of nerve damage and loss of dexterity for a time.

I must have told the story fifty times by the end of that week. The attack happened on November 28, 1978, the same day Harvey Milk and George Moscone were assassinated in San Francisco by ex-cop Dan White.

My assailant was caught within a day. He was a convicted rapist who had ravaged two other women in the neighborhood on his first few days out of detention for his last series of rapes. The police described him as a ''career criminal'' and I was asked to go to the police station to complete some paperwork for their records. They even sent a patrol car to transport me. I was never told what happened to the rapist-attacker. I assume he was or will be released again and will probably attack women and rape again.

The state of Florida victim's compensation fund sent me ninety-nine dollars for lost income and paid the hospital bills. My friends helped me get over the trauma by listening to me tell and retell the story until it was out of my system.

I pieced together the events: he had entered through the open unfinished cinder-block window at the back of the garage, come up behind me as I was painting, and was about to put his knife to my throat when I saw the sneaker and struck back with my paint-laden brush, screaming all the while. Later, the police said a rapist will run from a screamer, and I have a voice like a siren.

My hand was cut because it got in the way of the knife, or perhaps he struck for the hand intentionally, just to cut me. I think about it when the San Francisco assassinations are mentioned in the news and I am reminded that I was attacked on the same day. The scars on my hand have a positive value, reminding me that I fought back and didn't suffer rape or worse.

Fighting back came naturally to me. Instinct set me going, luck helped. My mother had taught me how to scream with force when I was quite small and, though I haven't often needed that skill, I have practiced it from time to time all my life. I have no inhibitions about letting loose with a bloodcurdling, forceful yell. Luck put a paintbrush in my hand—an unlikely weapon, but an effective one that served to mark my attacker and perhaps speed his arrest.

Other women might want to develop a good, strong yell that they can sustain. I think it is a good idea to practice fighting, too. Even before the attack, I had practiced escaping from an attacker, using friends as surrogate rapists. I've never studied self-defense, but I'm not afraid to hit back and I will again if I have to.

No Bluff

Laura Smith Turner

Laura Smith Turner lacks three hours on an honors degree in Scottish history and foreign languages. She runs a small business in the rural South.

"This event changed my life. I felt pretty crazy for a couple of weeks, because it was a grim act to shoot a man who hadn't yet laid a hand on his intended victim. But if he had gotten into my house, he would have raped me—certainly he threatened to—and beaten me badly. Having survived the emotional trauma and the uncertainty of the possible legal ramifications, I find the experience did a lot for my self-confidence and sense of autonomy. I continue to tell the story with relish, because it produces in my listeners an instantaneous surge of respect.

"If more and more women will defend themselves, maybe men will get the idea that it's a very chancy proposition to jump a woman. How terrible if we should have armed sex war in the streets, but the 'turn the other cheek' philosophy is not going to solve the problem."

As told to the editors in an interview: I was living in a tiny house out in the woods, with no electricity or plumbing. I was there all by myself. Nobody else was around. Since I was exhausted, I went to bed around seven-thirty. I'd been asleep for about half an hour when I heard somebody outside letting my dog off the chain. Toby would make friends with anybody, so I checked it out. It was this fella who'd been out to my place a couple of times before and I didn't particularly care for him. He used to get drunk and make a terrible mess, and I had told him not to come. But of course people do whatever they want to do, whether you like it or not.

I hollered at him, to find out who he was for sure, and he told me. He was looking for John, a fella who had stayed out at my place the month before, in a bus that he parked there. I said, "John's not here, go hunt for him somewhere else." Well, he didn't want to go hunt for him somewhere else; he wanted to aggravate me. He started hollering and carrying on, and I sat for about half an hour under some of the nastiest abuse I've ever heard in my life.

I was scared to death, and I knew from experience that since he was drunk, he would get even meaner. It usually took three or four of his brothers to settle him down and haul him off when he got out of hand. My little house only had screens on the windows; in the wintertime, we covered them with plastic, so there really wasn't much protection, and the dog didn't care what was going on. I had a rifle and I knew it was loaded, and I told him so. I told him to go away, but he would not go away, so I said, "I do have a gun and I do know how to use it." And he said "Aw, no you don't, you don't know what you're doing." So I shot the gun out the back door, out across an open pasture where it wouldn't hurt anybody. It didn't make any impact on him at all.

"I'm going to come in there and show you what a real man is," he said. It was something he had talked about before, so I knew it had been in his mind for some time. I wasn't interested in finding out what kind of a man he was. I think if he hadn't been so drunk, the gunshot out the back door would have made more of an impression on him. But he said, "Go ahead and shoot me, go ahead and kill me, I have a death wish, you'll spend the rest of your life in prison."

I was shaking all over. What an adrenaline rush! I was just terrified. I had a bell outside the back door that I use to signal to people, and I rang that until I broke it and it fell down. Nobody heard it and nobody came. This fella said he was coming in, and I said, "No, you're not." Then he swung his arm through the window in the front of the house. When his arm came through the screen window into the house, I went ahead and pulled the trigger.

There was no way I was going to let him come into my house and do whatever he wanted to, and if I had to shoot him, I would. It's not a rational decision. It's like the top of your head lifts off and your consciousness is expanded and your thoughts are flying by about thirty times faster than usual and you're scared to death the whole time, but it was scarier to let him in than to shoot him.

It was a .30-30 deer rifle, and I was standing about five feet from him. The bullet evidently went through his elbow from the outside and then into his body. He fell down and said, "Oh, I'm hurt bad, go and get me some help." I looked at him and he *was* hurt, so I said, "Okay, I'm going to go get somebody." Of course, I wasn't nearly that calm. I got some shoes on and took the rifle and a flashlight and took off across the country. It's about a quarter of a mile to my neighbor's house. I banged on the door and she let me in. She hadn't heard anything going on, and couldn't imagine why I was in such a fit, but I went ahead and called the sheriff's department. The Emergency Medical Service came and more or less patched him up and hauled him off. In the meantime, John showed up while I was gone calling for help. He was drunk, too, he'd been out drinking earlier with the fella I shot. He went nuts when he fell over this fella's body, didn't know whether I'd shot him or he'd shot himself or what. It took three or four deputies to subdue him and they hauled him off to jail. After everything settled down, they said they needed to take me in to make a statement.

There was one woman there, the wife of a constable who'd answered the call. She was really terrific, she kept me from going all to pieces. We went on in and I made my statement orally, and then they made me write it all down. They said, "Well, that's all, we'll let you know how he does in the hospital. You can go home now." Of course, you don't just go home and go to sleep after something like that. Fortunately, it was springtime and the hill was covered with wild flowers, and I got up around four or five o'clock and walked. The dog thought that was great.

That was one of the hardest weeks of my life. You don't realize what a shock it is. I still had to go to work, and there was blood all over the front of the house and all over the ground in front of the house. Blood stinks, in case you've never come in contact with it; it just smells awful. John was in jail, and I went to see him and said, "This is it, if you can't behave yourself and keep your friends under control you can't stay out at my place again." He wanted me to bail him out and I wouldn't. They finally got tired of feeding him TV dinners and let him out early.

The law enforcement people were very supportive. This fella I shot was a perpetual troublemaker. He was being hauled in for drunk and disorderly every night and frankly I think they were glad somebody finally stood up to him.

Three or four days later, I went into a filling station that was run by a local justice of the peace and I wrote a check out for the gas. He looked at the check and then he looked at me. My eyes were bloodshot and I had big black circles under my eyes. He said, "Are you . . . ?" and I said, "Yes." He said, "I hear you had a little trouble out at your place the other night." I said, "Well, yes sir, I did." He said, "Well, I just wanted to tell you," and all this time he's patting my hand, "I wanted to tell you that I think you did a real fine job and I'm proud of you." I knew right then it was going to be okay.

Nobody knew for several days whether or not this fella was going to live. They told me later that he had died once in the ambulance on the way to the hospital and twice on the operating table, but they revived him. I didn't want him to die because I knew I'd have to go to court if he did. It was another couple of months before the grand jury considered the case and I found out from an insider that they just couldn't decide whether to indict him or me, so they didn't indict either one of us.

This experience has made me a lot more radical about self-defense. I grew up in the late sixties, early seventies, believing in peace, love, you don't strike back, you turn the other cheek, there's no excuse for war and violence. But I decided that if somebody was going to threaten my well-being, I had a right to put a stop to it. This attitude helped me fit into the community a lot better than I ever had before. This is an old county—it's very "country," and here I came from a big city. They weren't too sure about me at first.

After the man who had attacked me had been in the hospital for three weeks, the fellas in the sheriff's office went up to see if they could get a statement from him, and he corroborated everything I'd told them. He didn't have to do that. He could have lied and made it a lot harder on me. But he backed up the story I told and even dictated a letter of apology to me. He said, "I called your bluff and I shouldn't have and you did the right thing and I'm sorry I made you do it." I have only had to speak to him once or twice since then. And he's never been back out to the property.

Part V

Life-Threatening Assaults

Introduction

Some of our worst fears involve weapons, attacks by groups, and situations that require a physical response to escape safely. The stories in this section deal not only with extreme violence, but also with correspondingly strong defenses.

In working with women who have been raped, one hears stories over and over again that involve death threats. "If you don't do this, I will kill you." Women are forced to participate in their own violation for fear of something worse. The greatest fear of the rapist or attacker is that someone will find him out, therefore his most common threat is "If you tell anyone this happened, I will kill you." Or "I will harm your family," or "I'll tell everyone you know that you loved it."

We know of a woman who opened the door of her trailer and was faced by an attacker with a gun. He said, "If you don't do what I want, I will kill you." She just looked at him, and said, "Well, then you will have to shoot me right now, because I'm not going to do what you want." Her will to defend herself was stronger than his will to hurt her, and he left.

We are misled by what we see on television and in the movies. The use of weapons, the frequency of group attack, and actual murders of women are all greatly exaggerated by the media, both in fictional accounts and in the news. Weapons are present in less than 10 percent of all situations reported to rape crisis centers. When a weapon is involved, it is often only used as a means of inducing fear, as a threat. In effect, the attacker is saying, "I have to have something in my hand with which I could kill you, in order to even get near you.'' This is an interesting psychological statement: the attacker clearly credits his intended ''victim'' with a good deal of power.

A threat of a weapon does not mean one is really there. Some women have challenged attackers, saying boldly that they do not believe there is a weapon. Having something stuck in your back does not necessarily mean it is a gun; it may be a screwdriver, or a finger.

You may ask, ''Well, what about the crazies?'' Although there certainly is a percentage of attackers who are psychotic, we venture to suggest that it may not be higher than that in the general population. Mass murders sell papers, but your chances of running into someone who truly is crazy are pretty slim, but not unheard of; sometimes survival means fighting with every ounce of strength and will you possess, using every skill you have ever learned, physically, emotionally, mentally, just to stay alive. Py Bateman tells one such story. A black belt in karate, a fit woman, Py Bateman (''Coming Out Alive'') ran into one of the crazier attackers we have heard of, who seemed genuinely interested in taking her life, and who had no previous acquaintance with her. Despite his obviously planned attack and his perseverance in trying to hurt her, she showed great courage and skill and is alive to tell about it. Kimberly Rosa uses willpower and fights just to stay alive in ''Adrenaline: A Hitchhiking Story.''

Keep in mind that most women are attacked by men whom they know, and who are mostly sane. This, of course, does not mean their actions make sense. Men in this country grow up with a horrible burden of negative ideas about themselves and about women, some of which they may act out in a rape. Some of these ideas are fostered by the multi-billion-dollar violent pornography industry—which makes more money than the record and concert industries put together—from the idea that women enjoy sexual humiliation and pain.

In reality, many women attacked by people with weapons do escape, although if the weapon is used, the degree of injury is sometimes greater. Yet even women who are injured get away with their lives. Survival does not always mean beating your attacker into the ground. Sometimes it means running. Or hiding until he goes away. Often it means verbally negotiating yourself into a safer position: ''If you just put the gun down, I'll do anything you want.'' After he puts it down, you can make your move.

We recommend that women take classes specifically labeled ''self-defense'' to learn practical, immediately useful skills. Please see ''So

What Do I Do Now?'' or "Self-Defense Programs," pages 255–292, for more information.

Half of defending yourself is sizing up the situation at the outset. How dangerous is it? Is there more than one person? Is a weapon visible? Or is the person who you think is following you just another woman or man hurrying home from work? Many women don't want to look. We are afraid to acknowledge that an attack might really be happening to us, not just to some actress on television. We try to ignore the potential danger, in the hope it will go away. Unfortunately, this sometimes means ignoring vital information in life-threatening situations.

All the women in this section use finely attuned assessment skills to size up the situation, and to prepare an appropriate defense to meet it. Sometimes there seems to be no time at all to see what is going on, yet there is enough to effectively fight back. There is often more than one chance, or opening, and it is important to stay calm enough to see it and take it when it comes.

In "Testimony of a Welfare Mother," Juana Maria Paz flees a life-threatening assault by her husband to build a new life for herself and her children. Over the past ten years, women's shelters have made escape for battered women more possible, although not easy. The dynamics of love and violence are complex, and, as in other attacks by known people, make "defense" more difficult. Often the dependence is financial and emotional, and the ties include common children. The recovery of self-esteem by a woman who has been battered is a major triumph.

Cindy Nakazawa's story, "Asian, Female, and Fierce," shows how a small woman learns to overcome what the police describe to her as a particular vulnerability in appearance. Asian women have often been stereotyped as fragile and exotic, but Cindy has a fierce fighting spirit, and years of aikido training to back her up. She has been attacked several times, and shows wit and understanding of the psychology behind the attacks, as well as physical prowess.

Claire Trensky, the national judo champion in "Does He Know Who I Am?," actually thinks of martial arts techniques during the attack. But it is her determination to protect her sister and nephew that impressed us as well. Many women say that they feel they would do anything to protect a child—but each of us is someone's child.

Marsha Hamm ("If at First You Don't Succeed . . .") uses her weight to her advantage and summons help, even while her attacker holds a jagged piece of window glass at her throat. Her sense of humor definitely helps her survive.

Group attacks may be planned, but are less likely to come from organized gangs than from impromptu groups of boys or men who are friends out drinking, perhaps daring each other to "go get a woman." In "Here Comes the Macho Woman . . ." Dora Gonzalez is confronted by a group of buddies at a party, who are totally floored by her physical defense.

In another group attack, Rashida, in "Battle in the Cemetery," uses a tremendous physical defense, first stunning the man closest to her, and then the next closest one, effectively dealing with the most dangerous threats first. She explodes into action and then flees, faster and more determined than her would-be kidnappers.

"Waiting for a Chance" by Leslie Bandle is difficult to read for several reasons: the attack is protracted and terrifying, and the story involves the issue of racism and feelings about race. Leslie is a survivor, and ultimately uses her wits and senses to avoid being killed.

Despite the severity of the situations you'll read about in this section, all of these women are alive to tell the tale. The key to their successes was often the variety of defenses they tried—from verbal, to physical, to wielding weapons themselves. Even the most confirmed skeptic will find these stories inspiring.

Here Comes the
Macho Woman . . .

Dora Gonzalez

Dora Gonzalez is a Spanish-English bilingual teacher who works with four-year-olds, mostly from low-income families in California. One of her goals as a teacher is to try to be a model of a strong woman.

"There was a little boy in one of my classes who was really angry with me because I went swimming in the ocean. He said women aren't supposed to be swimmers, they aren't supposed to do anything like that. He told me that when he grew up he was going to cut my arms and legs off, and then he was going to swim out further than I had. This was a four-year-old boy.

"That's the attitude some children have about women, but then they learn differently as they observe me and what I do within my job. I run and I race with them; that's showing that there are women who can speak Spanish, who can also swim, who can also run, and who can be very loving and nurturing at the same time."

As told to the editors in an interview: Santa Paula is a small town in Ventura County, California, where I went to high school. It's a town for high-schoolers—all the action happens around the school and the kids. There are a lot of parties, where people get drunk and rowdy. It's the kind of town where kids like to fight.

One night, my cousin Victor and I went to my friend's house for a party; it was a pretty big party and there were a few kegs there. There were people that I knew, mostly high school kids and a few older guys who liked to hang around the high school girls. Victor had just recently gotten out of the Marines. He has a pretty long history of aggression, and he was trying to get over that, but we went to this party and he immediately got involved in a fight.

What happened was that these three hostile characters showed up at the party and immediately picked on this smallish guy. No one knew the small guy and we didn't know the other guys very well, they were kind of peripheral characters who occasionally came into town. They started hassling with the little guy outside and then they took him inside the house and into the bathroom. They started beating up on him in the bathtub.

My cousin Victor, seeing this, couldn't tolerate it. He just had to go in there and defend this person. It was obviously the thing to do. People were just standing around not doing anything, not thinking about what should be done, and so Victor jumped right in and pulled the guy out. Immediately, the three guys turned on Victor and started going toward him, so I got near my cousin. He just stood his ground. I wanted to make sure he didn't stay and do anything that would cause him to be thrown back into jail, which had happened two times before.

"Victor," I said, "let's leave. We've got to get out of here." The guys were coming closer and closer to him and he was still standing there, ready to take on the three of them.

When they saw me get close to my cousin, their focus changed. They started coming toward me and I could see what they were about to do. One of the guys picked up a beer bottle, and I could see he was going to get pretty dangerous and I was scared.

I didn't think about anything except getting my cousin out of there. I had just taken a year and a half of karate, so I knew a few moves. The three guys were coming at us in a row. I decided to go for the nearest one, and I knew I had to be really fast, to catch them off guard. They weren't expecting retaliation, not from me, anyway.

I picked up my leg and kicked as hard as I could toward the first guy's groin. He doubled over with this look of shock on his face. He just couldn't believe what had happened to him. The other guy was getting closer, and I slammed the heel of my hand up against the bottom part of his nose, so that he got a bloody nose, and he stopped coming toward me. Once again, I remember noting this look of extreme shock on his face. By this time some other men had come and gotten the third guy and held him back.

What amazes me was how natural, how accepted, violence was. No one thought of going in and helping this guy in the bathroom. There were lots of us, and we could have grabbed the three guys and sat on them, but no one thought of doing that. So for me that was one of the most empowering experiences I've had, knowing that I could defend myself by just being real fast and accurate and not thinking that I would get hurt more if I hurt these guys. They were completely dehumanized in my eyes and they felt it. They didn't have a sense of power over me—it was quite the opposite—I had overpowered them.

My cousin was so surprised. He told the story everywhere. He was just incredibly proud that I could do this. It really changed our relationship. We had had an adversarial relationship, since we were the two oldest kids in the family, and after that we became buddies.

When the story got around town, at first the guys would make fun of me, like "Here comes the macho woman," but the women I talked to were really amazed that I could do this to those guys, because they had a reputation of going around causing trouble. I saw one of them later on and he didn't come near me, he didn't bother me.

Now I have no fear of walking anywhere because I know I can defend myself. I usually wear the appropriate kind of shoes—I wear clog boots if I'm ever out alone. But I avoid situations that are obviously dangerous. When I go to meetings at night, I go by myself and take my bicycle. I feel that the way I carry myself shows I can defend myself.

I would not have done what I did had I not been in a self-defense class. It wasn't even for self-defense that I took the class; I took it for exercise. I didn't even think that it would be of use later. But now I know that it is useful because it trains you; you know how to kick, you know how to hurt, you know how to defend yourself.

I wouldn't recommend going around hurting people, but women do get attacked and they have to know how to hurt back; they have to really seriously know how to hurt back, so that men don't think they can get away with that sort of thing. If attackers were so severely injured that they would have a hard time walking, for example, they would think twice about attacking someone, and they wouldn't feel that sense of power in attacking someone.

For Latina women, self-defense is a twofold issue. We are oppressed as a people by our society, because of race. And our own men oppress us, too.

It's a big issue and you have to come at that issue from all different areas: education and social work and nutrition. You can't isolate it in a self-defense class, because the women won't come to the classes. They're home feeding the children and their men are telling them they can't go anywhere by themselves.

Women work hard in Mexican families. They're raising their kids and they're also working in the fields. That makes strong people. They're not on a pedestal, so in some ways they don't feel as hopeless as a woman who has never had to *physically* support a family.

When you've grown up working in the fields, you do have a certain amount of power. You're strong, you've been throwing things onto trucks and picking up giant loads of food and carrying them around. Not all Latina women work in the fields, but many of them have seen their mothers labor, because we Latina women have been working in the fields throughout American history.

I've seen my grandmother yell back at people who've insulted her daughters, or herself, or me. I've seen her get at it with men, just bunches of men on the street corner, which is probably why I was not afraid to tangle with more than one man. I've heard her say, "You don't talk that way in front of my daughters," or her grandchild, or whoever she felt was being insulted. When someone has stood up for you often enough, you're eventually going to feel you're worth defending.

If at First You Don't Succeed . . .

Marsha J. Hamm

Marsha Hamm was twenty-two and living alone in the garden district of New Orleans, Louisiana, when she was attacked. She worked as a medical secretary in a city hospital, and "never thought that I would be the victim of a crime." Now she lives with her husband and child in Indiana, where she works with chemically dependent adolescents.

"I've always heard and read that you shouldn't fight back because you might be hurt worse. Based on my experience, I think I would fight back again."

I went to bed that night around 11:00 P.M., after first opening my bedroom window about three inches to let the breeze in. At about 3:00 A.M., I woke up because I had the feeling that someone was staring at the back of my neck. In the light coming in from the patio, I could see a man removing the screen and starting to come in my bedroom window.

The first thought that ran through my mind was, I have to get up in a few hours and go to work, come back some other night. Then I began to feel scared and decided I needed to get help. I got out of bed, ran across the room to the phone, and dialed my landlady's number before he got through the window.

He had a glazed look in his eyes and was probably on drugs. He got me in a corner and put a piece of broken, jagged window glass to my throat. I had been screaming all this time and was still hanging onto the phone. My landlady answered, and I screamed my name before the phone was knocked out of my hand.

He hit me several times in the face with his fists and threw me on the bed. Then he told me what he was going to do to me. He threatened that if I did not cooperate, he would cut me up good.

Still screaming, I told him I was pregnant. When that didn't work, I said I was on my period, hoping that I was talking loud enough for the man next door to hear me through the apartment walls. I knew this was possible, because we had talked to each other through the walls several times in the past. Unfortunately, he was not home that night.

When none of this deterred him, I slid off the edge of the bed between his legs and sat down on the floor. I weighed, at that time, about two hundred pounds. The thought running through my head was, If you can pick this fat ass off the floor, you can have whatever you want.

By this time my landlady was pounding on the door. She had an unloaded gun in her hand and several male tenants with her. The man fled through the window, as I ran to open the door. Several of the tenants chased him, but he disappeared into the night.

The police were called and several squad cars came to the apartment. I was apparently in shock and did some strange things, like hiding my dirty dishes in the oven so the police wouldn't see my messy house.

I am a talker, and I talked about this incident with friends, police, relatives, and anyone who would listen. I think that is why I feel the way I do about the assault today. When I think about the incident now, I do not feel violated as I did then. I think of the funny things I did, like hiding the dishes and flirting with the cute police officers.

Testimony of a Welfare Mother

Juana Maria Paz

Juana Maria Paz is a thirty-three-year-old New York-born Puerto Rican lesbian and "welfare" mother. She has published books, plays, and reviews, and has worked as a TV/radio announcer/producer. She runs a hand-sewn clothing business from her home. Her writing presently focuses on prison, poverty and literacy. She coordinates the Prison Reading Project in Fayetteville, Arkansas, where she lives with her eleven-year-old daughter Mary Ann.

"About ten years ago, the man I was living with began beating me with a frequency and intensity that caused me to fear for my life and that of my nine-month-old baby, Mary Ann. We lived in a small cottage on the Florida coast and I was supporting all three of us with my veteran's benefits, which enabled me to go to college for the first time."

One June, my lover Mark admitted some startling things—that he'd made sure he slept with me every day until I got pregnant and that he'd manipulated me during the entire relationship through an elaborate system of lies and deceptions. He laughed and said it was easy, that I had a moral code I lived by and he could always anticipate how I'd react to any situation. He also said he wasn't letting me go alive. I threatened to leave and he threatened to kill all of us, including the baby and the dog.

I knew he was serious the night he dragged me around the house, closing windows with one hand to muffle the noise, and covering my mouth with the other. I held the baby with one arm and tried to loosen his grip so I could breathe. I broke free long enough to scream bloody murder and the police arrived within minutes, then checked me for external injuries. They tried to get me to make a statement, but the inside of my mouth was cut and I couldn't talk. They assured me that my neighbors were looking out for me and urged me to yell if I needed help, so someone would call them.

They left, and Mark apologized. Actually, he wanted to have sex. I refused. He raped me the next day. As things went from bad to worse, I made plans to leave town. I was all packed and waiting for a ride to the bus station when he came home drunk and carrying a loaded gun. He held me hostage for four hours and slapped me and knocked me down so many times that I can't remember them all.

He wanted to kill me, but I think he was afraid to live without me. He raped me until he couldn't get an erection anymore. Mary Ann cried at first, but I closed the door so she couldn't watch, and she finally sat down in her crib to play her red toy piano.

Mark decided I should cook one more dinner before he killed me. I ran away from him on the way to the grocery store, despite his promise to shoot me in the back if I made any false moves. He disappeared when I started screaming. I got to a phone and called the police. Since I looked like a victim from a horror movie by then and I had called many times before, they had no trouble believing my story. They did think I might change my mind later and refuse to press charges. I explained that the only way for me to get out of town alive was for them to keep him in jail overnight. The bus to Los Angeles left once a day and I had already missed it.

I had to get to a major city with emergency social services. I chose Los Angeles because it was far away and on the West Coast. I knew how to survive on my own in a big city, but I didn't want to go back to New York.

I arrived in Los Angeles after three days on the bus. I didn't know a soul there. I got on welfare quickly, and no one had trouble believing my story. My bruises were starting to get large and purple and yellow. My face was sore and swollen. There I was, a young woman walking around a strange city with a baby, a suitcase, and signs of a recent beating.

"I know. I've been there," women on buses and street corners seemed to say to me with their eyes. Wherever I went people seemed to know I was on the run.

I spent nine months staying home, taking care of the baby. I needed to heal, to forget, and to let go. Some days I was too upset to leave the house. When I did, I often returned to my roach-infested apartment, my mind full of the dreaded image of my husband. I imagined him standing in the shadows, red-faced with beer and violence, holding a gun and sneering, "Hello, Honey . . . get undressed."

That it could come to this, I thought as I calmed down and assured myself that it was just my old fear, welling up again and making it seem so real. After the better part of a year, I was ready to face the world again: I went to a conference on welfare, and plunged headlong into welfare rights work.

When welfare rights became a never-ending fight to change a system that wouldn't budge, I went on to other things—women's land, school, feminism, writing, and lesbianism. I began writing for lesbian/feminist publications.

Collecting welfare gives me a lot of leverage in dealing with the rest of the world. If my books don't sell I don't have to worry about how to pay the rent. If the people I work with on a volunteer basis don't like my performance, they can't withhold a paycheck. I would never want to be financially dependent on a husband or lover again.

Coming Out Alive

Py Bateman

Py Bateman is one of the best-known women in the United States self-defense movement. She is the founder of the Feminist Karate Union (FKU) in Seattle, Washington, and was chief instructor there from 1971 until 1984. She is the director of Alternatives to Fear, a nationally known self-defense organization, and is the author of the self-defense manual *Fear into Anger*. She has dedicated sixteen years of her life to fighting violence against women.

On May 26, 1984, Py Bateman was assaulted in her home by a man who tried to kill her. What follows are two letters she wrote to her former students at the Feminist Karate Union, and to other women in the martial arts after the attack. Since the time of the first letter, her attacker was convicted.

12 June 1984

Dear Sisters,

As many of you have already heard, I was assaulted in my home some time ago. I am recovering rapidly, and am now out of the hospital. Let me just go over the events of the assault for those of you who have not heard, or who have heard rumors.

It was Saturday afternoon, May 26, around 1:30 P.M. I was on my way home after running an errand. As I walked up the back stairs to my house, a man who had been hiding in a corner of my porch grabbed me by the hair and immediately began to cut around my eyes with a knife. (Luckily, there has been no injury to my eyes themselves and my vision has returned to normal.) He forced me to unlock the door and let him in.

Once we were inside, his level of violence escalated. He tried to put the knife to my throat. I caught the knife as it was coming toward me and took it away from him. The knife fell to the floor at that time. Then I kneed him in the groin. He doubled over and fell on top of me, then got me by the neck and dragged me upstairs. I became concerned because he was not leaving, and began to be less conservative in my defense; I hit him. He hit back, and we fought all over the house. He outweighed me by ninety pounds and was fourteen inches taller than me. Many injuries were sustained during this fight—the cumulative effect of repeated blows, rather than one good blow.

A friend came to my house about thirty minutes after the assault began, and I now believe that he left because she scared him away. Due to her clear thinking and fast action by police and aid units, I was taken very quickly to the hospital. There I underwent plastic surgery for the damage to my face and brain surgery for a subdural hematoma, or swelling under the skin over the brain.

In addition to the fantastic support network that sprang up here in Seattle to take care of not only the practical details but also to give support to me as I'm recovering, there have also been cards and letters from around the country. It has been tremendously heart-warming to hear people's good wishes and concerns—and their own experiences and struggles.

My recovery is going very well and there is no expected permanent damage, to my eyes or my brain. In the time that I've been recuperating, I've done a lot of thinking about what happened and what it means for women in the martial arts and the concepts of self-defense.

At first I was sorry that I hadn't defended myself to the point that I had no injuries, as in my favorite fantasies. But then I thought about how he used the knife, so deliberately and quickly. And how I responded with some pretty risky moves when he put the knife to my throat. So I decided that I had done pretty well—in fact, saved my life by fighting.

My training—and the years I've spent teaching—served me well during the assault. There were a few seconds at the beginning when my mind was simply coping with the reality of what was happening. But after that, my mind was busy with plans for ending the attack. I was thinking the whole time, never overcome by fear. That has to be a result of my training.

Also important was a commitment to our approach to self-defense. We have always stressed determination as important, and it was determination that kept me fighting—and thinking—when he didn't give up, when he escalated the violence. Another factor, one that we didn't know so much about, was biology. I never felt any pain while I was fighting. Not even when I cut my hand grabbing the knife by the blade. My consciousness was dominated by the determination to come out alive and my plans for how to do that.

In addition to coming to grips with the difference between my hopes for myself standing over an assailant's inert body and the reality of the grim struggle, I had to think of whether we had been wrong to say that most attackers are easily scared off by an effective resistance.

I had to remind myself that one individual's personal experience, no matter how powerful, does not change what we know about violence against women. This man's level of violence was at the extreme end of the scale, as was the extent to which he was willing to continue despite my calls for help and my fighting back.

We have not been wrong in predicting that most assailants would give up in a struggle; we have the research that proves that beyond any individual experience. Even the police, who in many ways are not the most enthusiastic proponents of self-defense for women, are convinced that my assailant was one of a minority of criminals whose main goal is to hurt or kill someone, and who don't respond the way "normal" criminals do.

This realization, plus the cards and letters I've had from women who have successfully defended themselves after taking a self-defense class or taking karate for some time, has brought me full circle from doubt to a renewed commitment to the work I've done over the past thirteen years. [Letter ends.]

Spring 1986

Dear Sisters,

My assailant was captured two months later. He was apparently inactive for about six months. I hope it was to recover from getting hurt fighting with me. But then he started going after elderly people, attacking an eighty-six-year-old woman and her son, one other woman, and finally a woman in her mid-seventies.

It was this last woman who set him up for capture. She awoke one morning to find him sitting on her chest, strangling her with a nylon stocking. She somehow got the stocking off her neck. She couldn't tell me just how, but she did. Then he began to beat her and gouge at her eyes with his fingers. She kept her head in the course of this.

Then she gave him her bank card and told him that he could get cash if he went to the bank machine. She told him which branch to go to. When he left with her card, she called the police. They staked out the banks in the area, and when he turned up at the one she had sent him to, they arrested him. What presence of mind she had!

The man pled guilty just before I was to go on the stand to testify, saving me that grief. He got twenty years for two first-degree assaults and three first-degree burglary charges. I found out later he was a heroin addict, and I feel I interrupted him in a burglary attempt. I feel he tried to kill me so I could not identify him, as he lived just beyond my back fence with his girlfriend.

I've become much more passionate about self-defense now. I realize that self-defense is more than just one other choice that a woman might have in response to an assault. It's a necessity. If I had not known how to defend myself last year, I would not be here this year. The level of violence this man presented me with is rare, but in some situations, if you don't have fighting back as a choice, you don't have any choices.

I used to be afraid of pushing self-defense too hard. Now I see it as the bottom line. I tried a fairly conservative approach, allowing the man a lot of time to give up and leave before I started attacking aggressively. I yelled for help, and tried to escape, until it became clear that there was nothing else I could do to stay alive. If I had it to do over, I would have started hitting much sooner.

I am no longer as conservative in what I teach. The techniques are the same, but my strategy has changed to no longer give the man so many chances.

Self-defense training is a vital survival skill. My training brought me many things—the excitement of competition, the striving for excellence, the fun of working out to the maximum, the friendships I developed with others. It is important for those things alone, but it also saved my life.

In strength and dignity,
Py Bateman

Adrenaline: A Hitchhiking Story

Kimberly Rosa

Kim Rosa was attacked when she was in her late teens. Her assailant was acquitted. A few years after the assault described in her story, Kim moved to northern California, where she went to a university and majored in justice administration. In the course of writing a paper on rape, she contacted the Humboldt County Rape Crisis Center and began to volunteer there; now she is assistant director.

"I believe I stayed in sort of a shock state for about five years. The trauma of the trial and his acquittal was perhaps worse than the actual attack. After all, I did live through it, which was obviously a lot more than one other person intended.

"I've never thought of my experience or this incident as a success story, except that I did live and to this day I wonder why, because it really was a miracle."

First—and this is so important—I want to comment on the feeling I had right before I got into the car. I had this feeling that I can never really describe, except that something was saying to me, "Don't do it." At the time I didn't know or couldn't figure out what not to do. It was a confusing message and I ignored it. I had been hitchhiking for four years already; it was my sole means of transportation. I lived by myself and worked in the next town, Manhattan Beach.

I was hitchhiking over to a girlfriend's house to do my laundry in her parents' machine. I had a box of clothes with me. When a man finally pulled over to pick me up, everything was normal until, right as I was about to get in with the box on my lap, he pulled the front seat forward so that I could put the box in the back. That's when I had the feeling: "Don't do it!"

When we got to the end of the street where my friend lived, the man pulled over and took out a screwdriver, put it to my ribs, and told me to get down on the floor. I was so shocked at first that I grabbed the screwdriver and pushed it away from my ribs and reached for the door handle to get out—"the nerve of this guy"–type reaction. There was no door handle.

The screwdriver found its way to my ribs again and I got down on the floor of the car at his instruction with my head on the seat facing the door. He held the screwdriver at my neck while we drove away. We were just a few feet away from my girlfriend's house.

On the way out to the field where we ended up, he talked to me. In this conversation, it became clear that he was going to rape me. I asked him if he was going to kill me, and he said no, that he would even give me a ride back to where I was going. You know, I believed him!

As I sat hunched on the floor of the car, the only thing I had the presence of mind to do was to try to vomit by sticking my finger down my throat. It didn't work. Every time I moved, he pressed the screwdriver a little harder against the back of my neck.

When we got to where we were going, we got out of the car, and he started to beat me and kick me and pull me along by my hair. We got down to the bluffs and he raped me—and at this point I still really believed that he would do like he said he would do, and take me back to my friend's house.

When he took the screwdriver out of his pocket and started to stab my chest with it, I began to realize that I might have to do something besides try to endure this as best I could. At one point, when his arm came up to stab me again with the screwdriver, I saw that there was no longer a blade in the handle. I looked down and saw it sticking out of my chest. This all happened in a few seconds.

He did not realize what had happened yet, so I took the blade out of my chest and put it on the ground behind my body, trying to bury it as inconspicuously as I could.

When his arm came down and he realized that the blade was gone, he threw the handle off and put his hands around my neck and started to choke me. Now I knew that I was dying, and that I had to do something if I wanted to live.

I think it was adrenaline that gave me the strength to do what I did next, because I could literally feel the life leaving my body. I just gave a last thrust of my body, mostly with my legs, and threw him completely off of me. That strength has surprised me to this day.

I got up and tried to get away, but I remember not being able to walk very steadily; my legs felt weak. Next, I felt a strong, heavy thud on my head, then my body falling to the ground, and then another thud on my head. I remember nothing more until I awoke.

I came to, crawled to the road, and lay vomiting until some kids came by and took me to their mom's house. She called the ambulance and the police.

I work for a rape crisis team now. I believe that the feeling I had before I got into that car is of utmost value. Everyone has, I believe, a sixth sense, but we are not taught to pay attention to it, or it has been written off as ''women's intuition.''

I am proud of the strength I had at that one moment, and I know that it saved my life. I have never thought of my experience as a success story until now. I did live, and it really was a miracle.

Waiting for a Chance

Leslie Bandle

Leslie Bandle is twenty-nine years old and "in love with life." In the last eight years, she has traveled the world and had numerous adventures. She is presently the regional sales manager for an electronics firm, and entering into the fifth year of a joyous and fulfilling relationship with someone with whom she wants to grow old.

"At one point after the attack, I told a student intern that I should have never gone to the man's room. She immediately gave me a strong lecture, saying that if I was going to make it through the experience, I was going to have to realize that it was not my fault. I realized that she was absolutely right. From that point on, I never felt responsible for the incident again."

It was a great opportunity that I could not pass up. After many interviews and one long paper, I was finally chosen to be an intern for a Congressman. I would be going to Washington, D.C., to work directly with him and his staff. It was a political science major's dream.

I arrived in Washington, D.C., with very little money and a lot of enthusiasm for my new position. I immediately set out looking for a place to stay, but I found it difficult in a city I knew very little about.

After looking at several rooms that could only be described as slum tenements, I finally gave up and went to stay at a youth hostel. A friend of mine had stayed there for four months and had had a wonderful experience. But from the moment I walked into the place, I was afraid.

When I turned on the light in my room, I saw several cockroaches scurry into the cracks in the wall. The carpet was riddled with cigarette burns, and my bed consisted of the top bunk of an army-style bunk bed. Needless to say, I was uncomfortable, especially when I found out my roommates were going to be transients for the next four months. Evidently, there were no other female guests who would be staying as long as I had planned.

The hostel managers informed me that there was a male guest, also an intern, who would be staying at least three months. I met him in the stairwell my second day at the hostel. He was a welcome sight, since I was lonely and very uneasy about my new environment. He was holding a steam iron and he asked for a match.

His name was Mark, and he said he had been living at the hostel for a week and he was kind of lonely. This interested me. Here was a potential friend who was involved in the same kind of program as my internship. He invited me up to his room to watch TV and drink a beer. I said that I might just come up to watch some TV, since there wasn't much to do around the hostel at night, and I could really use a friend there. I emphasized the word "friend." I did not want him to get the wrong impression.

A while later, I knocked at his door. He opened the door in his boxer shorts, and I immediately decided that Mark was expecting something more than I was willing to give. Then I realized that he was in fact wearing a pair of cut-off polyester pants and not boxer shorts. I went in and sat on the bed across from where he was sitting.

Mark said that he couldn't offer me a beer, because he had drunk it all before he went to work. I remember thinking that it was strange that he would drink beer before going to work, and this added to my nagging apprehension. Then we dropped into casual conversation about the tremendous difference between my slummy room and his nice room.

"My room is nice, but it has just as many cockroaches!" he said. "I really worry that the maid or some of these guys just passing through will get into my things. Most of them are broke and don't look particularly honest." Of course, I immediately related to his fears.

Mark told me he was very shy, and did not invite many people to his room, but that his roommate in college was constantly having friends in and out of their dorm room. He went on to explain that his roommate got ripped off for everything as a result. He then re-emphasized his anxiety about leaving his luggage behind while he was working, since he was sure the maid or his potential roommates would steal it.

Then he expressed his surprise that I trusted him enough to come to his room, because he had thought his conversation with me on the stairwell made him appear like a man with the wrong intentions. I said I had trusted him because he was really polite, a fellow intern, about my age, and a potentially good friend to know during my stay at the hostel. He said I should never trust anyone.

Mark said he had met another girl at the hostel, but he did not invite her to his room because he just did not invite people to his room. He explained that I was different because I seemed so down to earth; it made him feel secure. He went on to say that he had just broken up with his girlfriend after two years. He also mentioned that a woman rejected him on the way to Washington. He had hitchhiked after missing his bus, and a woman stopped to pick him up, and then had second thoughts and tore off in her car. This seemed to really bother him because he felt she was unjustified in her actions.

We went on to talk about dancing, his "A" standing at his university, and our new jobs as interns. I was actually starting to feel comfortable with my new friend.

At approximately 11:30 P.M., I got up to leave, explaining that I had to go because I had to get up early to go to work. As I walked toward the door, I felt a huge bang on top of my head. I couldn't figure out what had happened. I initially thought the ceiling had fallen, so I looked up and around. As I turned around I saw that Norman had the steam iron in his hand and was coming down to hit my head with it again. BANG! I could hear the sound of the iron making contact with my head. I was so confused that, for a fleeting moment, I thought perhaps he was protecting me from something. Then he hit me a third time and the full realization sank in: this guy was really trying to hurt me.

I was flooded with emotion. I was stunned, terrified, confused, and in shock. I started using my arms to protect myself from the continuous blows he was raining on my head. I reached for the door-knob and started to turn it when he grabbed my left arm and jerked me away. It still bothers me to this day that I almost had that door open. He continued to hit me, and I could not figure out why I was not going unconscious. From the look on his face, I could tell he was also wondering. It did not seem to matter that I was using my arms to protect myself. Every blow hit me squarely on the head. Finally, after ten blows, I fell on the bed.

"Please don't hurt me, please don't hurt me, please don't hurt me," I pleaded, as I held his wrists while he leaned over me. "You're a really nice guy, I like you, please don't hurt me," I said in an effort to tame his violent attack. I thought that maybe he thought I didn't like him, and this was his reason for the attack.

"You can have my money, really, you can have my money," I said. I actually thought he wanted my money.

"I don't want your money. . . . Take off your clothes," he mumbled. I was absolutely stunned. It had not occurred to me that he wanted to rape me until this moment. Actually, it never occurred to me that I would ever be raped by anyone. It always happened to other women, but this would never happen to me. Welcome to the world, I thought to myself. I kept thinking about the movies where the women get raped and murdered. This thought was absolutely horrifying—it convinced me that I would never make it out alive.

I was still holding his wrists and he was still holding the iron in his right hand, when he pulled away and set the iron at the head of the bed. He then began to unbutton and unzip my pants.

"Hey, I'm on my period," I said, hoping to deter him from raping me. He ignored this and told me to move so I was lying lengthwise on the bed with my head at the foot. As I lifted my body to move over, I saw the pool of blood on the bedspread where my head had been. I put my left hand on the back of my head and said, "Oh my God, I'm bleeding." He ignored this.

He pulled my pants down below my knees, bent my legs upward, pulled out my tampon, and raped me. It seemed like he wasn't enjoying it. He looked and sounded like he was in pain.

I could still feel the blood from my head pouring down my neck and back. I started to breathe hard and fast until I began to slip into unconsciousness. Then I realized that if I was going to survive, I had to stay conscious. I held my breath for a second and told myself to calm down. Then I began to strategize about how to get out of this situation alive. I decided that a run for the door at the right moment would be my best bet. I knew I needed to calm him down a little so he would bring his guard down and I could make my move.

He was so quiet it was scary, so I tried to get him to talk.

"How do you feel?" I asked.

"Fine," he grunted. "How do you feel?"

"Fine," I replied.

"Have you ever fucked a black guy?" he demanded.

"No, I just dated them," I said.

He told me to put my legs up over his hips and lock my feet, which I did. He was hurting me. Then he said, "You better not tell anyone."

I said, "Oh, don't worry about it, I won't tell anyone."

"You better not or you know what will happen," he threatened. I said "Yes." I felt a little better because I had gotten him to talk, but his words were just as scary as the silence.

Finally, he finished raping me and told me, "Get on your stomach on the floor." I sat up and began to get down on the floor next to the bed nearest the door. "No, I want you on the floor between the two beds!" he demanded.

I got up and began to crawl over the bed to the area between the two beds, but I froze in terror when I saw the iron on the bed.

"No," I murmured. I was convinced that he was now going to finish smashing my head in if I lay between the two beds. He moved the iron onto the dresser, which relieved me tremendously. I continued onto the floor and he said, "Lie flat with your hands under your head and your head turned toward the right." He began adjusting my head this way and stopped for a moment to feel my face.

I just could not lie with my head flat, since in that position I couldn't keep a close watch on his moves. I was really sure that he was going to make a move to kill me. To calm myself, I decided to think of the worst thing that could happen, which would be to die. This somehow made me feel better. I drifted, thinking about my best friend, whose spirit would greet me, and of my dog, Bonnie, who had just died. Then I thought of VOID and I snapped out of the pleasant thought of death. There was still some doubt in my mind that there really was an afterlife, and I clicked back into survival mode. I also thought of my parents seeing police photos of me beaten and smashed to death between two beds in a slummy hostel. I couldn't stand the thought that they would have to imagine what I went through before I died.

He jammed my head down again and started walking toward the dresser where the iron was. I sprang up onto my elbows and turned to look because I was sure he was going to get the iron. Instead, he said, "Let's turn this TV off." Then he came back over and turned the light off on the nightstand. Looking back on the entire assault, the scariest moments were when he had the lights off. I could not see or predict what was to come. I was terrified.

He got on top of me and tried to insert himself from behind. Then he said, "This won't work," and he got up and turned the light on. "What do you mean?" I said. My hopes were starting to rise. Perhaps he was just going to rape me and then let me go.

"I'm going to walk you back to your room," he replied.

He started to get dressed and I asked, "Can I get up?"

"No," he replied. Finally, he brought my pants over to me and I got up and put them on.

"Pull your pants back down to your knees and lie on your stomach on the floor where you were," he suddenly commanded. All my hopes died, but I did what he asked.

As I was on the floor, once again he turned off the light and just stood between my legs. "Why did you turn off the light?" I asked. I just couldn't stand the light to be off; it scared me. I pressed my ankle against his leg, so I could tell if he moved toward the iron. Again he leaned over and adjusted my head and felt my face for a moment. Then he turned the light on again.

"Can I get up and get dressed?" I asked hopefully.

"Wait a minute," he said. I waited a minute, then got up and pulled my pants on. While I was putting them on, I commented, "Yuck, that tampon looks gross." He bent over and threw it away.

"Stop being so cool," he grumbled, my comment only irritating him.

"Look, if you don't hurt me, I swear I won't tell anyone," I reasoned with him. He didn't respond. He just stared blankly at me with his mouth slightly open.

"You better not tell anyone," he finally said.

"Let's shake on it," I said. This he responded to, and we shook hands.

I grabbed my jacket and put it on. As I put the hood over my head I told him, "I'm putting this on so that no one can see my head when I go outside." I wanted to reassure him that I was not going to tell anyone. I started to move forward and he said, "Wait a minute." In an effort to sound casual I asked him to find my purse and then I had him picking up all the items that had fallen out.

Suddenly, he turned off the light again. In desperation, I asked, "Why did you turn off the light?"

"I don't want anyone to see me come out of the room." My hopes were crumbling, because now I was sure he was going to try to kill me.

He put his left arm around my shoulders and put his left hand over my mouth. He was looking all around the room as we edged toward the door. I pressed the side of my body against his, so I could feel if he stretched over to grab the iron. As we neared the door, I felt his body stretch over toward the dresser, and I knew he was getting ready to make his move. I began preparing myself mentally and physically for the moment.

Suddenly, he thrust a hunting knife into my chest. My mind was a thousand miles away. I was thinking about all the movies I had seen; this is the scene where the girl is knifed and killed. Fortunately, my body was reacting while my mind was on vacation. My hands grabbed his thrusting hand just as the knife went into my chest. I struggled with him as he put a tremendous amount of pressure on his thrust in order to get the knife all the way into my chest. I started to pull the knife out, but I had to change my grip. As I did, he stabbed me again.

With both hands holding him off, I pulled the knife out and shoved his hand, arm, and knife back until my arms were fully extended. I slipped my left hand down and opened the door. As it opened, it pushed into him. I screamed for help and pulled away from the hand over my mouth. The scream startled him and he let me go.

I can't truly describe the feelings I had as I ran out of that room and down the hall. I knew I was going to make it. I felt so free, so happy, and so lucky. When I was running, it felt like I could run incredibly fast and far. It felt like I was flying with each step taken.

Postscript

Mark was apprehended by the police that day. One year later, in the trial, he claimed that she knocked on his door and said, "Have you ever fucked a white woman on her period before?" Then he claimed she took her clothes off and they had sex, after which he claimed she made a racial slur, which made him angry. He admitted hitting her over the head with the iron and threatening her with a knife.

The all-black jury convicted Mark on charges of assault with a deadly weapon (iron and knife). They did not convict him of assault with intent to kill or armed rape. The jury foreman stated to Leslie after the trial that they had believed her story, but did not want to put a young black man in prison for life.*

Mark has never been sentenced and is presently free due to technical problems in the criminal justice process preceding the trial.

*This verdict and the foreman's comment make us face troubling issues of race and racism in our society. The jury's decision must be understood against the backdrop of the racism inherent in the criminal justice system. In fact, we know from statistics that non-white men are convicted of rape at much higher rates than white men. See the Note on Racism (page xxvii) for more detailed treatment of this subject.

Asian, Female, and Fierce

Cindy Nakazawa

Cindy Nakazawa (a pseudonym) is a Japanese-American woman in her thirties, living in northern California. She holds a third-degree black belt in aikido, and teaches in several aikido schools in the San Francisco Bay Area.

"You don't have to learn a martial art in order to defend yourself. What's important is knowing when to fight and learning how to keep your mind calm in case of an attack. A lot of women can get that just from psychological training. Martial arts training is ideal because it trains both your body and your mind."

As told to the editors in an interview: The first time I was attacked I was about fifteen. I got off the bus and I was wondering if I should go to aikido training, or go home and take a nap because I was so wiped out. Then, bammo, all of a sudden this guy (I didn't even hear him, he had sneakers on) ran up and bear-hugged me from behind.

I was so tired that I just relaxed and bent over as soon as he hit me and he went flying right over me. I thought it was a practical joke, maybe my brother or somebody I knew. So I looked and I saw this guy on the street and I thought, That's weird, that wasn't my brother. He was looking up; I think he was just as surprised as I was. Then out of the corner of my eye, I saw another person coming and I thought, Jesus, I'm getting attacked. It's six o'clock in the afternoon and I'm getting attacked.

I was on a street corner, and nobody was getting out of their cars to say, "Hey, leave that lady alone." So I thought, Well, fight like hell.

The first guy was on the ground and I figured that he wasn't going to get up real soon, so I turned around and kicked the other guy in the stomach, which worked pretty well. I had a shoulder bag, and luckily that's all they wanted. The second guy yanked it away and they both started running and I figured they must not want to hang around and fight with somebody.

I had on platform shoes and I started running after them, using every foul word in the book. I was so mad that I started running to catch them, and that's when my better senses said, That's really stupid, for a purse. So I turned around and asked myself, Where are all the concerned citizens in this neighborhood? They're all just kind of driving by and watching, to see what happened.

When the police came, they said that two men who fit that description, about seventeen or eighteen years old, had attacked three other women that morning, but the men had beaten most of them up before they took their purses. Two of them were elderly, and were hurt and in the hospital. The other was another small Oriental like me. The policemen were wondering why I wasn't hurt and asked why I didn't get beat up.

I went back and told my teacher about it the next day and he said, "In two-person attacks, you have to use better sense. You should have taken the guy out on the street and then you would have had just one on your back." But he was real proud of me because I had not been hurt and I had used my judgment instead of running in there after my purse. That's when I decided not to wear high heels anymore, because I couldn't run or get my balance very well. I threw them away after that. I didn't like wearing them in the first place. In case I do get attacked again, at least I'll be able to do something other than just clomp along.

A couple years after that, I was working graveyard shift as an X-ray technician in a large hospital. I had always felt it was a little on the dangerous side, because the X-ray floor is totally isolated. It's open, people can walk in from maybe six or seven different entrances without ever being seen, and it's got all kinds of weird places and unlit rooms. I had to do everything in a darkroom, developing and running the film. The only other person on the whole floor was the radiologist, who slept in a locked room.

One night, I had just finished a case and sent the patient downstairs to the emergency room. I went back in to do my paperwork in the file room, and was sitting on a chair with other chairs right next to it. This guy, who must have been waiting in the file room, dropped a blanket on my head, grabbed my throat, and pushed me down on the chairs. The first thing that came to mind was, This is not Sid, the messenger, 'cause he wouldn't do that to me. And I heard this guy say, "Put your hands down by your sides." My natural reaction was to get my hands up to my throat because he was closing my airway, but he said to put my hands down by my sides.

So I said, "Fuck you, I'm not going to do that." I just grabbed his little finger and bent it all the way back to get him to let go. And I knew that I couldn't come up, because of the pressure coming down on my throat, so I'd have to go down. I kicked the chairs out from under me, fell onto the floor and rolled up in a ball. I was right in front of his groin, so I figured, I'm going for it. I punched him right in the balls, and he flew back about four feet into my wooden aikido practice weapons. I usually brought my wooden staff and my wooden sword to work because there was nothing to do except practice.

When he fell, the nearest thing that came sliding down was my sword, so I picked it up and starting knocking at him. I went after him and he saw me coming with a stick, so he made a beeline out of the file room and I ran after him. He went behind a curtain into an emergency exit that no one would know about unless they had worked there. So I thought, This guy knows something about this hospital. I called security, and I was lucky that they were nearby; they got there within seconds. I showed them the exit he had gone through. Later, I found out that he had run all the way down through the emergency room and out.

This is what makes me mad—they did not catch the guy; he outran them. He just ran straight into Golden Gate Park. The security guards had city police helping them, but he just lost them in the park.

When the police were taking my report, they said, "Well, do you want to go to the emergency room to get checked out?," because they thought I might have been hurt. And I didn't even feel anything because I had been knocked around in training much more than this before. I thought, Well, my neck kind of hurts but it's fine, and I said, "I have to do the rest of my work. I have to finish my shift, it's only five o'clock and I have three more hours to go."

I didn't realize that there's a lot of psychological junk that happens after an attack, until the police said, "We want to take down your report, so tell us what happened." I . . . it's really weird. I just started getting real shaky about telling people about it. Afterward, I thought, If he did have a knife, I would have been dead, or if he had had a gun, I might have been dead. I didn't really want to talk about it for about a year.

My teachers said, "You can't think about what might have happened, you have to think about what did happen and how you handled it and that, thank God, you're not hurt." It was just a very hard thing to go through. Not as much as if he'd gotten away with rape or something like that. I do have friends who've been raped and I thought, Thank God that has never happened to me. I get really angry, sometimes I think I would just kill the guy if I had a chance.

The police told me that I was in one of the very high-risk categories: small, Asian, and female. People kind of feed on that, because they associate Oriental with being submissive, and they look at small, that's another check, and they look at female, that's another check. So they automatically think, Easy. So if you are in that category of a small Asian female, I would suggest taking some kind of training, because it's a hard world. I hate to say it, but we get preyed on, and unless you've trained your mind and your body to deal with that, then chances are one day you're going to have to face some type of aggressive energy.

The police told me I probably have never been hurt because I've been very aggressive in my actions. When the attacker came in, all of a sudden he was faced with somebody who wasn't going to give in. Attackers would much rather go for an easier mark, so they'll just give up on you because they figure they might lose a body part.

There's a woman who's training with me now in San Francisco— she's very small, a Puerto Rican girl—and the first time I saw her, she walked into the school and said, "Show me something that I can use on the street right now." And I just looked at her and I said, "You know, there are women who have trained for seventeen years in martial arts and have not been able to handle themselves because within the first few seconds of an attack they froze. And if you don't react immediately, chances are you're not going to get away with anything. I can't show you any tricks. All I can say is, if you train with me or with any good instructor, you'll train your mind to react within a few seconds." Martial arts are good for small people because they work on timing and on learning to keep control.

Aikido is a part of my life now, it's something that I have to do to be satisfied with myself. That's really the only competition there is in aikido—the one that you wage with yourself about what your goals are and what you want to get out of it. That's another thing that I really enjoy about aikido, that there is no competition between persons.

You learn who you are and how strong you can actually be psychologically. When attackers feel that piercing quality in response to whatever they've put out, that makes them think a lot about coming back in. I used to be a real quiet person, very meek and very shy, and I think aikido has changed me quite a bit. Especially at work, I'm in much more command of myself and I know exactly what I do best and how to do it efficiently, so when doctors are being total jerks, when they come in and pull their trips and try to be dominant in my area, I just give it right back to them because I'm in control of the situation.

Battle in the Cemetery

Rashida

Rashida is thirty years old and is of Afro-Cuban ancestry. She is a lesbian, and a pagan. She is currently working toward a degree in counseling psychology and intervention, and is an intern/volunteer at Chrysalis, a women's center in Minneapolis–St. Paul, Minnesota.

"I believe that self-defense comes from awareness at all levels of being. I am learning martial arts, not only for self-defense techniques, but also for the mental and spiritual discipline they teach. I am also working on my emotional issues with a therapist who follows a holistic approach to health and healing—it's another way of defending myself and becoming the best I can be."

I was less than a block away from home that evening, when a car with five young men drove up beside me. Two of them jumped out, grabbed me, and pulled me into the backseat. There was one on either side of me, so I couldn't reach the door handles.

Once they had me in the car, I stopped struggling. I felt very frightened at first. I have always been a passive person, taught to compromise instead of use force—an unusual attitude in my rough neighborhood. But as I sat there, I began to get angry. These men had placed me in a situation where I felt there was no compromise. I had to either fight and get away, or submit to being raped repeatedly by ''men'' barely older than myself.

I sat quietly while we rode to an old cemetery behind the church and grade school I had attended. I don't remember what they talked about during the ride. My anger helped me to relax, slipping into a state I call my "battle awareness." When they stopped the car in the middle of the dark cemetery, I was ready.

Most of the guys got out of the car, except for the one on my right. He had put his arm around my neck to keep me in place. The others were outside of the car taking their pants down. When one of them climbed into the backseat and moved toward me, I snapped.

I bit the arm that held me, hit the guy behind me in the gut with my right elbow, and kicked the guy coming toward me, all at the same time. The one holding me let go, and the one facing me got out of the car, hurt. I got out of the car quickly and ran. The other men were so surprised, they didn't move fast enough to stop me. One did start to run after me, but I heard someone call him back.

Across the street from the cemetery was a house that had a high, thick, bushy hedge. When the car came out of the cemetery, I hid there, watching it from behind the bushes. The car stopped at the gate for a few seconds, and I heard the men arguing with each other. They finally drove off at high speed.

I waited a bit after the car was gone, then I ran to the house of a classmate who lived nearby, still watching for the car to come around the corner. When I got to the house, I pounded on the door. Elisa, my classmate, answered the door, asking me what was happening. Then she took a good look at me, saw that I was too winded to answer, and let me in.

Her mother, a tiny German lady, came into the room and listened as I told what happened. Before I was finished, she left the room and returned with a rifle that was almost as long as she was tall. When Elisa and I saw her with it, we both started to laugh.

Then the impact of what could have happened hit me. I began to cry. Since I had asthma, I had an attack of wheezing. Elisa's mom put the gun down by the locked front door, told Elisa to sit down with me, and went to call the police. When she came back, she had a cup of tea, two antihistamine tablets, and a box of Kleenex for me.

By the time the police got there, I had calmed down considerably. They filled out the report, asked if I needed medical attention, and took me home.

My mother worked nights as a custodian, so she wasn't home. I didn't tell her what happened, thinking that she would just get upset when it wasn't really necessary. But I didn't count on the plainclothes cop who came to the door the next morning. He told us that a young man had come to the emergency room with a severe human bite that required stitches on his right arm. Would my mother care to press charges?

My mother was angry at the whole situation, and at me for not telling her, but she decided not to press charges. She did not want to "make things worse." Although I never saw those men again, I am still angry that they got away with what they tried to do to me. I would never allow anyone to take my dignity and my control away from me now.

Does He Know Who I Am?

Claire Trensky

Claire Trensky (a pseudonym) grew up in Los Angeles. She holds a second-degree black belt in judo and has worked as a city bus driver for eight years.

"I never have any trouble on the bus, because I'm so tuned in to who's getting on. But I have had some vivid pictures in my mind of some guy reaching around to touch my breast and me breaking his fingers.

"The attack I describe changed my Pollyanna approach to life—always loving people and having so much good feeling for everybody. Knowing that I could have died was startling. It showed that I need to be more alert and maybe not so trusting. I need to be more centered and watchful when I'm in public."

As told to the editors in an interview: I was with my sister and her four-year-old son, Stuart, who was strapped in the car seat in the back. It was a Sunday afternoon, and we were parked in the Home Savings parking lot on Hollywood Boulevard and Edgemont. To use the automatic teller you have to park along the side street, shut off from the main street. Susan went off to get some money, and I was just sitting there in the passenger seat, singing and playing and chit-chatting with Stuart. We were playing this game where one person says "Yes" and the other person says "No," and you go yes, no, yes, no, and then trade.

A minute later, I saw this guy walking up to the car, casually, yet with an aggressive manner. I wondered, What's this guy want? He walked right up to the door, which was partly open to let air in. He didn't stand back a few feet and say "Excuse me," as if asking for help. I thought, What's going on? Maybe somebody's hurt and he needs some help. He was holding a paper folded over, and I could see this black handle sticking out, like an umbrella handle. He came right up to the door and said, "Don't do anything, I've got a gun."

My initial thought was, Well, show it to me. I didn't see a gun, only this sinister-looking black handle. The guy was looking around, giving off these terrible evil vibes, and I thought, This guy really means business and I'd better pay attention to what's happening here. So I said, "What do you want?" in a small voice. And he said, "What do you think?," making fun of me. I thought, What are the alternatives here? What do I have to give this guy? Sex? Money? So I thought, Money, that's better. I reached in my pocket, and happened to have two twenties. I was glad because I thought, Well, forty bucks, that's pretty good, so I looked at him and said, "Here's some money." And he took it.

Just then my sister came walking around the front of the building, probably twenty feet from the car, and I looked over and he looked over. Then he opened the door, and took out a knife, and it was big—about a five-inch handle, a six- or seven-inch blade, serrated on the top with a silver shiny point. It looked really scary. He said, "Move over," and held it against my kidney on the right side. I moved over into the driver's seat and he sat down in the passenger seat with the knife in his left hand. I instinctively looked down to see how he was gripping the knife, because I thought, I have to get out of this, but when and how?

Technically, I knew how to get the knife away. That's because I've been two times national champion in judo kata (prearranged forms), and have nine years of judo training. So I was thinking, This guy is nuts. Does he know who I am? But I was also really scared and thought, This isn't like the martial arts practice hall. I decided it would be better to hang out, because my sister was there and my nephew was strapped in his car seat. I didn't want to do anything wrong. What felt right, especially with the point of the knife sticking in my side, was to do exactly what he wanted at that point.

There was some doubt in my mind whether I would survive. Then my sister came out. By this time, the situation felt really serious, and I thought, This is life or death. His eyes were shifting around. I tried to look him in the eye and he would not meet my gaze. I was trying to contact him as a fellow human, but he wouldn't look at me. He was speaking with slurred speech, so I thought he might be on drugs. But he had pretty good coordination when he got in the car.

Then my sister came walking up and I tried to tell her something with my face—to calm her. She said, "Hey, what's going on?" Later she said she thought it was some friend of mine from high school. Then she looked in and saw the knife sticking in my side. She's an RN, so she was thinking about my perforated liver. He seemed to know where to put it, right under my ribs. It wasn't under the skin but poking, constant pressure, enough so that my entire focus was on it. Her face was totally drained, and she almost screamed, but she said softly, "Don't hurt my sister, don't hurt my son," sounding lost and real scared.

"Give me the money," he said, gesturing. She had seven twenty-dollar bills in her hand from the automatic teller machine. "Here. Don't hurt my sister and my son." He took it and said, "How much is it?"

"A hundred and forty."

Then he told her, "Go around to the other side of the car." When she started walking around the front of the car, he increased the pressure on the knife. I thought he might leave when he had the money, but all of a sudden he was pushing harder. And suddenly I thought, Oh my God, my sacred body, and my fear turned to rage. Something clicked inside me and everything slowed down, like underwater, slow motion. Time stood still and I felt I could live or I could die right then.

I was lucky that the handle of the knife was about five inches long, and his hand took up maybe three and a half or four inches, so there was that extra handle sticking out from his hand for me to grab. His ring finger and his pinky were semirelaxed on the knife—he wasn't gripping it tightly. The way the handle was situated I knew I could get my hand on it and pry it out from between his fingers. That's a pretty common self-defense technique, and I'm glad I know it. So when that click happened, I shifted my body to get a little bit away from the point, and at the same instant I reached with my right hand onto the part of the knife that was sticking out past his pinky. It wasn't much grip, but it was better than nothing. I pulled, then I tried with both hands. He then pulled back and fought for a second. He didn't just let me take it away, although I used quite a bit of force.

When I went for that knife, I just focused on the handle—I hardly noticed the blade. He pulled it in front of himself, with both of his hands, and I yanked it with the thought, This is it, I've got to get it, there's no choice. So I got it. I don't think he got cut, and I know I didn't. Then there was a slight pause and I had this elated feeling—this really worked and I'm free, I'm safe now.

He opened the car door and ran fast. Meanwhile Susan was screaming, "Claire, Claire." She saw this struggle going on in the car and she thought he was stabbing me, so she freaked out.

I was so pissed off and so enraged, I opened my door and started after him. I dropped the knife on the floor of the car. There's no way I would have thought of using it on him.

I yelled, "Fuck you, you piece of shit, fuck you, leave us alone," to release all those feelings.

I thought, Well, maybe he does have a gun, maybe he's got some friends around the corner, maybe I shouldn't chase him too far. Then I thought, Let me go back and take care of the living, not take care of this jerk.

I went back to the car, and calmed down my sister, who was getting hysterical. I was still pissed off, though, and jumped in the driver's seat and said, "Let's go get our money." We went up the street where he went and drove really fast trying to find him, but it had been a couple of minutes and he was gone. We saw one guy get in a car and drive off and we thought, There he is, and we chased him for a few blocks and then lost him.

Susan said, "Well, let's not report it, it probably happens every day, it's no big deal," and I said, "No way, we're going to call this in. We've got to do whatever we can to get our feeling of power back, and maybe catch the guy, who knows?"

So I called 911 and told the story and the dispatcher said, "Now, let me understand this, you got the knife away? Is this a kid who attacked you?" I said he was probably twenty-eight years old, about five feet nine, 165 pounds. She said, "How did you do that?" And I said, "Well, I have a black belt in judo so I know technically what to do in that situation." She said, "Oh, I see."

My nephew was completely calm and silent through the whole thing. When he talks about it now he says, "Oh, the bad man, we got the knife away and he ran."

Part VI

Teamwork

Introduction

We gotta fight back
In large numbers
Fight back
I can't make it alone
Fight back
In large numbers
Together we can make a safe home.

Holly Near, "Fight Back"

One of the myths about being attacked is that it is necessarily an isolating experience. The classic TV or movie image depicts a lone woman, clicking down a dark alley in high heels and a dress that restricts her movement. Suddenly, she is attacked by a masked stranger, who more than likely is holding a knife to her throat. If she does manage to scream, no one hears her cry. Or if people are nearby, they are only indifferent bystanders.

The stories in this section are by women who called on the resources of other people to help them defend themselves or actively deal with the aftermath of an attack. In the "Weapons at Hand" section, women used "found" weapons—ones that happened to be nearby—as well as intentional weapons that they consciously kept for use in a possible attack. Similarly, the women who use teamwork call on people who happen to be nearby, as well as friends and supporters.

An attack is always unexpected; but that doesn't mean your potential responses need be unrehearsed. Nobody wants to think about being assaulted. Violence is an awful reality of contemporary society, and it's understandable that we'd rather close our eyes to it. Yet, do you know what you and your best friend would do should you be attacked while walking down the street together? Certainly, you would want to present a united front to an attacker. Not that your responses can be mapped out and followed like a script when the moment arrives; your best defense is a flexible mind and body, armed with a repertoire of possible responses. Still, self-defense is also about being prepared. When you're with another person, there are two or more sets of possible responses—as well as two sets of limitations.

For instance, some women believe in nonviolence, while others would be willing to seriously injure or even kill in self-defense. It's important to talk about strategies with the people you spend time with. For instance, what would you do if a man walked up to you and tried to punch you? Maybe you would back up and then run away, while your friend would stand her ground, block the punch and punch back. If you live with other people, you may want to develop a strategy for self-defense in your home, too. For example, you can figure out together what might be the best escape routes, or how the various aspects of each room might be used to your advantage.

As in all areas of self-defense, there is no right or wrong answer. What is important is that you communicate with others and find out what your strengths and limitations are. Share your fears. Perhaps you fear attacks by gangs the most, while your friend is terrified by weapons. Not only can such discussions give you a good idea about what you can expect from each other; they also can break through the terrible fears we have about even imagining an attack. By visualizing an attack and your effective response to it, the attack loses some of its power. By imagining yourself and your loved ones actively resisting an assault, you can see a way out. Also, strategizing with another person can help you face your deepest fears and think of ways to work with and around them. Fear is a healthy response to danger, and can also be a powerful energizer—as long as it is *used* and doesn't freeze the mind and muscles. And even the most fear-inducing situations can be handled successfully. In 1985, two women in Placerville, California, "bit, choked and battered a rifle-toting man who robbed their campsite," according to Placer County sheriff's officials. There is safety and power in numbers.

What about bystanders? It's true that some people—particularly in cities where they may see an enormous amount of violence in their daily lives—may not want to get involved if they witness an assault. You can't *expect* to be rescued by anyone who may be in the vicinity. But there are also modern-day hero stories about bystanders who leap to the aid of someone in trouble. For instance, in January of 1985, the *San Jose Mercury News* reported that Monica Jones faced off an attacker who was about to rape a twelve-year-old neighbor in her St. Louis apartment building. "You don't think about getting hurt," she said. "If someone is getting hurt, I can't close my door."

There are also ways to encourage others to get involved. D. P. and her friend in "Rounding Up the Campers" manage to mobilize an entire campground to pursue a man. They were direct in their appeal to other people; they simply said they had been assaulted and asked for help, and then gave others clear directions about what to do. In "Two Gutsy Women," Chris Weir and her friend don't get a response at first from their neighbors when they are assaulted at knife point on the street. Porch lights begin to go on, however, when they actually call their neighbors by name. That, of course, means that they took the time and effort to get to know who their neighbors were—an important community self-defense tactic.

If you are attacked, think about other women and how you can help protect them from assault. This may mean reporting to the police, or calling your local rape hotline and giving a description. Some organizations post "street sheets"—descriptions of attackers in the area that include the man's identity and address (if known), what he did, physical description, and typical "hangouts." The sheet may include a drawing or photograph of the man, and must be carefully worded so as not to include any information that might identify women he has assaulted.

In "Elevator Escape," Tamar Hosansky gets away from her would-be rapist, but realizes quickly that other women are at risk and takes steps to see that he doesn't escape from her apartment building.

There are other ways to get help from others:

- Yell "FIRE!" instead of "HELP!" or "RAPE!" Some people might be too afraid to get involved when one human being attacks another, but most people are willing to do whatever they can in a fire—especially if it's in their building. It doesn't matter what you yell—just get their attention, then tell them what you need them to do.
- If you're in trouble on the street, run to the nearest house or place

of business. Bang on the door and let the people inside know you
need their help. Again—say and do whatever works to get you
in the door. If the people inside are reluctant to let you in, encourage them to call the police.

• Make a scene. Your life may be at stake, and this is no time to
observe the rules of polite society. If you're on the highway, you
could run into the street and flag down a car.

• Make a house self-defense plan with the people you live with.
Plan your escape routes, talk about what you would do if you got
separated, think about your potential weapons and whom you
might go to for help in the neighborhood. Keep a list of important
phone numbers in an accessible place.

• If your attacker is someone you know, or even a member of your
family, talk about it with others afterward. Tell your family, your
friends, his friends. Let them know you won't tolerate what's
happened, and ask their help in supporting you. If you're being
harassed at work, talk with your co-workers. You may not be the
only one who's experiencing trouble.

The last tactic mentioned above strikes at the very heart of an
attack. Men who assault women don't want attention from other people; they want to do their dirty deeds in isolation, hidden from the
eyes of society. That's why *confrontations*—a type of *planned* teamwork—are so effective.

A confrontation, simply explained, is a time for a woman to go
with a group of supporters and tell the man who attacked her how
she feels about it, and what she expects from him in the future. She
tells him he will not get away with this again, that the community
knows who he is and that he is being watched. The point is to empower the woman who has been attacked, and to deter the man from
raping or assaulting again.

Anti-rape groups who help women organize confrontations often
notice that they don't get repeat calls on men who have been confronted.
In fact, in one case in Santa Cruz, the man's lawyer called the rape
hotline to see if his client was behaving himself. The lawyer reported
that the man said the confrontation had been one of the most profound
experiences of his life, and that he intended never to do it again.

A typical confrontation works like this: A woman who has been
attacked gets together with a group of friends, family members, co-
workers, and/or other supporters. Together, they plan a way to con-

front her assailant. As in Nikki's story, "The Confrontation," it may take place in public—say in a restaurant or at his workplace. The power of a confrontation is twofold: it allows the woman to express her rage in a safe context, and it makes the man publicly accountable for his actions to his community—his peers. Ideally, the man should be confronted by people who know him, and to whom he feels responsible. Young children can confront adults. Women can confront attackers on the telephone, in their workplace, or at school.

Peer approval and disapproval are powerful behavior modifiers. In some other societies, such as China, community involvement in crime prevention is commonplace. In some parts of West Africa, women were and are the hut builders. If a man raped a woman, the women of the community would tear down the hut of the offending male. In our society, in which people are less involved with their communities on a day-to-day level, confrontations are a way to break down the isolation that helps make our lives so dangerous.

A confrontation is planned down to the minutest detail, all with the approval of the woman who was attacked. Before the confrontation takes place, everyone in the group decides how they will act and what they will say. It's very important that everyone understand what to do if, for example, the man tries to flee or becomes violent. One person needs to be responsible for grabbing his left arm, one for his right arm, one for his left leg, right leg, and one for his head, in case he threatens to hit or grab someone.

But confrontations generally involve little or no physical contact; most men who are confronted are too surprised and chagrined to react. And because a confrontation is brief—usually ranging from a few minutes to a half hour—the group is gone before he can formulate a plan to escape or hurt someone.

In most confrontations, the "confronters" are all women. This counters the myth that an assault on a woman can only by avenged by a gang of vigilante men—while the wronged woman stays at home, unable to contribute to her own defense. Supportive men can wait in the wings, perhaps distributing leaflets with the man's name, address, physical description, and the nature of his crime. The purpose of a confrontation is to empower the woman; it is *not* meant to be an argument between the attacker and the survivor. Nor should it be a forum for the man to rationalize his behavior. In fact, it's usually best not to let the man speak at all. The most powerful confrontations are brief and to the point.

An important result of a confrontation is that the attacker is no longer anonymous; he has been recognized, and he won't be able to get away with this kind of behavior again. Bring this information home with concise, pointed statements: "We know who you are. We know where to find you. You can't treat women this way. We won't stand for this anymore."

Although you don't need an organization to plan a confrontation, you may want to talk to your local rape crisis group to get ideas.

There are many ways we women can band together to help take care of ourselves and each other. Some of those ways are discussed in the essay "So What Do I Do Now?," page 257. Take Back the Night marches (marches that happen at night to protest and draw attention to the fact that women feel particularly unsafe after dark), safe houses, and self-defense classes are all ways of breaking the traditional isolation surrounding women who've been assaulted. If you want to do something in your community and there are no organized groups, take the initiative and start something yourself.

There is another aspect to self-defense besides the actual response to the attack itself: the aftermath. When a woman is raped or assaulted, she must live with the scars for the rest of her life. But it's never too late to get help in healing the wounds. In "Facing My Demons," Ann Simonton chose a self-defense class that would help her confront the residual pain and fear from her rape experience. She courageously chose teamwork over continued isolation.

We want to inspire you to break your isolation, too. Like the women in this anthology, you can share your stories with others. Get to know your neighbors. Talk about self-defense with your family and friends.

Here is one of the most popular Take Back the Night march chants:

Mujeres unidas
jamás serán vencidas

Women united
will never be defeated

Rounding Up the Campers

D. P.

D. P. has been working in the anti-rape movement for over twelve years. Recently, she has been involved in presenting the Child Assault Prevention Project to elementary school children.

The incident described here occurred the first time D. P. had been camping in almost ten years. It was also the first time in six years that her dog had gone swimming.

"There were two things I did that I didn't know I could do. One is yell. I'd been practicing it, but many years ago there was a situation where I really wanted to yell and hadn't been able to. So now I know I can yell. I also didn't think I was very good at running, but I was barefoot and I ran great, I ran really fast and I didn't run out of breath until after I was finished talking to the cops. Then I was exhausted."

As told to the editors in an interview: J. and I and my old dog had gone camping, and we were down at the river. I wanted to take the dog swimming, so I decided I would go back to our campsite and change into my swimsuit, which meant that I left J. watching the dog at the river. As I was leaving the beach area, I noticed a man standing back from there drinking beer. He seemed to be watching the women on the beach, so I was paying attention to where he was going and what he was doing. He started walking up the path behind me and I got a little suspicious of him because he took the same wrong turn that I did, although lots of people did that by accident.

Farther on, he was still staying behind me in a way that I wanted to check out, so as I got near the camping area, I made a point of turning toward a different campsite. I didn't want to identify which campsite was ours, and I also wanted to see where he was going. I waited to see if he would go by. He didn't. So I came back down that path a little and saw that he was standing on the other side of a large tree.

"Are you waiting for someone? What are you doing?" I yelled over to him. I wanted him to know that I saw him, that he wasn't doing a good job of hiding.

"I'm waiting for the outhouse," was his reply. I later figured out that the outhouse had been empty all along.

"Are you camping here?" I asked him then. I wanted to get as much information as possible about who he was.

"Yeah."

"Which campsite are you in?"

"Oh, I don't know, just kind of over there somewhere."

It looked like he was going to stay near the tree for a while, so I moseyed over near our campsite and looked for some kind of weapon. The only thing I could think of at that point was a round-bladed table knife that we had just recently been using to cut cheese—and it didn't do that very well.

I didn't want to be at the campsite if he was going to be around, so I went back out to the main path, to be where it was more public. I didn't want him to have a chance to rip off any of our stuff. Now he was crouching in the bushes. He tried crouching lower when he saw me. I don't know what movies he had seen, about how to blend into things, but he didn't do it very well.

As I walked farther away from the campsite toward where he was, he got up and came toward me. He was a big guy—I'm five feet two, and he was about six feet tall.

"I think you should leave," I said to him.

"Why should I?"

"Just leave."

Then he swatted at my breast, at which point I yelled, much louder, "Get out of here!" Then he punched me in the side of my head, which made me really mad.

I had my little table knife in my hand, down at my side, because

I was trying to figure out if there was really any way to use it effectively. I liked just having it—it kind of completed my process of thinking through and acknowledging that this was a dangerous situation. But it wasn't something that realistically would make a good weapon, unless I had five minutes to carve. But holding it in my hand meant that my hand was more in a fist and I was thinking along those lines.

I kept yelling at him to leave, and he started to move away and then turned around and kicked me, but I was not close enough to really get hurt. I used a basic yell that I had learned through the Child Assault Prevention Project, the loud martial arts yell that I had been teaching children, and then started yelling "Help!" He started to back off, and finally he ran off.

I ran after him, and discovered that "Help" was a pretty effective word for getting people's attention. As I ran past a couple of people, I yelled, "Help, this man assaulted me!" After a while, I realized that about eight people, mostly in groups of two or three, that I had yelled to were following us, which was just swell.

I came to a fork in the road and lost sight of the guy. By that time, a couple of men had caught up with me, and were looking around for him, too. There were a man and a woman playing Frisbee, and I asked them, "Did you just see a guy run by? He assaulted me." They said, "Oh yeah, he went that way," and pointed, and a little while later I noticed they had joined in the chase, too! It was kind of cartoonish, I think it would have made a great aerial picture.

I thought we had lost him, but as we went around another corner, we found him once again trying to hide. Basically, he had reached a dead end and he was trying to hide in some bushes—unsuccessfully.

When he saw the group of us, he made a dash for it and ran into some tall weeds, at which point some men who were right behind him stopped and looked around. And I said, "Go get him, he assaulted me." So these two men charged into the bushes and brought him out with his hands behind his back.

I wasn't quite sure what would be the optimal thing to do with him with all those people involved. It seemed the only real choice was to take him to the campground office, which we did. Along the way, I dispatched people. There were the two men walking ahead with him and I was walking right behind them. I asked some people to go down and get J. and let her know what was going on, and why it was taking me so long to get back. People started to feel like everything was taken care of and now they didn't need to stay any longer, but it didn't feel real safe to me to just have the two men and him, so I asked more people to stick around and they did. The ranger in the campground office called the cops.

There was one woman who came over because she had heard the word "assault." She put her arm around me and said, "I'm a survivor, and I wasn't sure what was going on." She sat and waited with me.

When J. came, she took a couple of photos of the guy, at which point he called her names. He was really angry. He tried hiding behind the top of a Dutch door to keep from having his picture taken, but that just meant she had to take his picture through the window. He got really upset about that. "I'll get those pictures," he yelled. I asked him if he had a criminal record. "It's no business of yours, it doesn't matter what my record is," he said.

The cops asked me at least four times if I knew him—that was the first question the cops and various other people asked. The implication of that is upsetting—that if I knew him, they would not have taken the assault seriously. So I was actually coming up with the line "I've never seen him before in my life." I knew if I said it that way, people would pay more attention.

People were saying things like "Gee, nothing like this has ever happened here before." One of the men who had grabbed him was telling me what charges I should be pressing. Everyone wanted to tell me what I should be doing and didn't pay any real attention to how I was or what I wanted to be doing.

People responded, but they wouldn't necessarily initiate anything. One of the women said, "Oh, yes, I had seen him crouching in the bushes," on her way down to the beach. But then she *didn't* say, "Gee, there's a guy crouching in the bushes, we should do something about this, this is weird." People didn't want to interrupt the fun time they were having.

You can get people to respond, but it doesn't necessarily mean that on their own they would have thought of doing that. I was saying, "This man assaulted me." I don't know if I was actually pointing at people, but in my brain I was saying, You there, help me get this guy. And I think it took that—the fact that I kept yelling.

The guy who caught him said, "We're in this campsite. If you have any more problems tonight, yell, we'll be listening," so they were being responsive in that sense. They were wanting to be helpful, but they weren't sure what they were supposed to do and how to react.

When the case finally got to court, the guy pled *nolo contendere* to assault. He's on one-year probation, and one of the terms of the probation is that he have no contact, directly or indirectly, with "the victim," and that he be given credit for time served. He had served one day.

I wrote to the DA and said, "Keep me informed. I really want to know what's going on with this. I'm more than willing to come testify if you want me to." I've never gotten any response. It's only because I called the court that I found out what happened.

At the time, and now, too, I sometimes wish I'd done more to hurt him. I don't like having those "should have done more" feelings. But I want to be practicing more of the self-defense that I know because I didn't feel as confident as I would have liked to. I'm glad that I found out who he was and that he didn't just disappear. I'm glad I got to show myself that I can have some effect and I could get people involved even when they didn't necessarily want to be. That was kind of fun—I really felt like a director.

Facing My Demons

Ann Simonton

Ann Simonton was a professional model for almost eleven years. She is now an active feminist who uses civil disobedience to effect social change. She has been arrested ten times for such crimes as "littering" her blood at beauty pageants, tearing a single issue of *Hustler* depicting a woman drinking a boy's urine on the cover, and for taking her shirt off at the beach. She is currently the coordinator of Media Watch, a group that focuses on the media's contribution to violence against women and children.

I am walking alone. Without warning, a man grabs me from behind. His stench invades the surrounding air. An unspeakable terror makes me feel like vomiting. My breath catches in my throat. This can't be happening again. My body goes limp. He forces me down. As we hit the ground, rage explodes from my chest. Every inch of my body cries, "No, I won't be raped again." I drive my teeth into his flesh. He jerks his arm away, cursing, "Your ass is dead, bitch." Twisting, I thrust my elbow directly into his face. He grunts. I free myself from his grip. Moving onto my side, I kick him squarely in the face. He falls back, then grabs my foot. I scrape away his clenched fingers with my free foot, then kick him again in the head. He looks stunned. I move in close and kick him in the face. Finally, he is quiet. I have knocked him out.

A sharp whistle and wild cheering pierces the void. I'm in a mat-filled training room. The "mugger" is a martial artist dressed in fifty pounds of protective equipment. I stand by his head making sure he's out cold. This is my first day of a self-defense class called Model Mugging. In this course, a heavily armored male assailant attacks the participants one by one. I am only two hours into the first class session. After being mugged, I stand in a line of women who are also training. Someone hands me a cup of water. My tears flow uncontrollably.

I am leery as I read and sign the waiver: "Course involves strenuous physical activity, physical body contact, simulated rape scenarios which can be physically harmful and/or emotionally stressful. Danger involved. You must promise to consult with your physician and/or therapist prior to taking the course." Although hesitant, I decide to take the risks.

The teacher begins by asking the new students why we want to take Model Mugging. The thought pulls tears down my face. When it's my turn to speak, my face burns hot. I gather my hands together, stretching my palms open. My words fall around me: "I am angry— resent being here. I'm here because I was gang-raped at knife point. I was blamed for my rape—felt guilt for too long. I'm a political activist. My goal is to stop violence against women. Men are the ones who need help! Why should I pay so I can live without fear in my life? This course should be subsidized by the state."

I had no idea that I would be mugged during the first class. I'm not ready for it. Each time he attacks me from the back, each time imitates my rape. The other women appear to take it all in stride. No one cries as I do. With a padded mugger, I realize what it feels like to hit someone full force. This is my first, all-out fight for my life.

I am in a stupor after the first class. At home, I fall asleep sobbing on my couch. Hours later I wake with a migraine headache. In two days, I will drive five hundred miles alone to San Diego to lead a protest against the Miss California Pageant, commit civil disobedience, and spend an unknown number of days in jail. Every June, I protest the Miss California Pageant and celebrate my birthday. The day after my birthday is the anniversary of my rape. It seems every year at the time of my rape I work on healing.

Through my tears I see this year's costume sitting on the table. It's a giant box of Kellogg's cornflakes with the bottom dropped out and fake cornflakes spilling out to create a skirt. My costume represents a pageant sponsor and symbolizes this year's theme, "Get Your Business off Women's Bodies."

How can I do this now? I need help. After talking to answering machines, I finally reach a good friend in Los Angeles. "Renee, I got mugged. It brought everything about my rape back to me. Tomorrow I watch a slide show on child porn. Monday I drive to L.A., then San Diego. I can't take it anymore."

"Don't do the course now," she offers. "You're too harsh on yourself. Do it later. The timing isn't right now." Her calm voice smooths my terror.

I put on my public mask, bury my feelings, and dive into the next five days. They are filled with the madness of preparing our float, media interviews with L.A. and San Diego radio stations, major newspapers and television stations all asking over and over, "Why do you do this? What's so bad about a beauty pageant? The contestants aren't forced."

On the final night of the pageant, they arrest me after only thirty minutes of demonstrating because I accidentally drop a rose from my bouquet on the sidewalk. Charged with littering, I'm taken away. I spend a long night in jail with women whose crimes range from being battered by their boyfriends to putting a cigarette out in the street.

We are released. When I finally reach home, there is a message on my answering machine: "Are you coming to Model Mugging tomorrow?"

June 19, 1986—Journal Entry

I want to finish it—is this the right time? Will there be a right time? I haven't any support, except a few women friends who understand. The mugger gets nastier every week. Am I crazy to torture myself? Am I sane to give myself a chance to let my anger out? I like the idea of letting it go—I try to get close to my anger. I was close three months ago when my therapist asked me to express it, but I was afraid someone in the next room might hear me. I want to fix it up before it comes out, clean it, polish it, and make it succinct. When I'm mugged, all hell breaks loose and I want to kill the mugger. Possibly for the first time I've allowed my raw anger to come out.

There is a dangerous edge I get to. During a live television interview, a male newscaster glibly asked, "Did the gang-rape affect your life—if so, how?" I force myself to intellectualize about my rape, pretending it's not a gaping wound. I also answered glibly, "Yes, it does." I drive myself to this edge—thinking I can do anything. If I can survive rape, I can survive anything.

There isn't room in this world for women to air their disgust about men's aberrant sexual behavior. I hate men's arrogance—hate the ways I've been raised to think they are so damned essential. My decision is yes, I'll finish this class. I'll go into a strange group of women and try to catch up tomorrow.

I feel alone. They have already had one class together. They all cry easily. They're able to talk about their lives. I love that. One frail woman, Darlene, is taking the class to protect her children. She was almost attacked at a bus station along with her children, as bystanders watched. Darlene is an inspiration. At ninety-five pounds, she is knocking out our two-hundred-pound "mugger," Tom, who is six feet four. On Friday, we're having a potluck to get to know one another better.

I come late to the potluck. I feel separate. An assistant instructor is telling the women how to talk an attacker out of raping. Her comments push every button I have. I can't listen to casual talk about knives and how to talk men out of rape. Tears drip onto my plate as other women speak. The other women must notice my tears. Why are they ignoring me?

The same instructor, who sits next to me, asks if I'm okay. "No," I say. "I am not okay." There is silence. Someone else speaks.

When my friend leading the group finally asks me to talk, I jump—want to break glass—want to smash my curried fish all over the room. I hate them all—hate her damned advice. You can't talk a rapist out of raping you. I feel crazy. I want to leave, but the women coax me to stay and speak. When I do, my words are barely audible. I warn the women, "Don't blame yourself, if you can't talk men out of it, like I believed I could. I am still healing, still ruined from guilt."

June 27—Journal Entry

It is unspeakable what I have to say. I want to talk about a topic everyone hates. The prejudice is unsurmountable. Why can't I be the ideal rape victim—one who's back to normal in two years? Why can't I get it off my chest in one angry ten-to-twenty-line poem? Why am I still crying in groups fifteen years later, trying to heal? Have I made some wrong turn?

Believing our culture's lies about a woman's worth was easy before I was gang-raped. Three knives at my jugular changed my life. I became a human bulldozer. My younger sister said my face never looked the same again. I must be tough. *I* was blamed by everyone, including the legal system. I became the victim, wearing the painful guilt around me like a collar of thorns.

Guilt is what we never deal with. Guilt and self-hate. Women must know they are worth saving, worth fighting back for.

Under such outrageous circumstances, it is amazing women keep striving to be heard. I shared my pain tonight. I so rarely share it. I keep it inside—feeling alienated.

Everyone in our class feels instantly connected during Susan's mugging. She reenacts being beaten by her boyfriend. The mugger growls at her, "I've had it with all your shit, Susan." During the mugging, she screams out, "I can't do it. Stop him!" We grab onto one another's hands. Will they stop him? He keeps coming at her. Every one of us is in shock. The instructor screams at her, "Don't give in to his power, Susan." She regains her strength, waits for the perfect opening, and knocks him out. Afterward, she's glad he didn't stop; it pushed her beyond her limit. After this class, Tom, the mugger, cries. It reassures me that it is hard on him to do this.

We arrive for our public graduation physically and emotionally wrecked. The Model Mugging proverb seems to be "If you can fight when you feel lousy, you'll be able to fight anytime." I have the flu: fever, headache, sore throat, cough, mucus coming out of my ears, and the first cramping flood of my period. I am the first one out to be mugged before an audience. It is a "psychotic attack" by our "guest mugger." From a pinned position on the floor, I have to deliver five knockout blows in a row to pass, because he acts like he is on drugs or crazy. I stay with the fear of reliving my assault and channel that energy. His energy is quick and erratic. I don't remember what happens. My blind rage takes over and succeeds.

Each of us claims our identity as we are attacked. We aren't objects; we have a center to move from. I know what it means to be a warrior. I feel deeply bonded with the other women in the group and receive incredible support from our instructors. We fight for our lives and we win. My parents, younger sister, and friends are all at the graduation. Afterward, Mama cries and tells me, "For the first time I understand what it was like for you to have been raped." She also seems to understand for the first time what fighting back means.

September 4—New Moon Journal Entry

I walk into an ominous sea at night. The sky black as the sea, wind blowing huge waves. "You knew what you were doing when you modeled, Ann. You knew you were selling sex—five, even eight, years after you were raped, you kept doing it." I stand, ankles entangled in seaweed, fingers stretched into the darkness. I am exhausted from the guilt that pushes its masochistic nightmare into my face. "You knew you promoted rape, Ann." Guilt is just unresolved anger. I take the sweet, icy water and wash my hot, swollen face.

I am not to blame. I will no longer carry this pain with me. I pluck off my thorns and heave them into the arms of an angry sea.

The Confrontation

Nikki

Nikki (a pseudonym) is a successful businessperson with her own accounting business. She is an incest survivor from a violent family, and now says she's "happily in love and investigating new and exciting things."

"I had to go through a lot of growing to find enough self-love to transform my history into strength."

As told to the editors in an interview: In the mid-seventies, I was involved in a relationship with a man who would hit me when he was angry. At that time, I was young and confused and unable to defend myself in any way except to remove myself from his vicinity and the relationship. Six months after moving out of his house, I found out that he was renting to other women. One woman he was renting to was part of my circle of acquaintances, and confided in me what was happening.

Over small incidents, David would get angry and hit these women. They were not involved in a sexual relationship with him, as I had been. The reasons for his anger were things like someone not doing the dishes when he wanted them to and small roommate-type conflicts. She was very embarrassed to tell me about this, as I was when he battered me. You go through a period of reluctance to speak about what's happening, because it just is so shocking that it could happen.

Now that I'm older and a little more cynical, I'm much more willing to speak up and defend myself.

When I was relating to him, there were many threats. In fact, he threatened my life and attempted to kill me by running me over with his truck when I was pregnant with his child. I just got myself safe and dismissed his behavior. But when I heard that he was exhibiting similar behavior with roommates and it was getting more and more dangerous, I had to do something. She gravitated to me as someone who could understand and know that she wasn't crazy. I validated her fears and I said, "Get yourself safe." It took her a month or two to find another housing situation. During that time, I decided to confront him on his behavior.

I needed to express the anger that I had bottled up from the way that I had been treated and also to let him know that his behavior needed to stop, that there was a community of people that were aware of his behavior and were asking him to stop. So a month after she had moved from the house and was safe and I knew that she was going to be okay, we held a public confrontation. She also asked that I not mention her in the confrontation and asked not to participate because she was still too frightened.

I organized the confrontation with the help of Women Against Rape in the community where I lived. I had heard that the women involved in confrontations were able to control the confrontation and express their anger and ask the individual who had hurt them to change. I wanted to walk away and feel that I had done my bit to contribute to my own sanity and my own release from the nagging belief that I should have fought back, I should have made him change, I should have done this or that or the other thing. I wanted to relieve the guilt of having been a victim of violence.

The first step was to get together a group of people, including some people from Women Against Rape, to discuss what a confrontation was and if I wanted to do it in this particular circumstance. They gave me their feedback and validation for my feelings at the first meeting. That was a real important step. People were shocked. Talking about what happened was a hard step to take because people are usually shocked about violence and surprised that it happens. I never really accepted that I was a victim, but something had happened to me that I didn't want to happen again.

I told them my personal history with David. I explained that because some other people had gotten messed up with him, I had gotten motivated to ask him to change. And that's the irony in my situation: it was not when *my* life was being threatened that I decided to do a confrontation, but when other people were threatened and abused. That's what it took for me to recognize my own history and validate it. That's what it took for me to say this needs to stop. I came out of that meeting feeling, yes, I want this confrontation to happen. The nice thing about the design and the structure of the confrontation is that I was pretty much in charge. I asked for cooperation from my friends and from Women Against Rape to structure it in a way that I felt safe, so that I could powerfully voice my objections to this person's behavior.

I asked that men be in the background during the confrontation and not to speak with David because I didn't want them to take over and run the confrontation. Other women who were unhappy with his treatment of women got to say some things, but basically I had the most to say since it was my confrontation. I asked other individuals to tell him it was his turn to listen, that he needed to hear what I had to say. They repeated that to him when he tried to talk.

The confrontation was in a public place, a café. David had a counseling business which he at times conducted in the café and so it affected his public image and his ability to keep secret his private behavior.

One woman volunteered to contact him and to ask for an appointment at this café. So he came to the café expecting to meet with a future client. When he entered the café, I stood up to meet him. He sat down on a bench and was surrounded by several other women.

There were ten to fifteen women who participated in the confrontation, who knew of his behavior through their contact with this other woman or through myself. They surrounded me in a horseshoe and kept him from just walking away from me. I asked him to stop, to listen to me, and then I said what I had experienced out loud in public for the very first time.

"I want you to stop what you're doing. I don't want you to hit one more woman. You battered me and you've battered other people and it's got to stop. You tried to kill me and you can't kill me and all these people know and understand about your behavior and find it unacceptable." In the beginning, he said, "You're crazy, you don't know what you're talking about." But the entire group told him it wasn't his turn to talk and his protests died out. Then he began to look for ways to physically escape from the situation.

I saw his eyes roving around in the café looking for someone he knew. My eyes weren't roving, so I don't know what he found there, but I don't think he found any support.

There were men on the periphery that were handing out leaflets that explained to people what was going on, who this person was, and something about what I had to say to him and what his behavior problem was. They did not identify me in any way. One woman took his picture with a flash as well.

I didn't want him starting to have a fight with another man. In fact, I saw him lock eyes at one point with one of the men who was leafletting. That person stayed peripheral, which was very important. David also tried to attempt to argue his way out of what I had to say. At one point, he did try to engage one of the men in conversation, as if that man had something to do with what I had to say, which he didn't. He needed to hear what I had to say, because I don't think he had ever heard my hurt or my anger before.

The whole thing lasted about half an hour. It seemed very long while I was in it. Afterward, I remember being amazed at how short it actually was. I felt like a whirlwind had just passed through me and cleaned me out.

Afterward, the group that did the confrontation with me met and rejoiced that we had successfully pulled off what we wanted to do, which was to confront him in a nonviolent way, but still to have him hear what I had to say.

I felt very good afterward. A group called Men Against Rape contacted him and asked him if he was interested in doing counseling or dealing with his behavior, being accountable for his behavior. I felt great. I felt cleared of the anger that I had stowed. I believe that when someone does violence to another person and that person has no way of releasing the anger that has been discharged on them, it can turn two ways: it can be destructively displayed in society by the victim going out and displaying violent behavior, or internally, self-destructively. Confrontations are some of the most critical and useful tools for expressing rage. Violence must be stopped in its tracks and not be passed on as a social disease. Confrontations are a nonviolent and yet strong way to do this.

Elevator Escape

Tamar Hosansky

Tamar Hosansky was born and raised in New York City. She took her first self-defense course when she was eighteen. Now thirty, she has been training in the martial arts ever since. She co-founded, along with two other women, the New York–based Safety and Fitness Exchange (SAFE). SAFE travels throughout the United States, doing personal safety programs for women and children. Along with Flora Calao, Tamar is the author of a children's self-defense book, *Your Children Should Know.*

"That's really been my life commitment: to help people be safer and to help them recover if they've been attacked. Martial arts study helps keep me healthy and sane and helps me continue the work I'm doing. I don't think I could hear the thousands of abuse stories I hear without letting it out on a punching bag."

I was riding the elevator in my office building with one other person who was a messenger in the building. Somewhere in the middle of the ride, he just lunged at me. He screwed up his face like he was going for a kiss, but his expression was totally cold. I was wearing a skirt and heels and makeup, so I'm sure he thought that I was an easy mark and had no idea what he was getting into. I hit him in the chest to back him off so he wouldn't grab me. I assumed that I was going to have to really take him out because we were trapped in a little tiny elevator. But he backed right off and said, "I'm sorry, I'm sorry, don't hit me.'' I took a fighter stance and yelled, "Get off the elevator!'' I kept pressing buttons on the control panel, and he kept saying, "Don't hit me, don't hit me.'' I kept looking at him, thinking, You make one move and I'm going to really have to hurt you.

He got off the elevator and I rode up to my floor and got off. I became extremely worried that he was going to attack someone else who didn't know how to defend herself. I ran into my office and sort of fell apart. My partner said, "We have to call security, we have to call the police,'' and sort of got me functioning again. I called downstairs to building security. They locked the building and they asked me to come downstairs and identify him on the way out, which I did. They held him there until the police came. The police really couldn't do anything because he hadn't put his hands on me. I hit him before he touched me, and he hadn't said anything like "I'm going to rape you, I'm going to kill you.'' But they did tell me later that he was on parole for something, so I asked that they tell his parole officer what had happened.

There was a series of elevator attacks in midtown-Manhattan office buildings a couple of years ago. It really scared people because a lot of people have this idea that midtown is safe; if you're in a business area, you're in some kind of safety bubble. I think the man had a knife and he was raping women. A number of the women got away by screaming. When they screamed and they made a scene, he apparently took off. There were a number of media reports about these women getting away—which is unusual, with New York media, anyway. A similar situation for suburban women is parking garages, which are trapped spaces similar to elevators.

It was an extraordinarily dangerous situation, being inside the elevator with somebody who could be armed. A friend told me not to underestimate the effects of the attack. Even though I defended myself, there were some traumatic effects afterward.

I had defended myself before verbally, but I had never had to hit anybody. It certainly helped me believe in what I was teaching. I responded without fear and with the certainty that I was going to handle the situation no matter what it took—that I wasn't going to let him rape me.

Two Gutsy Women

Chris Weir

Chris Weir was born in New Jersey in 1952, the second daughter in a blue-collar family. After college, she worked as an elementary school teacher and a community organizer. Chris has recently begun a new career in computer science and is active in local politics and gay rights issues. She says she may be "the only lesbian who doesn't like cats, but I am partial to chickens."

"My self-defense experience is minimal: a few one-day workshops and a summer of judo lessons. Learning to say no was the most important lesson I learned. Whether it's asking the person at the next table to stop smoking, or confronting verbal harassment on the street, saying no is the best first step we can take."

It had been a fine afternoon Christmas party—warm with friends and laughter and good food. Sally and I declined a ride home. By six o'clock, the rain had slowed to a light drizzle and we wanted to walk the three blocks to our house.

After crossing the busy main street, we linked arms and continued our walk through the dark and deserted medical complex that flanks the access street to our block. Stepping out from the lighted walkway to a dark stretch of road, we saw a figure walking toward us silhouetted in the streetlight at the end of the block. Continuing our talk, I speculated vaguely about which of our neighbors the person might be, and started to veer to one side of the street so he could pass on the other side. He didn't veer away. He came directly up to us. I thought, Oh no, this guy's going to hassle us for being lesbian and walking arm in arm. What will I say now?

Instead of delivering the expected insult, he suddenly grasped my arm, brought something up to my stomach, and said, "I have a knife." Sally let go of my other arm and jumped a few feet away. While part of my mind was trying to figure out a way to reverse time and do this walk a different way, another was deciding this must be a robbery, and the way to handle it at this point was to treat his actions as something short of ridiculous.

"We don't have any money," I stated, in a tone that implied he wasn't too bright to have chosen us, that we were too poor to be worth robbing.

"I don't care. Get over there," he said quietly, motioning with his head to the overgrown bank of ivy that bordered the road. Oh, I thought, as I felt my body go still with fear, it's rape. What do I do now? Do I go along and hope I don't get too badly hurt? NO! I emphatically rejected the idea. In the back of my mind, I could hear snatches of a talk given by a woman from Women Against Rape, saying that resistance works most of the time, that fighting back is usually successful. I thought he just might stab me right here in the street for resisting, but I knew I'd be hurt if I went anywhere with him. I was not going to let him take me into the bushes without a fight.

I took a deep breath. "No," I said. Summoning up my best authoritative schoolteacher tone, I continued. "I won't do anything you want me to do. I am not going anywhere with you. This is my neighborhood and you can't get away with this. I'm going to yell and people are going to come out. You'd better get out of here right now. Go away! Leave us alone!"

Sally picked up my cue and joined in the assertion that he had better leave. I knew Sally was probably considering running for help, just as I was considering asking her to do so. But I needed her there to help me continue my offensive. She was a part of my strength, and a touchstone for the reality that we were going to get out of this. In the five years we had been together, we had gotten through some tough times. Our trust in each other, and familiarity with each other's responses and attitudes, made us good partners. We would get out of this.

He motioned with the knife and told Sally to move over with us, but she kept away and circled behind him, continuing to talk, distracting him. He tried to pull me to the side of the road, but I refused to go. He didn't seem to know what to do. I decided it was my turn to move. I wanted to get near the streetlight I could see over his shoulder.

"I'm not taking any more of this," I told him. "I'm leaving." And I moved toward the light, and into the knife. He backed away, and let go of my arm.

But it was not over. Moving to my side, he took hold of my other arm to walk beside me, and transferred the knife to his other hand. That was the first time I really saw the knife—a six-inch hunter's blade. I kept walking, kept telling him to leave.

When I got close to the lighted area, I again said, "I won't take it anymore," and jerked my arm out of his grasp. This time he stepped back several feet, and now that we had some space between us, I was ready to raise my voice and really yell. While he was so close to me, I hadn't wanted to startle him with loud shouts or quick moves. But now Sally and I both started to call loudly for neighbors to come out, that there was a man out here with a knife. He started walking quickly down the street, and we followed, shouting after him. We never did call out for help. We both kept on the offensive, choosing to snarl at him rather than show vulnerability.

Now he was looking like he wanted to get away very quickly. When Sally yelled, "There's a man with a knife out here!" he turned and lunged back toward us with the knife pointed at us again. We decided we needed to approach the neighbors more directly, since no one had showed up yet. We yelled the names of specific people, and porch lights began to go on. The man took off running. We ran screaming after.

When people came out, I slowed down, overwhelmed with relief that it was over. It was over, he was almost gone. But Sally was still chasing after him, angry now that he was going to get away. She finally stopped and came back when he turned a corner and headed into a deserted warehouse district. People were out on the street, and now the fear and tears started pouring out as we told what had happened.

Sally and I held on to each other, terrified of what could have happened, and amazed at how we had saved ourselves. We had done it well, we had fought back, we had chased him out of the neighborhood. We said no, and it worked.

As a postscript to this account, I'd like to add that the man was caught, and convicted to fourteen years in prison. He had been out of jail only months when he attacked us, having served six years for multiple rape charges. When his defense lawyer argued for the minimum sentence, since he had not actually committed rape, the judge snapped back that he should hardly be rewarded for failing in his attempt just because he had "run into two gutsy and determined women that night."

Part VII

Life Strategies
and Self-Defense Tips

Introduction

In this last section of *Her Wits About Her,* women share what they have learned about self-defense from a variety of life experiences. The tips they give will be useful to any woman, not only in violent attacks, but in everyday life. Their courage in choosing strategies that help them survive extends to more situations than sexual assault.

These stories range from the practical to the philosophical. Joan Joesting gives us "Ten Commandments: How Not to Get Raped When Bicycling Alone" from her years on the roads of the United States and Australia. Donna Sirutis, in "A Groundhog with Gumption," reflects on general principles to keep in mind when faced with danger. As an "older woman," she encourages others to study self-defense and martial arts.

Patricia Searles, in "Showdown in the Corridor," shares a wonderful tale about using intuition. Her self-defense instructor's tips and strategies echo in her head as she faces a potentially dangerous attack on campus.

Life experience comes from many sources, and every woman who has been attacked has learned something unique about survival. Most women have experienced powerlessness or have been warned by well-meaning friends to take precautions that limit their freedom. But humans are risk-taking animals, and in order to live a fully human life, women act in free ways.

Women who take risks and are raped are accused of provoking or even wanting attack. Yet even women who do all the "right" things, wear the "right" clothes, stay indoors at night, and depend on men to protect them, get attacked. The truth is that no woman, no matter what her life-style or sexual activities, wants to be brutalized or to live in constant fear.

Some women are at higher risk because attackers view them as less able to defend themselves. Two women who fall into this category are Sandi Collins ("Self-Defense on Wheels"), who lives in a wheelchair and has defended herself while sitting in it, and Autumn ("The Getaway Bike"), who has cerebral palsy and is differently abled as a result. They share ideas about learning self-defense for women with disabilities.

In "A Test of Faith," Barbara Richmond is attacked by a mob that sees her as an outsider and an enemy. This is not a sexual assault, but one that happens because of a clash in ideas. The calmness that Barbara musters typifies the "eye of the storm" feeling many women in this book have experienced when their intuition starts working.

Women in this section did not turn away from suspected dangers, but took concrete steps before and during the assaults. Tips and strategies can be picked up from friends who have used them, from self-defense or assertiveness classes, and from the authors in this book. One can never learn too much about stopping an attack—the more options open in your mind, the more likely you will be to find the most useful one when the time comes.

You can rehearse successful self-defense with your eyes closed or with your friends, so that strategies will come as second nature. Many women defend themselves using good common sense, but there's no law against improving our common sense. The resource section and bibliography of this book can give you additional ideas.

Her Wits About Her was written not only to be good reading, but to directly improve your chances to escape if you are attacked. We believe that there is always an opening, always a chance for escape, from even the most threatening situations. We hope all of you will use your wits, and the ideas here, to devise creative responses that will keep you strong and safe and free. Remember that self-defense is a flexible, living set of choices, not one or even ten techniques. Keep your choices open and do whatever works. Good luck! Fight back!

Showdown in the Corridor

Patricia Searles

Patricia Searles is an associate professor of sociology and women's studies. She is also a certified self-defense instructor. Her most recent research has focused on sexual assault, rape law reform, the self-defense movement, and pornography. In the spring of 1980 she decided to begin self-defense training. She wanted to reduce the daily fear and insecurity she felt living as a woman in a violent society. She also thought that self-defense training would improve her skills as an educator.

"I had no idea, however, how significantly the study of self-defense would transform my concept of self and my sense of personal power, strength, and independence.

"I had been working for years to help women understand how traditional education has devalued and obscured women's history and experience, but what self-defense taught me in a very personal, firsthand way is that I have 'learned the lessons of patriarchy in my muscles and sinews, as well as in my mind and soul' (Emily Culpepper, Womanspirit, Summer, 1976*)."*

After attending a lecture on campus one evening, I decided to drop in on a friend of mine who was working late at the office. I was excited by the lecture I had heard—a feminist interpretation of some Biblical passages—and I couldn't wait to tell Nan about my discovery. Nan and I had offices in a long mazelike building that was supposed to be closed to the public after 6:00 P.M. But tonight, as was often the case, the entrance was still unlocked at nine. As I entered the building, I wished I had thought to use the bathroom before I left the crowded student union. But now, in Willits Hall, where the never-locked rest rooms were rumored to be scenes of numerous "incidents," from voyeuristic to violent, I decided to wait and ask Nan to accompany me. Several years ago, I would have found this kind of "buddy system" ludicrous and certainly unnecessary for self-sufficient adults, but self-defense training had given me not only a real gut-level understanding of the reality of sexual assault, but also the confidence that my precautions were sensible, not paranoid.

On my way to find Nan, I decided to stop briefly at my own office to pick up a book I'd forgotten earlier in the day. I approached my door, keys ready in my hand, and reached for the knob. I had been trained to be alert at all times, not only to prevent being taken by surprise, but also to avoid appearing an easy target.

A noise caught my attention and I looked around to see a young, sandy-haired man, casually clad in sandals and cut-off jeans, exit from a hall that intersected my own and proceed down a staircase a far distance from my office door. As I turned to see him, he looked at me, paused momentarily at the staircase door, then opened it and went out.

I felt a flash of discomfort. He had paused only momentarily. He had focused his eyes on me for no more than a second or two. There were plenty of rational, nonthreatening explanations for his presence and for his glance at me. Perhaps he was a student who had wandered up to check a professor's office hours or to deposit a note or paper under a door. Perhaps he was a graduate student working late. Perhaps he was a janitor leaving for the evening.

Perhaps he was startled by me, not expecting to find someone else in the building after hours. All these explanations flashed through my mind, but they didn't quell the sense of uneasiness that had come over me. "Trust your intuition," I had been told in self-defense class. "Don't pass off bad vibes as paranoia." It was only a momentary glance. It wasn't at all sinister. But somehow I had the sense that that sandy-haired man was taking note of me and my whereabouts. "If you think something might be wrong, believe it, and act accordingly." The lessons came back to me.

Something inside told me to get out of the corridor as soon as possible. I decided to head in the opposite direction, away from the staircase where I had last seen the man.

I moved quickly and assertively down the corridor, through the vestibule, and into the next corridor toward Nan's office, carefully noting the crack at the base of each office door for any trace of light or other sign of occupancy. I knocked firmly at Nan's door. No answer.

Perhaps she was typing in the main office. I made my way to the other side of the building, then peered in the window of the department office. There was no light on inside, no sign of Nan or any other late-working colleague. I decided to leave Willits Hall as quickly as possible.

I was now a good distance from where I had seen the man enter the stairwell. Since the man seemed to have left the building, I thought it best to stay inside until I was as close as possible to my car. I felt more secure traveling these well-lit corridors than I would have outside on the dimly lit bush-lined path.

I walked at a quick, determined pace, alert for noises or movement or any evidence of inhabited offices. My heart was pounding, my adrenaline pumping. My gut told me something wasn't right. It was a strange, unexplainable sense that I had, but I trusted it implicitly.

The building was long, and I moved quickly through the office-lined corridors and connecting vestibules. In reality, only a few minutes had elapsed since that first flash of discomfort, but my journey seemed endless. Now, at last, I was almost to the end of the building!

As I pushed open the corridor door and began to enter the vestibule, I saw a figure moving in my direction, about to open the opposite corridor door and enter the very vestibule I was approaching. It was hard to see clearly, but I caught a glimpse of sandy hair and cut-off jeans! This was the same man I had seen moments before, supposedly exiting at the far end of the building! What was he doing here now, back on the third floor?

"Remain calm. Center yourself. Review your options." I could turn abruptly and retrace my steps. I was several yards ahead of the man and unless he started to run, he wouldn't overtake me. But in that direction there were no open offices to run into, no one to scare the man off, to assist me, or to call for help. And, besides, I didn't want to appear frightened.

What would the man think if I suddenly turned and hurried back in the direction from which I had just come? That I'd just happened to recall that I had forgotten something in my office? Not likely. He'd think I was fleeing in fear. If this guy was going to try to harm me, he was going to have one mean, angry fight on his hands. I wanted him to know that. Deciding not to turn back, I continued into the vestibule.

Other options flashed through my mind. I could walk assertively past the man and continue my path down the corridor to the far end of the building. If I looked him straight in the eye and walked with a strong, forceful gait, perhaps he would sense my power and determination and decide to find an easier victim. This seemed preferable to retreating, but I didn't like the idea of getting that close to this questionable character. If, on the other hand, I veered off to the side of the vestibule, I would be putting greater space between us, and then be in a position to enter either a perpendicular corridor or a stairwell leading outside. Since both these paths lay ahead, neither would signal retreat. It was very important to me that I not appear frightened or confused.

My mind was working quickly. Only a second or two had passed since I caught the glimpse of the sandy hair and cut-offs. I decided to make my way toward the perpendicular corridor. The stairwell, an enclosed concrete structure, seemed too risky. If I had to defend myself, I preferred to do it on a flat surface. There was little chance anyone would see or hear a struggle going on inside the stairwell. The short perpendicular corridor, on the other hand, would quickly lead to more offices and a well-lit windowed hall. Anything that happened there would be clearly visible to passersby outside.

Still traveling toward me, the man began to push open the corridor door. "Focus your mind, body, and spirit on the situation confronting you." My view was partially obstructed by the door, but I saw the man hesitate briefly and move his hands toward the crotch of his pants, making a slight gyrating motion with his hips as he did so. Something was going to happen!

There was no doubt in my mind now. "Don't panic. Review your options. What body weapons do you have available?" I knew my possible escape routes. My arms and hands were free, my legs unconstrained. Self-defense drills flashed through my mind—an instant replay of kicks and blows.

"Keep your presence of mind. Channel your fear into energy. Be prepared to act." I took a deep breath. Energy surged through my body, radiating outward in warm, pulsating waves. My heart was pounding, my extremities tingling. I threw my shoulders back, and my body seemed to expand as if to make room for this unleashed store of energy. I felt large and strong as I advanced. I felt my power in every step.

The man pushed the door open, and focused his eyes on me intently as he made his way toward me. I was walking with purpose and determination, subtly edging toward the vestibule and the perpendicular corridor that awaited. I caught a glimpse of unzipped pants, exposed genitals. "Gather your power. Direct your energy through your target." I riveted my eyes on his as he approached, careful not to signal in any way that I had noticed his exposed body. My expression conveyed neither anger nor fear, but a ferocious intensity. My gaze bored through him, giving him notice that he wouldn't want to mess with me. He never took his eyes off me, searching my face for some hint of reaction to his pathetic display. I held tough and miraculously he passed by, entering the corridor from which I had just emerged.

I breathed a deep sigh of relief and veered off in the planned direction, out of his sight once again. Never letting down my guard, I made my way quickly to the end of the building and to my car. The relief was immense, though I was trembling and shaken. The words from my self-defense class came back to soothe me. "Expect to be shaken, even traumatized. But remember: You did not ask for what happened to you. You did the best you could to cope with the situation. You're a survivor, and that's what counts most!''

A Groundhog with Gumption

Donna Sirutis

Donna Sirutis was born in 1946. She grew up in a working class family in La Mesa, California. She was a law student at the time of the incident described in her story, and is now an attorney employed by the Massachusetts Board of Conciliation and Arbitration.

"I continue to study karate. There are hardly any of us "older women" in the martial arts, and I would be very happy if I could do something to encourage women, regardless of age, to study self-defense."

It was 10:30 P.M., and I was out jogging alone, as usual. My route took me through an urban industrial area that had been the site of a vast fire several years before and was still uninhabited and poorly lit. Was it unsafe? Sure it was. But I like running at night better than in the morning, because I'm not so stiff then. And I also like running where I don't meet many people, because I'm not exactly built swift and lean, like a greyhound. More like a groundhog. A groundhog with cellulite. I don't like people to see me out there waddling along.

So here I was, about a year and a half after I had started studying karate, out jogging by myself through the dark, empty streets, when I heard a faint noise behind me.

I looked over my shoulder and saw a man wearing street clothes—and a palpably hostile expression on his face—running behind me. This was no jogger. I stopped in my tracks, and in a strange state of tranquility I watched him approach, thinking, Well, this is it. Have I learned anything or haven't I?

Why did I just stand there? you ask. First, any possible help was at least a quarter of a mile away. Although I am a fairly faithful jogger, I am certainly no sprinter. I know from many playful races that I can almost never outrun a man over even a short distance. Second, I was damned lucky I'd heard this guy behind me so I could see him in time. Why on earth would I want to turn my back on him again?

He drew near. His hands went to my throat. The instant he touched me, I twisted out of his grasp (one of the first moves my karate instructor had taught me) and gave him a few straight punches to the face (again, basic strikes, nothing fancy). Then, holding him by the hair, I forced his head down, watching to see what he'd do next.

What he did was give up! He actually started whining about how he hadn't meant anything, he just wanted to ask for some directions.

After I subjected him to a torrent of profanity and a number of threats to his life, I left him. Accidentally, but gratifyingly, I stepped on his eyeglasses as I walked away. I had knocked them off his face when I'd hit him. I heard them crunch like eggshells under my Etonics. (My own glasses were undisturbed.)

I finished out my run in a state of high euphoria, returned home, showered, dressed, and went to the police station to report the incident.

On reflection, it seems to me that there are some general principles in this episode that are worth keeping in mind.

- *It's possible to face danger without panic*. I said that I experienced a feeling of calm, standing there alone, knowing that an attack was inevitable. It was positively uncanny. My karate teacher had once told me that in a fight you get this sense of heightened perception, as if everything slows down, like the slow-motion fight scenes on that TV show "Kung Fu." Needless to say, when he told me that, I was more than a little skeptical. But that *was* how I felt when I was attacked. And, believe me, I am not an innately calm or brave person, so this was a learned response.
- *Simple techniques work*. Although I had been studying karate for a year and a half, the techniques I used were literally the first I'd learned. Granted, eighteen months of training had built up my

confidence and had contributed to that wonderful lucidity I experienced. But my success did not depend on complicated advanced skills. (However, it is important to know that even the simplest techniques demand brisk execution and good form. For example, there is a correct way, and many incorrect ways, to make a fist. Striking with a sloppily formed fist will hurt you more than your attacker.)

- *Not everyone thinks you have the right to defend yourself.* The cops were pleasant, courteously concerned, and found the outcome amusing. My colleagues at the karate school didn't think I went far enough. Some said they would have broken part of his anatomy, or at least left him bleeding and unconscious. They made me feel that I'm either admirably self-controlled or a sap for letting the guy off so easy. At the other extreme was one of my law professors, who seriously thought I should have tried to run away instead of fight. In other words, he was telling me I should have worsened my odds by making myself more vulnerable. That anyone could suggest that with a straight face is beyond belief, but there it is. I just think we can't worry about pleasing people like him, and we shouldn't be too surprised when we encounter them.

- *Fighting back is fun.* That night I'd had to drag myself out to run. I'd been at work all day and sitting in class all evening, so I was feeling sluggish and lazy. After my little adventure, I was flying! It must have been some kind of adrenaline high, I guess. Would I do it again? You bet!

- *Beware of overconfidence.* This is the dark side of what I just said. Here's the problem: since I thwarted an attack and escaped completely unharmed, I now suffer from a delusion of invincibility. I have to remind myself that my attacker was alone, unarmed, not under the influence of drugs, not large, and basically a coward. Had any of these conditions been different, I might not have fared so well. Still, given the choice between seeing myself as a helpless, pathetic victim, or thinking I'm probably Wonder Woman, I'll take the latter any day.

Ten Commandments: How Not to Get Raped When Bicycling Alone

Joan Joesting

Joan Joesting has run and cycled over thirteen thousand miles in the United States and Australia. At the age of forty-five, she began to chronicle her own adventures. She presently lives in Tampa, Florida.

"I refuse to stay at home because of fear of going 'about my business' alone in this world.

"My own father told me that I was raped because I was seductive. My answer to him was: What bank robber has been considered innocent by a judge, when the robber said the bank was so rich-looking that it wanted to be robbed?"

Many people have asked me about the main problem for a woman bicycling, running, and camping alone. In Australia, women asked me, "Aren't you afraid of getting hit on the head?" I answered, "If they hit me, they will only get a battered bicycle and some traveler's checks." In 1978, when I first talked about my plans to run from Tampa to Tallahassee, a distance of 242 miles on isolated roads, I was repeatedly warned that I would get raped. I had been raped by my husband in my own bedroom, so the nightmares of rape were nothing new to me. I had also read everything about rape prevention and thus formulated the following commandments that work well for me on bicycling, running, and camping trips.

One: Thou shalt not be afraid to bicycle/run/camp alone with cautious courage when your body and schedule permit, wearing ordinary but appropriate clothing. I don't believe in deliberately standing out by wearing a bikini top or a tight sweater. Loose clothing seems more comfortable in all kinds of weather. Nevertheless, the idea that women's sexy clothing excites men to rape is like the bank robber's defense that the bank made him take the money because it looked as if it wanted to be robbed.

Two: Thou shalt vary thy route and thy schedule. Many times, rapes are planned, with the rapist patiently waiting for the vulnerable victim to bicycle/run by him. When talking to local people on trips, I am often vague about my next day's travel plans. I hate sticking to a tight schedule, so I begin and end my travels and training at different times each day.

Three: Thou shalt not bicycle or run at dangerous times or in dangerous places. Dangerous times for any bicyclist/runner are after dark, particularly when bars close, which may vary in different locations. This is when the drunks get loose, and many rapes occur when the rapist is drunk.

Both dangerous times and places are not as dangerous when one doesn't appear to be a woman. I am flat-chested. When I wear baggy clothes, with my long hair braided under a cap, it is difficult to determine my sex.

Touring on a bicycle means that my tent/sleeping bag/foam mattress are heaped on the luggage rack behind my bicycle seat, hiding my wide hips in black cycling shorts. While bicycling in the isolated Australian outback, people at camping areas who had seen me while they were driving watched to see which rest room I would shower in, because they couldn't tell if I was female or male. They teased me, saying that I should wear a T-shirt stating, "I am a girl."

Once, just outside of Ozona, Texas, a man in a pickup truck pulled up beside me and asked, "Son, do you want a ride into town?"

"No, thank you, sir," I replied. He responded, surprised, "By God, you're a girl."

As Louise Sutherland says in her book about her solo thirty-three-country bicycle ride, *I Follow the Wind,* "People just don't think a woman would bicycle alone, and always automatically assume that a woman is a man."

Four: Thou shalt bicycle/run with assurance. Rapists prefer a vulnerable, weak victim, because as one bicycle-store owner in California told me, "No one likes to mess with a bicyclist, because bicyclists are fit, and the mugger feels he might get hurt."

Five: Thou shalt not be afraid to be friendly with men who have women with them. Without exception, men with women, in Australia, New Zealand, and in the United States, were very polite and kind. I always avoided men in all-male groups, saying "No speaka English." At campsites, I avoided single males, but was careful to "get to know" families or married couples camping near me, telling them if they screamed during the night, I would come to their aid with my bicycle pump. This usually led to conversation and discussion of crime in the area.

Six: Thou shalt train thy senses to be aware of unusual people or vehicles. I have normal hearing, but I can tell exactly what is behind me, even if it is a nonbarking dog sneaking up to attack, or a quiet motorcycle. If a woman knows what is in her immediate vicinity and it bothers her, she can always sprint, or get out of the way and keep from getting grabbed. If a man can't grab a woman, he can't rape her.

Once, before I began "doing the roads" alone, a young man on a picnic date with me pulled a gun, aimed it at me, and told me to submit to sex with him or be killed. I told him that someone would hear the gun go off, and that he would go to jail. He said no one would be able to hear the gun. I asked him if he was so sure, and if he had talked with the criminals in prison who had thought the same thing.

When running, I am always afraid of vanloads of men who pull up beside me and ask for directions. I am careful to stay out of close range and usually do not talk to them, even when they ask for directions. I say I don't know, or tell them to ask the police.

Seven: Thou shalt mentally practice strategies for getting help, or if completely alone, for coping with problem men. Once when I was jogging in an isolated area, a man parked his car and chased after me, yelling, "I know you did it!" I ran to a group of houses, yelling, "Fire!" and the people came out to see if their houses and cars were burning. "Fire" gets more attention and witnesses than "Rape."

Another time I was running across a deserted field next to a road at midnight, and a carload of men propositioned me. I screamed, "I'm a boy!" and they turned their car around to have another look. My appearance must have convinced them, because they sped away, and I set an Olympic record getting to lights and people. When I get really scared, I pretend to have an epileptic seizure. When I was jogging from Tampa to Tallahassee and arrived after dark in a small town, four men in a car began bothering me, so I began shaking, spitting, and sticking my tongue out. They said, "That woman's weird, man. Let's get out of here," and they drove away. Other women have picked their noses, or defecated on potential rapists.

Eight: Thou shalt always carry paper and pencil and change. The paper and pencil can be used to record license-plate numbers and both person and vehicle descriptions, and the money used to call the police or sheriff to report suspicious drivers.

Once I was bicycling in Tampa to a foot race at seven-thirty on a Sunday morning, with my long hair hanging in a braid down my back. A male driver deliberately swerved into me, but I braked to a stop. He was clearly masturbating and calling, "Come on, baby." I noted his license number, yelling it out as a memory aid device. I sprinted on my bicycle to a busy intersection, where I got off and recorded the license number. I reported him to the police, and with police and district attorney cooperation, got him thirty days in jail.

Nine: Thou shalt report any suspicious persons to the police, sheriff, or to their employer. I see no reason that I should be yelled at or honked at by men when I am riding my bicycle or jogging. If they are driving a commercial vehicle that is labeled with their employer's advertisement, I simply report the time and location of the offense to their employer. If they are paying attention to women, they are not concentrating on their driving or their job, and their careless accidents raise insurance rates. If the employer isn't cooperative, I then call the employer's insurance company. I have been able to get at least one man fired for not paying attention to his work.

Ten: Thou shalt remember that even by verbally fighting back, you are saving others from a worse fate than yours. In Australia, I bought a button that says, "A wolf whistle ends in a rape." I do my best to stop the wolf whistles and get the creeps off the street, by any method possible.

I sometimes carry a spray with which to fight attacking dogs. Although I have never had to spray it into a car window or at a person,

I would do so to keep from being raped. Yes, I know that it might damage the eyes of the rapist, but he might kill me, and that is what defense is all about.

For ten years, I have jogged and bicycled in areas ranging from the best to the worst neighborhoods in Florida, and in isolated rural areas in Georgia, North Carolina, New York, Australia, and New Zealand at all times of the day and night. During this time, I have run an average of about fifty miles a week. I have bicycled over 13,000 miles in three countries in all types of areas. Using these ten commandments, I have avoided rape while on the roads and have had much more fun than I ever dreamed possible. If I had listened to all the people who had warned me about rape, I would have missed the experience of a lifetime.

Self–Defense on Wheels

Sandi Collins

Sandi Collins contracted polio when she was three years old. She uses a wheelchair. Sandi took a self-defense class for physically challenged women in 1986.

> *"I'm not a stick-in-the-mud stay-at-home, that's for sure. I'm a mother even though they said I could never be one. I live in the country even though it's a lot easier in the city, because I have more fun out here in the country. I'm a lousy housekeeper, but it's not because of my disability, it's because I hate housekeeping.*
>
> *"My best defense has been a good story line. I enjoyed the self-defense class I took. I had thought about some of the techniques before, but I wasn't sure exactly how to do them. I used to read books about self-defense, but it helps if you actually have somebody there showing you that it really does work, even in a wheelchair.*
>
> *"I ran into one of the other girls who took the class in the grocery store. She asked if I'd been attacked. I said, 'No, have you?' and she said, 'No, darn it!'"*

As told to the editors in an interview: I had polio when I was three, so I grew up with a disability. My legs are very weak. I can use my right leg very little, mostly just for steering my chair. My arms are weaker than an average person's, except for certain muscles that I use all the time. There's a lot of people that I know who don't have any use at all from the waist down, but they're really beefy from the waist up.

The first time I ever had trouble was with a guy who decided he was going to go a little farther than I wanted to go. I was really in need of love right then, but I didn't want that kind of love.

We were in his trailer, and he offered me a drink. I said no; at seventeen I didn't drink. He just kept talking and the next thing I knew he was behind me with his hands down my shirt. I started talking a lot.

I pretended to be very well experienced, like I was really a girl about town. I said I had gotten an infection from the last guy I was with, darn him, he was just such a louse, and I talked and talked and talked. And I said you don't want this infection, I'm broke out right now so you don't want any part of this.

I told him he was really a neat guy but I just didn't want him to get any of this thing that I had, and I sort of flattered him up a bit like I didn't really want to leave but I didn't think he really wanted to have my problem. And he let me go.

I didn't really know anything at all about herpes or VD, but I sure faked it a lot. That got me out of that one. I learned a little about men and what you say and what you don't say.

The other time that I really had a problem I was at the store where I worked. It was really early, like seven in the morning, and I was trying to catch up on some paperwork. The boss had been gone and it was about time for her to get back, so I had to get caught up.

I was in the front of the store behind this tall counter when I heard the back door unlock. I assumed it was the other girl who worked with us, and so I didn't pay much attention. I was wearing a scarf at the time, a bandanna, and the next thing I knew somebody had a hold of the scarf and was choking me. He shoved me out of my chair, and put my arm in an armlock. My right arm is double-jointed, so when he put me in the armlock, I just let him do it and then I grabbed hold of his *gazmachis*.

He let go of the scarf for a little while and I thought I'd finally gotten loose, but then he grabbed my scarf again and got into a different position so that I couldn't reach him. But all he was interested in was cash or whatever he could find.

The worst part was that he stuck an old, dirty, yucky paint rag in my mouth, so I couldn't holler for anybody. I was spitting paint chips for days after that.

Since then, the only person who's ever tried to pull my wheelchair over is my husband. When we get in a good knock-down, drag-out fight about once every four or five years, he tends to turtle-ize me; he takes my wheelchair and tips it back on the back wheels, and from that position I'm sort of stuck. I can get out of the wheelchair, but I'm definitely down on the floor at that point. I've also had friends turtle-ize me just for the heck of it, you know, just being smart. It's a very vulnerable position.

If I've got my feet straight up in the air and I'm on my back, I can't use my legs to kick, unless I'm on my side. If they're just holding on to my feet, I can't get out of the wheelchair by turning one way or the other, I'm stuck. That is a really good way of corraling me. It definitely gets my attention. I do have the use of my arms, though.

Recently, I took a self-defense class for disabled women. It gave me a lot of ideas about things I could do. Before I took the class, I always wondered about what would work. Now I know what's effective. Like from down on the floor, I now know different ways of disabling somebody. If I get in that position again, I know how to get them down on my level. Once they're down at my level, I'm on more even terms with them. As long as they're up above me and taller than me, I feel considerably at a disadvantage.

If I had to give advice to other women in a wheelchair, I'd say: Take a self-defense class so you have some confidence, and then think about it ahead of time. If you were in a dangerous situation, what would you do? Become a good liar, a convincing liar. In the situation when I was a teenager, he wasn't sure whether I was lying or not, but he sure didn't want to take the chance. It was very effective. But if I were to be in a situation where there would be a need for physical self-defense, lying wouldn't be adequate.

For instance, in January I had a run-in with a neighbor lady who was being very obnoxious; she had my car blocked down at the bottom of the hill and she kept reaching in the car and I just kept pushing her hand out. At least I knew I wasn't going to get in trouble. She couldn't say I had started anything. So I left the area and drove to the nearest safe place, which just happened to be the church. I saw one of the head deacons down there. Otherwise, I would have headed to the fire station. I figured there was no way she was going to be able to start something in front of a bunch of big burly firemen.

Afterward, I thought of all these things I could have done. I could have just stuck her head through my steering wheel and been through with it.

I don't take a lot of chances. Like I don't go shopping downtown with a purse hanging over my wheelchair. I usually have my credit cards tucked in a shoe or somewhere that isn't too visible. There have been times when I've been working at night and I've had to park the car someplace and go in my wheelchair; I'm very conscious of where people are. I'm very aware of where every crack is, where every curb is, where every rock is, you know, what's available as far as curbs. If you're trying to get away from somebody, it's a lot better to have a ramp handy than a curb, because a ramp will pick up your speed for you. And I watch for lights in windows in case I need help.

When I was a teenager, I used to do a lot of stuff just for the heck of it. Like go out at night and park as far away as possible from where I was going to be working. I used to take all sorts of chances like that that I don't take anymore. That little lesson there with the guy in the trailer really brought things home. I thought I was immune, you know, that in a wheelchair nobody would bother me.

The Getaway Bike

Autumn

Autumn is a thirty-year-old physically challenged lesbian who has cerebral palsy. She is planning to ride the getaway bike in a team of disabled lesbians in the 1987 Gay Games triathlon.

"Especially when I'm riding the bike, I like everybody to know I defended myself. Everybody says, 'Aren't you worried that he might see you on it?' I feel like he should be worried if he sees me."

my arms spin lopsided cartwheels
as hundreds of crystal sweat drops merge into chlorine
blood and wind pulsate brain chambers
sparking dormant cells back to life
the rhythm pushes   faster faster
stroke by stroke   lap after lap
legs jerk up and down as my twisted body splashes thru the water
i follow the black line in serious concentration
knowing i am in training for something more
than the cerebral palsy swim meet next month
alongside swims a womon with very strong arms
her legs do not kick much at all
i always like sprinting backstroke at the end of class with her
we cue ourselves with the tall trees
or the moon when she's waxing

sometimes she pulls me in her wake
and sometimes i pull her in mine
arms propelling wildly in and out of the water
we always arrive together
this work is so good for my heart
the pool begins to empty
and a split second glance of approval from my coach
is enough to get me through the next month
guess she's been watching me struggle with the flip turns
my legs struggle up the ladder
and i catch myself staring in admiration
as wheelchairs crutches and the hydraulic lift
shift into movement

i climb up the high bleachers
where i can think about what i have gotten myself into
i try to fight off visions of drowning or getting caught up in the
    line

before thousands of spectators at the meet
and gradually i see myself solidly diving in
and flying across the water with great speed
sweeping the length of the pool over and over
and suddenly i have found the right spot and ride the wave into
    shore
the crowd is wild screaming and cheering
and pounding the bleachers down
and in the end i am standing very straight and steady
alongside the other wimmin with
lots of colorful ribboned medals hanging from our necks
dozens of anxious photographers and news reporters surround us
this new stream of seriousness and determination
makes me giggle to myself
but as i stand to head for the showers i can't help noticing
strange little bulges on my arms and legs
they were not there four months ago
my mother always said patience and determination would make me
    strong
lately i thought it would be my beard and nonmonogamy

there is a very large bike leaned up against the wall
just outside the wimmin's locker room

must be a giant amazon inside
i should remind her to lock it up
or bring it in even though no one's around
it's quiet inside as i pass the stalls
only the sound of a toilet running
i am alone there will be plenty of hot water

when like a bolt of lightning out of nowhere
a big thick hand grabs my arm
and is pulling me into one of the stalls
the tile is cold and wet
and in a split second i have lost my footing
and am not sure what's happening
there is a long handrail
i grab on and my feet gain their grounding
i take a good look
he is smelly and ugly and his thing hangs out open pants
like a slimy lumpy worm
i might throw up
my arms and legs are tense and jittering
hot blood floods my brain
his grip remains tight on my arm
and he stares at me blankly
with his other hand on his thing
i have got to do something
for a minute it occurs to me he may be disabled himself
maybe someone from my class
but then he asks me if i like candy
and my rage finally explodes
so what if he is disabled
it all comes back that lesbian self-defense class last winter
all in one breath my arm spins around
breaking through his fingers and thumb
shouting a fierce NO into his face
and keeping constant eye contact
i see he is as surprised as i am
as i step out of the stall
i actually think i'd like to hit him
but realize i am shaking inside my shaking
and run for the door my steps weak and wobbly

afraid he may be behind me
and there outside the locker room is that same unlocked bike
the perfect getaway
i ride off as fast as i can
two months later i sit naked under a tree
at the wimmin's music festival
addressing an envelope to my mother
inside is a picture of me taken by my coach
there are two red ribboned medals around my neck
nearby there is a pool full of hundreds of laughing wimmin and
    children

i stare at the wimmin of every size and ability
spinning and weaving through the water
it is safe
for four days we are thousands of wimmin and children
in the woods
there are no men hiding out in the bathrooms

After the assault, I felt really powerful, that I had taken care of myself. I had just come out of a relationship that lasted for three years, which was very dominating on both sides. We were very dependent on each other. I had been away from this woman for only three months and it had been a struggle to see myself as being strong and on my own. This incident was a big turning point, when I found myself being able to take care of myself again. I was shaking bad, but underneath it I felt good and so incredibly shocked. Probably the biggest fear in my life is that I'm gonna be in some room with some man and he's gonna try to rape me. And it happened, and somehow I got clear of it. I can't really even believe it now. It makes me angry, too.

I think I was very lucky, because he wasn't as aggressive as he might have been. I think he might have been scared of me. I like to tell some of the women that I know what happened.

I took a lesbian self-defense class the spring before the attack and it was the most empowering class I've ever taken—a room full of lesbians finding their power. The women teaching it were so supportive—it was phenomenal. One woman came up to me after the first class and asked me if she could get together with me privately and talk about any special needs I might have. I thought, I can't believe this is happening, somebody is really taking me seriously and wanting to teach me this important thing. I took the class knowing that it was probably going to change my life. It was one of the hardest things I ever did, staying in there and feeling weak when I was punching the foam against the wall, but knowing that I needed to keep on with it until I felt strong.

On the street, I depend more on psychic energy than my physical body. I feel lucky that I haven't been attacked more than I have. I think it has to do with not focusing so much on my physical strength all these years and being spiritually or mentally oriented. My advice to another woman with a similar disability who wanted to learn self-defense would be just to do it and stick with it, using the methods that she usually learns anything else by. I had to go through the class step by step and break everything down. Like with the wrist escape, which is the only thing that I feel I learned well in the class, I had to first think about learning what to do with the arm and then, when I got that right, I had to just do the body movement and then the legs. That takes a long time. Usually, I think a disabled woman's process takes more time.

The special challenges I face because of the cerebral palsy include new situations and situations where I'm not sure how much comfort there is between me and someone I don't know very well. For instance, when I take a new class, especially if it's a physical class, I'm not sure how comfortable the teacher is with me and that usually makes me nervous. I feel responsible, as if I should be the one to make her comfortable with me. Last week, I started a T'ai Chi class, and I was really insecure and thinking, What am I going to do in here? I'm so incredibly ungraceful and you're supposed to move like everybody else and of course I don't and I'm really sad about it. I was just about to walk out the door when the teacher came up behind me and said, "You're doing really well and I hope you stay."

A Test of Faith

Barbara Richmond

Barbara was born in New York. Her journey has taken her throughout Latin America, where she lived for eight years. Her interests, concerns, and commitments revolve around peace and justice issues, with particular focus on Central America.

"Now when I hear about violence and beatings and forced confessions in Latin America, it's part of my own story. And it changed who I am.

"I have a sense now of the strength that is available to all of us, whoever we are and whatever situation we happen to be in. It's almost like the strength of all people's struggles are available to us, whenever we need to call on it."

As told to the editors in an interview: I had been in Mexico since 1966, and in 1974, when this incident happened, I started working near Temisco, not far from Acapulco. I was working with a movement called *comunidades de base*—basic Christian communities. It's a community-organizing tool that was started through the Catholic church in Brazil; the movement has spread throughout Latin America. Traditionally, the church in Latin American countries has been allied with the powerful, and the message a lot of people got was "You're poor now, but you'll get your reward in heaven." People used to be very much resigned to their fate in life. *Comunidad* is a way to create a kingdom of justice and love *now*.

We worked in the villages and got to know people, talked about what was going on in their lives, in the factories and in the fields.

I was there with a Chicana friend, Lola. Crisoforo was another friend—my *compadre*—and his two daughters were my godchildren. We were working with the priest in the area, Padre Morfim. There had just been some changes in the diocese. The priest who had been there before Morfim, Padre Cornello, had been there for twenty-seven years, and had been in cahoots with the local authorities and landowners in milking the people. If it was Holy Week, or a fiesta or Christmas, Cornello would go around collecting money, then just pocket it.

Padre Morfim was very supportive of *comunidades de base*. One of the first things he did was tell the people at Mass that during Holy Week, he did not authorize anyone to go collecting from door to door for flowers or anything else.

The *caciques*—the big landowners—were all furious, because they had done this for years and had collected a lot of money. They were determined to get Padre Morfim out and Cornello back there again so they could continue the way things had been for the last twenty-odd years. They started telling rumors that Padre Morfim was bringing outsiders into Temisco to take away the people's religion—that he wanted to destroy their way of being and their saints, that he was a Communist.

One night we were having a meeting in the church in Temisco. We were almost finished with the meeting when we heard a knock at the door. Before any of the five of us at the meeting could get up, someone burst in wearing a white shirt and a straw hat. I could see people milling around outside—men with this very serious look on their faces.

"What are you doing here?" the guy asked.

We told him we were having a meeting.

"Well, we're Catholics here," he said, "and we don't want any of this stuff, we like our faith. We like our religion, and you're going to get in trouble."

He was so strong about what he was saying. I didn't know him and I hadn't seen him before. It was very scary, because I didn't know what he was talking about.

"We don't want to run you out," he added. "But . . ." And he went out and closed the door.

I thought, That's strange. I had a terrible feeling. I looked over at Padre Morfim.

"Who was that?" I said.

"Jorge Sanchez."

At the time I didn't know who Jorge Sanchez was, but as it turned out, he was the head *cacique* in Temisco.

Padre Morfim said, "I think we better stop this meeting." As we said a prayer that ended our meetings, I heard the church bell ringing. Jorge Sanchez had gone into the bell tower, and the bell was ringing, bang bang bang bang.

It was getting dark, and my heart was pounding. We walked into the street, and suddenly people started running. I could see people running down the nearby streets. There was a kind of buzz. I heard people talking, everybody was talking at once and coming toward us.

There was a crowd, but I couldn't tell how many people were in it. Later on, they calculated there were about five hundred people against the five of us. I really and truly didn't know what the hell was going on, but the feeling I had was just terrible.

There were crowds of people milling everywhere. We were about a half block from the road that goes to Acapulco. Buses went on that road. So I said, "Let's walk down." I thought maybe we could get on a bus and get out of there.

A woman came toward me. "We're Catholic and we like our faith, and you can't take our faith away."

I thought, What is she talking about? I had a Bible in my hand at that moment, and a notebook. I tried to talk to her, tried to ask her what did she mean, could she tell me what was going on? She was just so furious. There was an absolute rage going on among this group of people. As more people gathered, the anger escalated and then exploded. I started to feel rocks hitting me, and people were hitting me with sticks.

Right before we turned the corner, I saw Padre Morfim maybe ten feet in front of me. On one side of him there was a *campesino,* a man with *huaraches* and a straw hat, with one of those big machetes they cut sugar cane with, holding the machete over his head, and on the other side someone was sticking a gun into his side.

We went around the corner. My friend Don Lupe was sticking up close to Padre Morfim, and Lola and Crisoforo were next to me. As we got to the corner, I saw a store across the street with a light on, and I said, "Let's go across the street." In other words, get away from the mob.

I thought I was walking across the street with Lola and Crisoforo, but as I walked across the street, I realized that only Crisoforo was with me. I turned around and looked and Lola was still across the street, walking with the mob, *in* the mob. We called her to come across the street. "Lolita, Lolita, *vente acá, vente acá!*" She wasn't that far away from us and we were screaming at her. She was just walking, walking, walking. It was like she couldn't hear or see. It was too much for her to face. Crisoforo and I looked at each other and just went back across the street, into the mob.

Up ahead we heard a gunshot. Someone came running back toward us, saying, "The priest shot against the people." Someone else said, "*Ustedes van a pagar.*" You're going to pay for it. People really started hitting and punching and grabbing us. They were knocking me off balance. We just tried to take people's hands off us. I tried to take people's hands off Lola. She looked totally dumbfounded, she didn't have any expression on her face. People were twisting her arm around up near her neck, and I took their hands and tried to pull them off. At one point, several people were choking me, and I distinctly remember opening my mouth to bite the person who was choking me, but then stopping. It was almost like there was something in me that said, Don't do it, because you're going to give them more reason to strike out. I remember that very clearly.

Suddenly, the realization hit me that they wanted to kill us. I wasn't sure why or how this had happened, but they were so angry that they were going to pull us apart right there on the street.

Then I saw a bus coming down the road. Someone yelled, "Get out of the way, a bus is coming." And one of the people who had me said, "*Qué bueno.*" How good that a bus is coming. Then they threw me down in the road in front of the bus.

I remember going down, then looking up and seeing headlights. I heard people gasp in the background. I was just trying to get my balance again and get myself up. The bus stopped about a foot away from me, and I know it was very close because when I went to get up, I put my hand on it to steady myself. I pounded on the door of the bus and yelled, "Let me in, let me in, they're trying to kill us." But the driver wouldn't open the door because he saw what was going on, and there were passengers in there.

All of these things happened in a split second. It was the kind of situation where you don't have time to think, but there's just something that happens from within you. You just act, you just do what you have to do at that moment. I kept pounding at the door, and with my right eye I saw someone in a white car coming from the other direction, looking at this mob and hearing the shouts, going slowly. I started to run to my left to go around the back of the bus, hoping I would be able to meet that white car that was coming from the other direction. Just as I started to do that, I heard people saying, "*Mátenla, mátenla.* Get her, get her, kill her, don't let her get away."

For a very split second, I had that bus between me and the mob as I ran toward that car. The one thing I remember thinking at that point was, I hope the back door isn't locked. I ran over to the car, opened up the back door, threw myself in, closed the door and locked it, then told the driver, "Get out of here, step on it, get out of here."

I heard the thud of people landing on the car who had been running right behind me, to get me. The driver put his foot on the gas and took off, and as I turned around, I felt a surge of anxiety. I had left Lola behind, Lola and Crisoforo. I didn't know where they were.

As the car pulled off, I heard more gunshots and I saw, I actually saw, the explosion of guns going off. Here I was getting away, but I had left my friends. I didn't want to leave them, but I had to get some kind of help.

So here I am in the car and I'm talking and talking and talking and trying to think out loud, trying to center myself somehow. The driver was saying, "What happened, what happened?" and I was going over what had happened.

I saw a patrol car and I stuck my head outside the window and screamed at them to stop. Then I told the driver not to leave me alone until I knew the police were going to go back with me, and he said okay.

So I got in the car with the police, and they drove with me to a gas station. Time just seemed eternal. They had to have a Coca-Cola, they made a telephone call, they put gas in the car, all the time telling me to calm down. Finally, we went down near the government office. Sure enough, there was this whole mob of people down there. We pulled in, and when people saw this police car pull in with me in the back, they circled the car, still holding those clubs. They wanted to take me out and finish me off.

Then I heard a siren. I turned around and saw the Red Cross ambulance.

I wanted to go see what was going on and who was being put in the ambulance, but I couldn't get out of the car, because there were people right there with clubs wanting to get at me. Someone was being put into the ambulance, and people were shouting. I found out later that it was the priest, and the mob was still trying to finish him off. The ambulance pulled out, and so did the car I was in.

I realized at that time that I was holding my left arm. It turned out that my elbow was dislocated and my arm was broken. But I wasn't aware of it. When I look back on it, I was holding my arm like that the whole time, but I didn't feel pain, and it didn't stop me from running and doing the stuff I had to do.

Then one of the policemen said, "You're being accused by the people."

"Of *what*?"

"You are being accused of celebrating a Black Mass. These people said they went into your meeting and you were celebrating a Black Mass, and you were having sex with the priest, and there were drugs involved."

"Well, that's not true, that's not what we were doing."

"You have to tell the truth."

"I *am* telling you the truth."

"Well, I don't know, I've been told to come and get a confession out of you."

I had been in Mexico for eight years, and by that time I knew what that meant. That means you get beaten until you say what they want you to say. He pulled over to the side of the road, and we were at a place called Puerto de la Muerte—Bridge of Death. I don't know how it got that name and I don't want to know. We were on a mountain road in the middle of nowhere at ten or ten-thirty at night, it was dark, nothing else around. He stopped the car. I thought, I know I'm going to get beaten. In the front seat one of the police had this big piece of wood, a club. He got out of the car, came around the side, and opened the door in the backseat on my side.

It was an incredible thing, but at that moment I became calm. And I can pinpoint it to that moment, because I knew there was nothing I could do to get out of that situation physically. Up to that point, there was always something I could do. I could talk to someone, I could run, there was a car coming, I could get away, I could do this or that. But now there was no place I could go, nothing I could do.

My heart stopped pounding and this calm just came over me. I had the conviction inside me that I was *not* going to say we were celebrating a Black Mass and doing all those other things. I was not going to do it.

He told me to get out of the car, and I started talking again, but differently this time. Before, it had been this kind of frantic talking about what had happened. This time, I started talking in a much calmer way about the experience I had had in Mexico, that my experience had been so deep and so beautiful, people had been so good to me, and I had learned so much, that I had so many *compadres* and *comadres.* And I realized as I was talking that he was listening. He wasn't hitting me. So I kept talking.

After all this, I still had the Bible and my notebook in my hand.

"What's that book?" he asked me.

"It's the Bible." I opened it, started showing him that it really was a Bible.

He was looking at the Bible and he wasn't hitting me. So I kept talking. I was just groping at that point for things to say.

I was talking about the *comunidades,* and at one point I said, "*Muy pronto voy a regresar a mi tierra.*" Very soon I am going back to my land, my country.

"Where are you from?"

"I'm from New York."

"You're from the United States?"

"Yes."

It hadn't occurred to me to say that. You would have thought they would have known, but they didn't—maybe because of the dark, the confusion, and, sometimes to my credit and sometimes not, I spoke Spanish with the accent of the people from that area and even from that village.

"Do you have a passport?"

I had my visitor's permit with me, and I showed it to him. He stepped back, closed the door, went around to the front, sat in the driver's seat again, and said, "I didn't know. You'll have to forgive us. My people are fanatics." He apologized.

Right then a car came along the road, another police car. They opened the door and a little light went on inside, and I saw Lola and Crisoforo in the backseat. I grabbed a flashlight that was in the backseat and turned it on in my face so my friends could see I was okay in that car. As it turned out, they thought I was dead, because the last time they had seen me was when I had been thrown in front of the bus.

Then they were put into the car with me. Crisoforo was badly beaten. Lola looked scared, but she didn't look beaten to me. They took us to police headquarters in the city, and they put us in a cell. I asked Crisoforo about Padre Morfim, and he said he had been shot and beaten. Don Lupe's head had been broken open with big rocks. They let us out of jail later that night.

A lot of good came out of all this. The priest is alive; he still limps, but he's okay. Two years ago, he left Temisco. He could have left right away, but he said he was going to stay. If he had left, it would have been admitting he was doing something wrong, and he knows he wasn't.

The bishop canceled Mass in the village; there was no religious service or Eucharist allowed. That had a tremendous impact on the people. He said, "It would be hypocritical to celebrate the Mass here. Mass is a living symbol of communion, of community and love among people, and that's not here in Temisco. When you show me that what you seek is community and love in the kingdom of God, then I myself will come and celebrate Mass with you again."

One of the things he required of the people was that they find out what our meetings were about. They had been told the meetings were Black Masses, but he said people should go and see for themselves.

Some people were advising me to call the American Embassy and try to get some protection, or try to get Jorge Sanchez thrown in jail. But I thought: Suppose we throw Jorge Sanchez in jail. Suppose we call on the American Embassy. I can call on the American Embassy to protect me, but what kind of example is that going to be for the people in that village? Who are they going to call on in time of need? Can they go to the American Embassy? Can they even go to their own local authorities? No. We have to give them the example that there are other ways to be powerful and that we don't have to always call on some big shot to help and protect us. If we throw Jorge Sanchez in jail and the people in Temisco remain ignorant about what was going on, any old Jorge Sanchez can come back and the people will believe him.

When I left, there were about four different meetings going on every week. Within a year, there were twenty-five. This whole event sparked a lot of awareness. People realized how they had been exploited, how they had been lied to—for generations.

This episode wasn't something I would choose to have happen, but when I look back, it was an honor to have been part of something that was going to make people more aware of the oppression they had lived in and take some real control over their lives. My sense of faith in the struggle I'm involved in deepened a whole lot. I think it's one of those kinds of things where you either feel, Forget this, this is too scary and I don't want to do it anymore, or you just get totally convinced that this is what you want your life to be about. That's what happened to me.

So What Do I Do Now?
Ways to Learn More
About Self-Defense

How many times have you said, "Someday I'll take a self-defense class . . ." and not done it? If you've been assaulted before, a self-defense class can help you regain your confidence. If you haven't been attacked, self-defense is great preventative medicine: you don't have to wait until something terrible happens to start learning skills.

Self-defense can be fun. You can learn about your own power, physical and mental. It's good exercise, no matter what your physical condition, a good place to meet friends, and it can change your outlook on life. Whether you're skinny or fat, old or young, on your feet or in a wheelchair, you can learn self-defense.

If after reading this collection of stories you want to learn to yell effectively, practice ways to talk your way out of a dangerous situation, or try out some new physical skills, there are lots of ways to learn more about self-defense. Here are ten of the best:

1. Take a self-defense class. You can probably locate a course in your area by calling or writing a group listed in "Self-Defense Programs," pages 263–292, or by calling the rape crisis center or battered-women's shelter in your area.

Although one-day workshops can be a valuable introduction, a longer class—usually eight to ten weeks—will give you a good grounding in basic skills.

One way to get yourself to go to that first class—and to keep going—is to go with a friend. Mothers and daughters can take classes together as well. You can encourage each other when you're feeling lazy, compare notes, and practice techniques. Experiment: you'll probably come up with new and useful variations on the techniques you've learned.

There may be special self-defense classes for disabled women, girls, seniors, lesbians, Spanish-speaking women, or other special groups in your area. Many classes are low-cost or free. Most are taught by women.

After all, why wait to take a self-defense class? You can do it now, and have a better chance of preventing a possible attack. For specific self-defense resources for your state, see the Self-Defense Programs (pages 263–292).

A NOTE ON MARTIAL ARTS VERSUS SELF-DEFENSE. If you want to learn self-defense, take self-defense classes. Most strictly martial arts classes are not taught with rape prevention in mind, but as sports or with an emphasis on philosophy, rather than practical applications. There are exceptions: some women's martial arts schools *do* emphasize self-defense. By and large, though, self-defense courses are more likely to deal with the particular feelings and psychological issues women face about fighting back.

Many self-defense teachers have studied martial arts, and once you have taken a basic self-defense course, you may want to continue your training through martial arts. Martial arts will definitely extend your ability to defend yourself, but self-defense and martial arts are not the same thing. Some martial arts schools are listed on pages 263–292.

2. Take an assertiveness class. Most attacks begin on a verbal level and can be stopped there, by knowing what you want and saying it. You don't have to justify yourself to an attacker. It's okay to yell or "make a scene," too. An assertiveness class can teach you useful techniques and attitudes basic to sticking up for yourself on a verbal level. Such classes may be available through your local community college, the YWCA, women's center, or private instruction. If you can't take a class, at least read *When I Say No I Feel Guilty* by Manuel J. Smith, listed in our Bibliography. Speaking of books . . .

3. Read books about self-defense and violence against women. You can start with some of the ones listed in the Bibliography in this book. Most of these are widely available in bookstores and libraries, and can also be special-ordered. In some cases, we give books negative reviews, so you will have an idea about which ones to steer away from. All self-defense books have their shortcomings, but many of them are extremely interesting and good tools for learning. Books are especially useful if you are currently taking a self-defense course, or have taken one before. The pictures can help remind you how to do techniques.

4. Take a martial art. Particularly if you've already had a general self-defense course, martial arts can be a fun way to learn more about yourself and improve your physical abilities. Most martial arts emphasize using your mind and body in harmony for maximum effectiveness, a concept basic to good self-defense.

In many parts of the world, martial arts were developed by people who were forbidden to carry weapons, often when faced by conquering forces armed with swords or guns. Thus they are a fitting weapon for women in today's world.

You don't need any particular level of physical skill to try martial arts. Your desire to learn is enough. Each person starts as a beginner and learns safety and easier skills first. If you are interested, try a class and see if you like it.

Many people who practice martial arts will tell you that their art or school is the best, but we firmly believe that all martial arts can be valuable and fun. Which art or teacher you choose is a matter of personal preference.

A NOTE ON CHOOSING A CLASS OR SCHOOL. The best way to choose is to visit a school. Watch a class, notice how (women) students are treated, and decide whether you like the instructors. If there are women instructors in your area, they may be more aware of women's needs in terms of self-defense. Be wary of teachers who stress aggressiveness and competition over practice skills.

Avoid schools that are not willing to let you observe a class, or that ask you to sign a contract or make a financial commitment. No school should have anything to hide from you.

In any school, women should be represented in all belt ranks or colors. The belt colors generally go from white (basic beginner) to black (first rank), with several colored belts in between. The colors vary, depending on the art or school, but generally get darker with more experience. For example, in our women's judo class, they went from white to green to purple to brown to black, with ten degrees of black.

If women are only in the lower ranks in a school, talk to them about the instructors; they may be discouraging women from advancing.

MARTIAL ARTS TO CONSIDER. Most self-defense techniques are adapted from martial arts techniques. Each art emphasizes different qualities and approaches. For instance, one art may rely heavily on kicking, while another may emphasize joint leverage techniques. Here is some very basic information on the difference between arts, focusing on arts that have become widely available in the United States.

Karate or tae kwon do: Karate (meaning "empty hand") is Japanese, tae kwon do is Korean; both are similar forms of fighting that emphasize punching, kicking, and other ways of striking to vital points on the opponent's body. Techniques are sometimes practiced as kata, prearranged sequences usually performed alone. There are competitive forms of these arts, and thousands of different schools with different names.

Kung fu: Popularized by Bruce Lee and also by the popular television series, kung fu is a conglomerate art of ancient Chinese origin. Legend has it that many of the techniques in kung fu are based on animal movements. It includes striking and kicking, pressure points, and throwing and falling in versatile patterns. Although it is similar to karate and tae kwon do, the strikes and blocking movements tend to be more fluid and flexible.

Jujitsu: The mother of modern Japanese arts, jujitsu is a very diverse martial art that includes throwing, falling, the use of very painful pressure-point techniques, and some striking and kicking, as well as prearranged forms originally practiced stiff-legged in armor, by Samurai women and men.

Judo: Judo began in 1882 in Japan as an offshoot of jujitsu. Judo means "the gentle way," and its mottos are "maximum efficiency, minimum effort" and "mutual welfare and benefit" between partners. The aim of judo is to use the attacker's strength against him, via a system of throws, falls, and wrestling techniques.

Women's judo, a separate branch of the art, also teaches kata, or prearranged forms of movement. In judo, katas are usually practiced with a partner.

Aikido: Aikido began in the 1920s in Japan, growing out of jujitsu, judo, and Shinto, the nature religion of Japan. Aikido is a system of throws, pins, and joint leverage techniques developed by Ueshiba. It also incorporates practice with wooden knives, staves, and swords. Aikido is also a philosophy aimed at world peace. "Ai" is harmony or love, "ki" is spirit, and "do" is way or path, thus aikido means the way of harmony of the spirit.

Aikido is a purely defensive art; there are no competitive forms.

T'ai chi ch'uan: T'ai chi is Chinese in origin and is many thousands of years old—it is sometimes called the great-grandmother of all Asian fighting arts. Most T'ai chi forms are fairly slow, individual movements learned in a series, then performed in a prescribed sequence. This meditative art systematically and gently exercises the whole body. Some people say you must study T'ai chi for years to use it in self-defense, but if you have already taken some self-defense, the deflecting, turning movements and blows and kicks will be familiar. There are no ranks in T'ai chi, but Gail once saw a woman who had studied T'ai chi for years "defeat" a karate black belt in sparring by deflecting her every blow. She simply was not there when the other person advanced on her.

Naginata: A Japanese art developed specifically for Samurai women. The naginata is a six- to eight-foot pole with a long curved blade at the end, used for cutting off the opponent's feet in battle.

There are literally hundreds of arts that were developed in Japan and other Asian countries, but most have not spread to the United States. You may have heard of kendo (Japanese archery), iaido (Japanese sword work), and ninjutsu (the art of the assassin).

Capoiera: A Brazilian art developed by African slaves. This art is a composite of dancing, music, acrobatics, stick fighting, and fantastic kicks erupting out of handstands. The music and dancing provide rhythm, as well as disguise the art from the eye of the oppressor.

Penca silat: From Indonesia, this art is often performed to the music of the gamelan. It includes sword work and beautiful leaping kicks.

There are many more arts and schools than those mentioned here, and we apologize to anyone who practices an art not covered. Explore the arts that are available in your community.

5. *Learn about your body and mind in other ways.* Jogging, aerobics, dance classes, strengthening your body through weight lifting, push-ups, pull-ups, sit-ups, playing baseball or any other sport, joining an exercise group, walking every day—all of these are ways to strengthen your body and mind. If you have trouble sticking with an activity, try it with a friend or in a group.

6. Join a project for stopping violence against women. The rape crisis center or battered-women's shelter in your area may need help in working with women and children who are survivors of violence. If reading this book made you want to do something to help, please contact one of these organizations or start your own. And encourage your friends and family to take self-defense classes and to fight back so that more of this violence will be prevented.

Many communities also have organizations like Men's Alternatives to Violence, which offers support to men trying to change their violent behavior. Men who are concerned about this problem can volunteer as peer counselors or group leaders, or attend the support groups available.

7. Become a self-defense teacher. Although there are few formal training programs, many women become teachers by apprenticing themselves to their own teachers, or by studying martial arts and adapting them to self-defense. Talk to self-defense teachers in your own area to find out how they learned to teach.

8. Change your community. Some communities now have a Commission for the Prevention of Violence Against Women, which receives funding to sponsor free self-defense classes or child assault prevention projects in the schools. If there isn't such an organization in your area, you can put pressure on your local government to initiate such a program. Encourage your employer or your college to sponsor self-defense workshops at the workplace or on campus.

Other communities have started a Sexual Assault Response Team, to coordinate services for women and children who have been raped. The Response Team is often made up of staff from hospitals, rape crisis centers, police and sheriff's departments, victim/witness programs, and battered women's shelters.

As the general public has become more aware of the problem of child sexual abuse and incest, more and more school districts have welcomed groups like the Child Assault Prevention Project, which teaches basic defense skills to children. The project was originally developed by Women Against Rape in Columbus, Ohio, and has spread to other parts of the country.

Still other communities have safe houses similar in concept to the block parent program. Community members who offer their homes as safe houses put a sign in their windows indicating that they will help people who are being hassled or attacked in the neighborhood. The people participating in this program are trained to provide immediate help, and also are knowledgeable about related community resources.

9. Spread the word. Talk to everyone you can about the good news that women can and do defend themselves. Be willing to argue with skeptics, and encourage other women who are afraid. Strategize with your friends; play "What if?" Talk about what you can do to help each other if, for example, you're walking down the street together and you are harassed. Isolation breeds fear. Let other women know they're not alone.

10. Consider the boundless possibilities. You can create far more than we could suggest. Many women are preventing rape and assault every day, using their wits and whatever skills they already have. You have taken one more step by reading this book. Women can defend themselves—and we are worth defending.

We encourage all of our readers to take that next step, whatever it is for you, and learn a bit more about living your life fully, with "your wits about you."

Self-Defense Programs in the United States and Canada

If you cannot find a self-defense class near you in the following list, or if the number has become obsolete, try your local women's center, martial arts school, YWCA, community center, college, or rape crisis center. Or write Victim Prevention, Inc., P.O. Box 5957, Wheat Ridge, Colorado 80034—they have instructors all over the country.

If you are particularly interested in child assault issues and wish to contact the CAPP (Child Assault Prevention Project) office nearest you, please contact the national office in Columbus, Ohio, or, for California readers, the Oakland office.

United States

ALABAMA

Montgomery

Chung's Taekwondo
465 North Eastern Bypass, Sunshine Village, Montgomery, Alabama 36109
(205) 277-2627

Some emphasis on women's self-defense. Children's classes.

ALASKA

Anchorage

Kung Fu San Soo
549 West International, Suite A-1, Anchorage, Alaska 99518
(907) 562-0902 CONTACT PERSON: Bruce Bibee

Martial arts classes for women and men, self-defense for women only. No women instructors yet, hopes to have some soon as several are working toward their black belts. Street-fighting style, no competition. Bibee also counsels violent men, very supportive of women.

ARIZONA

Phoenix

Roberta Trias Kelley
P.O. Box 9817, Phoenix, Arizona 85068
(602) 829-4202

Self-defense, women instructors, some women-only classes.

YWCA
755 East Willetta Street, Phoenix, Arizona 85257
(602) 258-0990

Classes in self-defense and judo combined, plus martial arts classes in karate.

ARKANSAS

Fayetteville

Fayetteville Dance Center
25 East South Street, Fayetteville, Arkansas 72702
(501) 443-7897

T'ai chi classes for women.

Tae Kwon Do Ozark Karate Academy
32045 Thompson, Springfield, Arkansas 72764
(501) 751-0005

Tae kwon do karate classes with self-defense emphasis.

CALIFORNIA

Berkeley

Rape Prevention Education Program
Women's Resource Center, Building T-9
University of California, Berkeley, California 94720
(415) 642-7310 CONTACT PERSONS: Sallie Werson, Roberta Friedman

Self-defense classes for women only, all women instructors. Students learn skills for dealing with potentially dangerous situations, including how to assess situations, verbal and psychological resistance strategies, effective body language, physical techniques.

Carpinteria (Santa Barbara area)

Model Mugging Inc./Women's Self Defense and Empowerment
1330 Vallecito Place, Carpinteria, California 93013
(805) 684-8228

Self-defense classes with live mugger. For women only, all women instructors with male model mugger assisting.

El Cerrito

Women's Self-Defense Council
5621 El Dorado Street # 9, El Cerrito, California 94530
(415) 525-9265 CONTACT PERSON: Denise Leto

Self-defense classes for women only, all women instructors. Emphasis on psychological aspect of self-defense, i.e., awareness and self-confidence. Also includes basic effective physical techniques. Feminist approach. Sincerity, sensitivity, plus some political analysis.

Eureka

Humboldt County Rape Crisis Team
P.O. Box 543, Eureka, California 95502
(707) 443-2737 CONTACT PERSON: Kimberly Rosa

Self-defense classes for women only, at least one woman instructor. One-third psychological preparedness and awareness, one-third assertiveness training, one-third physical techniques.

Los Angeles

L.A. Commission on Assaults Against Women
543 North Fairfax, Los Angeles, California 90036
(213) 655-4235 CONTACT PERSON: Rosanna Hill

Self-defense classes for women only, all women instructors. Taught at the YWCA near UCLA.

Almut R. Fleck Poole, c/o Southern California Rape Hotline Alliance
Self Defense Certification Program
3827 Effie Street, Los Angeles, California 90026
(213) 661-1053

Self-defense classes for women only, all women instructors. Small classes, alternate physical techniques with discussion, take into account each participant's individual needs and background. Also training classes for instructors.

Monterey

Model Mugging Inc./Women's Self Defense and Empowerment
801 Lighthouse Avenue, Monterey, California 93940
(408) 646-5425/659-2041 CONTACT PERSONS: Danielle Evans, Mary Tesoro

Central office. Self-defense classes with live mugger. For women only, all women instructors with male model mugger assisting. Now offered in cities throughout the country.

North Hollywood

Model Mugging Inc./Women's Self Defense and Empowerment
12055½ Burbank Boulevard, North Hollywood, California 91601
(818) 509-8166

Self-defense classes with live mugger. For women only, all women instructors with male model mugger assisting.

Oakland

CAPP Training Center of Northern California
1727 Martin Luther King, Jr. Way, Suite 108
Oakland, California 94612
(415) 893-0413

Northern California office for Child Assault Prevention Project. Classes to train children to protect themselves from assault.

Dirty Fighting Self Defense
3928 Magee, Oakland, California 94619
(415) 482-0635 CONTACT PERSON: Bev

Self-defense classes for women only, all women instructors. Focus of class to teach women and girls how to avoid attack and, if they are forced to fight, to use serious, damaging techniques capable of stopping anyone. Practice strikes on bags and releases.

The Dojo
3718 MacArthur Boulevard, Oakland, California 94619
(415) 530-5043 CONTACT PERSON: Elise Prowse

All classes are for women only, all women instructors. Classes include a six-week self-defense class designed to increase awareness and give women usable techniques in a short period of time. Also ongoing traditional jujitsu classes.

Trouble House
3212 San Pablo Avenue, Oakland, California 94607
(415) 658-8375 CONTACT PERSON: Sensei

Self-defense and rape prevention classes are for women only. No women instructors, but great sensitivity.

Palo Alto

Model Mugging Inc./Women's Self Defense and Empowerment
3790 El Camino #2032, Palo Alto, California 94306
(415) 494-2611

Self-defense classes with live mugger. For women only, all women instructors with male model mugger assisting.

Pasadena

Pasadena YWCA Rape Hotline
78 North Marengo, Pasadena, California 91101
(818) 793-5171 CONTACT PERSON: Rachelle Coffey

Self-defense classes for women only, all women instructors certified by Southern California Rape Hotline Alliance. Teach rape awareness, prevention, simple self-defense methods.

San Diego

Model Mugging Inc./Women's Self Defense and Empowerment
5019 Santa Monica Avenue, San Diego, California 92107
(619) 298-1698/222-5085

Self-defense classes with live mugger. For women only, all women instructors with male model mugger assisting.

San Francisco

Brinkman & Associates
1300A 12th Avenue, San Francisco, California 94122
(415) 661-4040 CONTACT PERSON: Trisha Brinkman

Self-defense classes and workshops provide information about assault, safety tips, verbal and body language skills, and realistic physical techniques. All women instructors, some women-only classes.

City College of San Francisco
Ocean & Phelm, North Gym, San Francisco, California 94112
(415) 564-9140 CONTACT PERSON: Judith Fein, Ph.D.

Self-defense classes for women only, all women instructors. Physical, prevention, and psychological skills to prevent and, if necessary, to counter an attack.

Ron Dong's School of White Crane Gung Fu
4010 Balboa Street, San Francisco, California 94121
(415) 668-8086 (evenings)/668-9366 (days) CONTACT PERSONS: Lynda Cence, Ron Dong

Classes are White Crane gung fu (ancient, classical form) with self-defense emphasized. Graceful, elegant, yet deadly defense against larger or more numerous people. Small classes, individual attention. No classes for women only, at least one woman instructor.

San Francisco State University, Department of Physical Education
1600 Holloway Avenue, San Francisco, California 94132
(415) 469-1258 CONTACT PERSON: Jean Perry, Department Head

Self-defense classes for women and men, both women and men instructors.

Self Defense/Tae Kwon Do for Women and Children
178 Anderson Street, San Francisco, California 94110
(415) 647-4300 CONTACT PERSON: Nina Jo Smith

Classes in martial arts and self-defense. The one instructor is a woman. Adult classes are for women only, children's classes for both female and male.

Women's Self Defense and Martial Arts Club
c/o Women's Center
1650 Holloway Avenue, San Francisco, California 94132
(415) 469-2486 CONTACT PERSON: Nina Jo Smith

Self-defense classes for women only, all women instructors.

Worthington-Fein Associates
P.O. Box 27352, San Francisco, California 94127
(415) 564-9140 CONTACT PERSON: Dr. Judith Fein

Self-defense classes plus tear gas certification classes, some for women only, all women instructors. Assault prevention and rape resistance training, emphasis on integration of psychological prevention and physical skills, and on fighting back and winning.

San Pablo

Rape Crisis Center of West Contra Costa County
2000 Vale Road, San Pablo, California 94806
(415) 237-0113 CONTACT PERSON: Gloria Sandoval

Self-defense classes for women only, all women instructors.

Santa Cruz

Santa Cruz City Commission for the Prevention of Violence Against Women
City Hall, 809 Center Street, Santa Cruz, California 95060
(408) 429-3546 CONTACT PERSON: Susan Strehlow, Commission Staffperson

The commission acts as a funding body and sponsor for a variety of activities in the city, including free self-defense classes, development of domestic violence prevention curriculum for the schools, art and theater productions relating to violence prevention, mass mailings of informational brochures to households in the city, and other innovative educational prevention activities that decrease the likelihood that women will be attacked. The commission also monitors police response to sexual assault cases. "Imagine a World Without Violence" is the commission's motto.

Santa Cruz Women's Self-Defense Teaching Cooperative
135 Serra Court, Santa Cruz, California 95060
(408) 427-0176, (408) 426-5724 CONTACT PERSONS: Gail Groves, Rachel Harwood

The Coop teaches eight-week self-defense classes for women and girls, incorporating concepts and techniques that include vital points, escapes, ground techniques, verbal defense, defense against weapons, and defense against multiple attackers. We also teach special classes for girls and teenagers, seniors, disabled women, lesbians, and intermediate students. Eclectic, feminist approach. All classes are free at this time due to funding from the Santa Cruz City Commission for Prevention of Violence Against Women.

Women's Self-Defense Council
P.O. Box 8312, Santa Cruz, California 95061
(408) 427-2184 CONTACT PERSON: Toni Crossen

Self-defense classes for women only, all women instructors. The eight-week class addresses both the psychological and physical aspects of self-defense.

Santa Rosa

Association for Shotokan Karate (ASK)
1804 Piner Road, Santa Rosa, California 95401
(707) 575-1681 CONTACT PERSON: Susan Joiner

Classes are martial arts, with self-defense emphasis (traditional Japanese shotokan karate). Some classes for women only and at least one woman instructor. Offer special women's programs and teach with awareness and sensitivity to women's issues.

Sonoma County Women Against Rape
P.O. Box 1426, Santa Rosa, California 95402
(707) 545-7270 CONTACT PERSON: Cindy Dickinson

Self-defense classes for women and girls fourteen and over, all women instructors, with male sparring partners. Six-week course on street fighting and physical self-defense skills. Practical, easy-to-learn information. Step-by-step teaching method to develop confidence and a sense of control. Empowering.

Take Nami Do Karate
1220 Eva Avenue, Santa Rosa, California 95407
(707) 544-2361 CONTACT PERSON: Stephanie Snedden

Mixed classes are martial arts only, women's classes incorporate self-defense. Some classes for women only, at least one woman instructor. Take Nami Do karate provides creative nonviolent conflict resolution for children as well as self-defense and traditional karate classes for adults.

South Gate

Southern California Rape Crisis Hotline Alliance
Self Defense Instructor Training Program
Box 2272, South Gate, California 90280
(213) 861-1600 CONTACT PERSON: Dr. Betty W. Brooks, Director

Classes to train women self-defense instructors. All women instructors. Program requires seventy to ninety hours of individual skill training, methods of how to teach self-defense, rape and sexual assault information from a feminist perspective, and practice teaching activities. Instructors are certified by a team of master teachers (for other instructor-training courses, also see Almut Poole, L.A. Rape Crisis Hotline, and Pattie Giggins, L.A. Commission on Assaults Against Women).

Stanford

Everywoman's Self-Defense Collective
P.O. Box 6553, Stanford, California 94305
(415) 326-1235 CONTACT PERSON: Becky Fischbach

Self-defense classes for women taught by women, using techniques from a variety of martial arts. Working from the assumption that women have the right to fight back, the collective teaches a combination of physical and verbal skills necessary for self-defense.

Women Defending Themselves, c/o SWOPSI
123 Sweet Hall, Stanford, California 94305
(415) 723-4305

Self-defense classes for women taught by women. Includes both discussion of societal causes of and support for violence and physical and psychological techniques of self-defense.

Stockton

Women's Center of San Joaquin County
930 North Commerce Street, Stockton, California 95202
(209) 941-2611 CONTACT PERSON: Pat Tinker

Classes emphasize self-defense, are for women only (twelve years and up), all women instructors. Aikido and karate principles and techniques are used, street-fighting strategies and assertiveness skills. Class is six weeks long, one one-and-one-half-hour class each week. Learning progression designed to take participants from a general awareness through specific strategies for handling a variety of different assaults.

COLORADO

Wheat Ridge

Victim Prevention, Inc./Women's Self Defense Course
P.O. Box 5057, Wheat Ridge, Colorado 80034
CONTACT PERSON: Helen Groom Stevens

Self-defense classes for women only, all women instructors. Focuses as much attention on the mental underpinnings of self-defense as on protective body maneuvers.

CONNECTICUT

New Haven

Women's Self Defense Alliance
614 Orange Street, New Haven, Connecticut 06511
(203) 787-0031 CONTACT PERSON: Dawn S. Evans

Self-defense classes for women only, all women instructors. Feminist perspective. Eight classes, one and one-half hour long, includes twenty-minute discussion period.

DELAWARE

Dover

Dover Isshinryu Karate Club
54 Beechwood Avenue, Dover, Delaware 19901
(302) 674-3339

Martial arts plus self-defense tactics.

Milford

Milford Isshinryu Karate Club
12 Nelson, Milford, Delaware 19963
(302) 422-4290

Martial arts plus self-defense training.

FLORIDA

Jacksonville

Florida Junior College, Physical Education Department
Jacksonville, Florida 32205
(904) 387-8311

Self-defense classes.

GEORGIA

Atlanta

Self Defense for Women
324 Elmira Place N.E., Atlanta, Georgia 30307
(404) 688-5280 CONTACT PERSON: Ellen Teeter

Self-defense classes for women, all women instructors. Emphasis on avoidance
of attack situations by developing "radar" to inappropriate/threatening individuals, plus fundamentals of where to strike, what to strike with, etc., for the most
devastating response to attacks.

HAWAII

Honolulu

Victim Prevention Inc./Women's Self-Defense Council
500 Lunalilo Home Road #28H, Honolulu, Hawaii 96825
(808) 395-6164 CONTACT PERSON: Ginger Russell Reznik

Self-defense classes, all women instructors with male assistant at end of course.
Some classes for women only—mostly women, but some men do take it. Objective of the course is to give the woman a new awareness of her capabilities
and the dangers around her as well as a practical working knowledge of physical
tactics useful in all phases of personal safety.

IDAHO

Boise

YWCA Women's Crisis Center, Rape Crisis Alliance
720 West Washington, Boise, Idaho 83702
(208) 343-3688 CONTACT PERSON: Lou Hamill, Director

Occasional self-defense classes when an instructor wishes to present one. The
last class was for women only with male instructor.

ILLINOIS

Chicago

Budokan/Illinois Aikido Club
1103 West Bryn Mawr, Chicago, Illinois 60660
(312) 271-2870 CONTACT PERSON: K. Choate

Classes are martial arts only (aikido, judo, iaido), taught in the traditional Japanese manner. Classes are women and men together, at least one woman instructor.

Chimera, Inc.
10 South Wabash #602, Chicago, Illinois 60603
(312) 332-5540

Main office. Self-defense classes for women by women. Students learn effective physical techniques plus warning signals and the attacker's tactics. Practice in an atmosphere of cooperation. Emphasis on practical, effective solutions. Women of any age, athletic ability, or previous experience.

Women's Gym
1212 Belmont
Chicago, Illinois 60657

Offers an ongoing, ten-week course in self-defense, teaching defenses against various types of attack. By women, for women.

(312) 549-0700 CONTACT PERSON: Dr. Pauline Bart

Peoria

Chimera, Inc.
1323 East Dean, Peoria, Illinois 61615
(309) 692-1790 CONTACT PERSON: Cathy Corl

Self-defense classes for women by women. Students learn effective physical techniques, warning signals, and the attacker's tactics. Practice in an atmosphere of cooperation. Emphasis on practical, effective solutions. Women of any age, athletic ability, or previous experience.

INDIANA

Bloomington

Oyama Karate School, Bloomington Headquarters
2116 Rockcreek Drive, Bloomington, Indiana 47401
(812) 336-7203/332-8499 CONTACT PERSON: Peg Strain

Self-defense emphasized, some classes for women only, all women instructors.

Teach traditional Japanese karate, self-defense, and nonphysical self-defense skills (violence prevention). Weekly classes and seminars, teacher training available.

T'ai Chi Chuan Association of Indiana
P.O. Box 1834, Bloomington, Indiana 47402
(812) 332-9911 CONTACT PERSON: Laura Stone

Martial arts classes (t'ai chi), some self-defense classes, for women and men, at least one woman instructor. Students of all ages, including teens and seniors.

IOWA

Des Moines

Iowa Coalition Against Sexual Abuse
25th and Carpenter, Illinois Hall, Des Moines, Iowa 50311
(515) 271-2918 CONTACT PERSON: Carole Meade

Class is for women only, women instructors. The preventive personal safety course utilizes: open discussions, lectures, demonstrations, role-plays, films, and individual practice time. Avoidance, precautionary measures, communication/negotiation techniques, and physical techniques are taught. Also includes wellness and becoming physically fit, relaxation and stress management techniques, assertiveness training, identifying anatomical control points on the body and hypothetical situations.

KANSAS

Emporia

S.O.S., Inc.
P.O. Box 1191, Emporia, Kansas 66801
(316) 342-0548 CONTACT PERSON: Susan K. Moran

Classes for women only, all women instructors. Self-defense classes emphasize that 90 percent of self-defense is self-protection, but also demonstrate vulnerable body areas to strike using appropriate movements with sufficient force to escape.

KENTUCKY

Louisville

Bellarmine College
2000 Norris Pl., Louisville, Kentucky 40205
(502) 452-8211

Self-defense classes.

University of Louisville
2301 South 3rd., Louisville, Kentucky 40208
(502) 588-5555

Self-defense classes.

LOUISIANA

Metairie

Louisiana Karate Association
2563 Metairie Road, Metairie, Louisiana 70001
(504) 835-6825

Martial arts with self-defense emphasis for women, men, children.

Yang Moon College of Taekwondo Karate
3330 Lake Villa Drive, Metairie, Louisiana 70002
(504) 887-6835

Martial arts with self-defense emphasis. Classes for women, men, all ages.

MAINE

Portland

American Martial Arts Foundation
70 Cobb, Portland, Maine 04102
(207) 772-1512

Martial arts, including some self-defense.

Villari's Studios of Self Defense
500 Congress Street, Portland, Maine 04101
(207) 761-0114

Self-defense plus karate, kung fu, t'ai chi.

MARYLAND

Germantown

White Lotus Taekwondo
14125 Berryville Road, Germantown, Maryland 20874
(301) 869-5518 CONTACT PERSON: Karen Lunquist

Martial arts classes, some self-defense. Some classes for women only, at least one woman instructor. Traditional and sport tae kwon do. Free newsletter called "Girls and Women Taekwondo."

Silver Spring

D.C. Self Defense Karate Association
701 Richmond Avenue, Silver Spring, Maryland 20910
(301) 589-1349 CONTACT PERSON: Carol Middleton

Classes include self-defense only, martial arts only, or a combination. Some classes for women only, mostly women instructors. One-month women's self-defense class, beginners' karate class emphasizes self-defense, continuing classes in tae kwon do combine traditional values and modern techniques. Also serve blind, hearing-impaired, disabled. Feminist, focus on empowerment.

MASSACHUSETTS

Cambridge

Chimera, Inc.
153 Hamilton Street, Cambridge, Massachusetts 02139
(617) 576-0722 CONTACT PERSON: Pam Frorer

Self-defense classes for women by women. Students learn effective physical techniques plus warning signals and the attacker's tactics. Practice in an atmosphere of cooperation. Emphasis on practical, effective solutions. Women of any age, athletic ability, or previous experience.

Sanchin Women's School of Karate and Self Defense
595 Massachusetts Avenue, Cambridge, Massachusetts 02139
(617) 868-3554 CONTACT PERSON: Debbie Karlan

Classes include both self-defense and martial arts (gojo-ryu), all are for women only, all women instructors. Feminist approach, empowerment of women. Respect for traditions of gojo-ryu, but reject the authoritarian aspects of it. Noncompetitive.

Chicopee

Kanku School of Karate
154 Grove Street
Chicopee, Massachusetts 01020

Easthampton

Valley Women's Martial Arts, Inc.
P.O. Box 1064, One Cottage Street, Easthampton, Massachusetts 01027
(413) 527-0101 CONTACT PERSONS: Janet Aalfs, Beth Holt

Classes emphasize self-defense, all women instructors, for women only. Some children's classes (girls and boys) and some special seminars for women and men. Shuri-ryu Okinawan karate, self-defense, and arnis (Filipino stickfighting).

Orleans

Willys Gym and Indo-American Karate
225 Cranberry Highway, Orleans, Massachusetts 02653
(617) 255-6826 CONTACT PERSON: Barbara Niggel

Separate martial arts and self-defense classes. Some classes for women only, at least one woman instructor (woman head instructor). Classes are taught with mutual respect and love for the art and its practitioners. Emphasis on effective self-defense and karate training, remembering each person must be trained according to individual ability.

South Hadley

Bushido-Kai Karate Club
P.O. Box 1030, Mount Holyoke College, South Hadley, Massachusetts 01075
(413) 538-2304
CONTACT PERSON: Barbara A. Arrighi, Sandan, Chief of Security

"We teach all aspects of karate, including self-defense, kata, and kumite." Several women instructors, some classes for women only through PE department. "A lot of emphasis on basic techniques, without which the rest does not work."

MICHIGAN

Ann Arbor

Okinawan Karate & Self Defense Club
409 Pauline, Ann Arbor, Michigan 48103
(313) 665-2840 CONTACT PERSON: Barbara Christensen

Classes include separate self-defense and karate classes for women only, all women instructors.

Detroit

Alkebu-lan Martial Arts Federation
8411 East Forest, Detroit, Michigan 48214
(313) 342-8688 CONTACT PERSON: Michelle D. Bradford

Martial arts classes (jang soo do) with self-defense emphasized. Some classes for women only, at least one woman instructor. Classes are very structured and disciplined. Strong value and code of ethics.

Catherine Daligga
138 West Dakota Street, Detroit, Michigan 48203
(313) 865-5848

Self-defense classes, women instructors. Most classes for women only, but senior and children's classes are open to males. Not only physical techniques, but also mental awareness and preparedness. Supportive atmosphere.

Mejishi Karate Dojo
494 West Greendale, Detroit, Michigan 48203
(313) 869-4286 CONTACT PERSON: Jaye Spiro

Classes include self-defense only, martial arts with self-defense emphasized, and martial arts only (traditional ai mute shoto-kan karate and modern arnis). There are some classes for women only, and all instructors are women. Children's classes, too.

East Lansing

Michigan State University Project for Personal Safety
105 1M Sports Circle, Michigan State University, East Lansing, Michigan 48824
(517) 373-0728 CONTACT PERSON: Jayne Schuiteman

Three ten-week self-defense classes for women only are offered through the PE department each term. Women instructors. MSUPPS also offers programs ranging from one- to four-hour workshops to ten-hour seminars in self-defense and personal safety for the entire campus community.

Lansing

Movement Arts
230 Bingham Street, Lansing, Michigan 48912
(517) 485-3868 CONTACT PERSON: Joan Nelson

Classes are martial arts, self-defense, and health- and fitness-related programs, all women instructors.

MINNESOTA

Eden Prairie

Chimera, Inc.
10300 Riverview Boulevard, Eden Prarie, Minnesota 55344
CONTACT PERSON: Anara Guard

Self-defense classes for women by women. Students learn effective physical techniques plus warning signals and attacker's tactics. Practice in an atmosphere of cooperation. Emphasis on practical, effective solutions. Women of any age, athletic ability, or previous experience.

Minneapolis

Anderson Community School
2727 Tenth Avenue South, Minneapolis, Minnesota 55407
(612) 627-2310

Offers both martial arts (judo and karate) and self-defense, especially karate for women. Some classes for women only, some women instructors.

Midwest Karate Association
1819 Nicollet Avenue, Minneapolis, Minnesota 55403
(612) 871-1101 CONTACT PERSON: Master Robert L. Fusaro

Martial arts classes, self-defense emphasis. Karate means "empty hand"—karate *is* self-defense. Several women instructors, no classes for women only, but classes are 40 to 50 percent women—a good supportive place for women. Children's classes, too.

Women's Self Defense Empowering
P.O. Box 10119, Minneapolis, Minnesota 55440
(612) 827-4813 CONTACT PERSON: Tom Washington

Self-defense classes for women only with women co-instructors. Emphasizes physical techniques and psychological awareness in three areas of self-defense: street safety, intimate relationships, self-destructive behavior.

St. Paul

Bendix & Brandell Self Defense
762 East 7th Street, St. Paul, Minnesota 55106
(612) 771-7901 CONTACT PERSONS: Anita Bendix, Mary Brandell

Self-defense classes, some classes for women only, women instructors. Philosophy that avoidance is much better if possible. Teach women how to use their bodies, how to analyze situations. Skills include recognition of dangerous situations, verbal assertiveness, physical techniques.

Woman's Karate Club
762 East 7th Street, St. Paul, Minnesota 55106
(612) 771-7901 CONTACT PERSONS: Anita Bendix, Mary Brandell

Shotokan karate classes for women only, all women instructors.

MISSISSIPPI

Jackson

Dragon Martial Arts Academy
3522 Terry Road, Jackson, Mississippi 39212
(601) 372-3962

Martial arts classes with some self-defense emphasis.

Gober's Karate and Fitness Center
McLaurin Mart, P.O. 5614, Highway 80, Pearl, Mississippi
(601) 932-3397

Both women and male instructors. Self-defense classes.

MISSOURI

St. Louis

YWCA
1015 Locust, St. Louis, Missouri 63101
(314) 421-2750

Self-defense classes, some women instructors. Many branches throughout the city.

MONTANA

Dillon

Eric Strausser
234 North Idaho, Dillon, Montana 59725
(406) 683-2692

Self-defense classes, some for women only. Includes martial arts, kendo type emphasis, and spiritual training. Also combat techniques. Eric is very involved in the men's anti-violence movement.

NEBRASKA

Omaha

ATA Taekwondo Center
151 North 72nd Street, Omaha, Nebraska 68114
(402) 556-9812

Self-defense for all ages.

Omaha Kung-Fu Institute
2308 North 72nd Street, Omaha, Nebraska 68134
(402) 391-1014

Self-defense for all ages.

NEVADA

Reno

Sierra Kenpo
135 Vesta, Reno, Nevada 89502
(702) 322-1756

Self-defense, martial arts.

Sparks

Bushidokan Martial Arts Temple
311 Ninth, Sparks, Nevada 89431
(702) 358-1518

Self-defense, children's classes, the gentle way.

NEW HAMPSHIRE

Concord

Bob Meserve's Health and Self Defense
89-F Fort Eddy Road, Concord, New Hampshire 03301
(603) 224-9844

Self-defense, karate, kung fu for women, men, children.

Villari's Studios of Self Defense
3 North Main Street, Concord, New Hampshire 03301
(603) 225-7499

Self-defense, karate, kung fu, t'ai chi.

NEW JERSEY

Morristown

Robin Robertson/Constance Fraser
94 Elm Street, Morristown, New Jersey 07960
(201) 538-5686

Self-defense and karate. All classes for women only, both instructors are women.

Mount Holly (Philadelphia area)

Chimera, Inc.
2461 Fostertown Road, Mount Holly, New Jersey 08060
(215) 569-0347 (days)/(609) 261-8252 (evenings) CONTACT PERSON: Mary
Partin

Self-defense classes for women by women. Students learn effective physical techniques plus warning signals and attacker's tactics. Practice in an atmosphere of cooperation. Emphasis on practical, effective solutions. Women of any age, athletic ability, or previous experience.

Pleasantville

The Way of One School of the Martial Arts
108 West Mulberry Avenue, Pleasantville, New Jersey 08232
(609) 645-8397 CONTACT PERSON: Robert R. Murie, Director

Classes are street-oriented martial arts, practical self-defense emphasized. Some classes for women only, no women instructors.

NEW MEXICO

Santa Fe

Ja-Shin-Do Studio, c/o Joan Chernock
702 Felipe, Santa Fe, New Mexico 89501
(505) 982-4083 CONTACT PERSON: Joan Chernock

Women's school: women students, women instructors. Ja-shin-do was designed specifically for self-defense and is an extremely good self-defense method. Every move is intended for self-defense.

NEW YORK

Brentwood

Brentwood Karate Club
169 Ocean Avenue, Brentwood, New York 11717
(516) 435-0677 CONTACT PERSON: Judith T. Scaglione, Director

Karate and self-defense classes for women, all women instructors. Women of all ages, including seniors, many older women. Children's classes for both girls and boys.

Brooklyn

Brooklyn Women's Martial Arts
421 Fifth Avenue, Brooklyn, New York 11215
(718) 788-1775 CONTACT PERSON: Annie Ellman

Offers four-week self-defense-only class and also goju karate classes that include self-defense. All for women only, women instructors. Encourage all women to work at their own pace. Sliding scale fees, free child care.

Ithaca

Wind and Water Martial Arts, c/o Women's Community Building
100 West Seneca Street, Ithaca, New York 14850
(607) 257-2716 CONTACT PERSON: Cassandra George, Director

Formal, coed karate classes year-round, self-defense emphasized. Classes are twice a week with beginners' classes started every eight weeks. Also four- and six-week self-defense classes for women one to two times each year. Beginners' classes include safety and prevention information, verbal confrontation techniques, and defenses against frontal attacks. Intermediate classes include defenses against rear attacks and evasive techniques against weapons.

New York City

Karate School for Women
149 Bleecker Street, New York, New York 10012
(212) 982-4739 CONTACT PERSON: Roberta Schine

Serious, nonintimidating approach to traditional karate, with an emphasis on how women best develop and use their bodies. Self-defense classes also. All classes for women only, women instructors.

New York University Department of Athletics
Coles Sports Center, 181 Mercer Street, New York, New York 10012
(212) 598-9324 CONTACT PERSON: Gail Stentiford

Self-defense classes, all women instructors, no women-only classes. Karate, judo, jujitsu techniques taught in street-oriented manner with emphasis on psychological aspects of vulnerability.

Person-to-Person Karate
465 Lexington Avenue, New York, New York 10017
(212) 599-1966 CONTACT PERSON: Robert Scaglione

Karate with self-defense emphasized. No classes for women only, some women instructors.

Safety and Fitness Exchange (SAFE), Inc.
541 Sixth Avenue, New York, New York 10011
(212) 242-4874 CONTACT PERSON: Tamar Hosansky

Supportive, noncompetitive classes in realistic self-defense. Classes are for women, men, and children (age two and up), some classes for women only; women, men, and children instructors. Women-owned. People of all ages, physical abilities, and life-styles welcome.

Women's Center Karate Club
243 West 20th Street, New York, New York 10011
(212) 663-7108 CONTACT PERSON: Susan Ribner

Martial arts (shotokan karate) classes with periodic self-defense courses. All classes for women only, all women instructors. All-women's school, but affiliated with a male-run school, some students take classes there in addition. Serious but supportive atmosphere.

Queens Village

Self Defense for Women
P.O. Box 28-462, Queens Village, New York 11428
(718) 776-8257 CONTACT PERSON: Susan Bartelstone

Self-defense classes for women only, all women instructors. Males can be taught separately or privately. Classes are designed to teach how to safely resist and escape from the most common types of attacks. They combine practical street-fighting strategy with modified techniques from various martial arts and army commando tactics and can be successfully learned regardless of the participant's age or physical condition. Classes deal with the psychological aspects of self-defense as well.

Rochester

Personal Prevention and Defense Skills
115 Alliance Avenue, Rochester, New York 14620
(716) 442-4466 CONTACT PERSONS: Bobbie Majka, Patti Follansbee

Self-defense classes and crime prevention workshops taught by victim prevention specialists. All women instructors, some women-only classes. Classes emphasize personal skills to reduce crime risks. Classes, workshops, and training programs for children and adults.

NORTH CAROLINA

Carrboro

Triangle Women's Martial Arts Center
P.O. Box 381, Carrboro, North Carolina 27510
(919) 682-7262 CONTACT PERSON: Kathy Hopwood

Classes include both self-defense and traditional martial arts courses. All classes are for women only, all women instructors. Emphasize learning at an individual pace in a supportive atmosphere. Goal is to make both martial arts and self-defense training accessible to as wide a range of women as possible, including physically and financially disadvantaged and survivors of assault.

OHIO

Athens

Careline Sexual Assault Prevention Program
(Tri-County Mental Health and Counseling, Inc.)
28 West Stimson Avenue, Athens, Ohio 45701
(614) 593-3344 CONTACT PERSON: Cheryl Cesta-Miller

Self-defense emphasized. Some classes for women only, some women instructors. Education and prevention modules covering general awareness, self-defense, and direct care services for survivors of sexual assault. Also programs for adolescents concerning date rape and prevention.

Columbus

Child Abuse Prevention Project (CAPP)
P.O. Box 2005, Columbus, Ohio 43202
(614) 291-2540

National office. CAPP is a community prevention project that teaches children how to prevent verbal, physical, and sexual assault.

FIST (Feminists in Self-Defense Training)
28 East Northwood Avenue, Columbus, Ohio 43201
(614) 299-4443 CONTACT PERSON: Sunny Graff

Both self-defense and martial arts classes (Korean tai-kwo do, hap-kido) for women only, women instructors. Practical skills and training to all levels.

Ohio Women Martial Artists
1462 Summit Street, Columbus, Ohio 43201
(614) 299-0725/421-2019 CONTACT PERSONS: Judy Beckman, Julie Harmon

Classes for women and girls only (ages eight and up), women instructors. Classes consist of practical self-defense training as well as aspects of traditional tae kwon do.

Rape Education and Prevention Program
408 Ohio Union, 1739 North High Street, Columbus, Ohio 43210
(614) 422-8473 CONTACT PERSON: Mary M. O'Melia

Self-defense classes for women only, all women instructors. Also confrontation training and feminist rape prevention theory, including a women's redefinition of rape. Classes are designed to help women develop strategies and skills to take control of their personal safety and to prevent rape in their lives.

Women Against Rape
P.O. Box 02084, Columbus, Ohio 43202
(614) 291-9751 CONTACT PERSON: Debra Seltzer

All women instructors, seif-defense techniques for women only, other informational classes for both men and women. Basic self-defense classes offer simple techniques and confrontation skills.

Tuppers Plains

Personal Safety and Assault Prevention
P.O. Box 173, Tuppers Plains, Ohio 45783
(614) 594-7452 (Athens) CONTACT PERSON: C. C. Miller

Self-defense classes for women only, all women instructors. Classes include awareness, verbal and physical skills for women and girls, stranger and acquaintance assault. Four two-and-one-half-hour classes offered three to four times per year, beginning and advanced.

OKLAHOMA

Oklahoma City

YWCA
129 North West 5th Street, Oklahoma City, Oklahoma 73102
(405) 232-7681

Self-defense classes for women. Karate for ages six and up.

OREGON

Eugene

Amazon Kung Fu
1002 West 2nd, Eugene, Oregon 97401
(503) 345-6490

This collective teaches kung fu with some self-defense. All classes are for women and girls, all instructors are women. In the future, children's classes may open to boys as well.

Rape Crisis Network
358 West 10th, Eugene, Oregon 97401
(503) 485-6700 CONTACT PERSON: Nadia Telsey

Self-defense classes for women only, all women instructors. Also workshops for getting at the stages of assault and trying to interrupt those stages before confrontation is necessary.

PENNSYLVANIA

Ardsley

Ardsley Karate Club
Ardsley Community Center, Spear & Center Avenues, Ardsley, Pennsylvania
19038
(215) 576-1630 (evenings) CONTACT PERSON: Teresa Galetti

Classes include both self-defense only and tae kwon do with self-defense emphasized. Self-defense classes include some classes for women only, martial arts have no women-only classes. All instructors are women. Martial arts: traditional emphasis on self-empowerment. Self-defense: street real, rough.

Philadelphia

Amulis Women's Self-Defense Training
P.O. Box 58845, Philadelphia, Pennsylvania 19102
(215) 438-5712 CONTACT PERSONS: Linda Adams, Libby Harman, Pat James,
Esther Miller, Joan Levin

Self-defense classes with women instructors, most are for women only except for classes for children, seniors, and disabled—males are allowed in these classes. Feminist approach, practical and effective self-defense skills. Emphasis is on finding the individual's strengths and building on them. One-day workshops, six- to eight-week classes for beginners and intermediate students.

Pittsburgh

School of Martial Arts for Women
1334 Wightman, Pittsburgh, Pennsylvania 15217
(412) 787-2759 CONTACT PERSON: Peggie Buckland

Formal karate classes with self-defense emphasized, self-defense classes for women only, children's classes for girls and boys. New style—quan yin—best approach from various styles for women.

Wilkes-Barre

Victims' Resource Center
132 South Franklin Street, Wilkes-Barre, Pennsylvania 18701
(717) 823-0765 CONTACT PERSON: Carol L. Lavery

Classes in rape prevention, some classes for women only, all women instructors. Classes are lecture-style and group discussion on rape prevention tactics, emphasizing potential situations (location), type of assailant, preference or abilities of woman to protect herself, role-playing as practice.

RHODE ISLAND

North Kingstown

Cerio's Kenpo Karate Studio
7610 Post Road, North Kingstown, Rhode Island 02852
(401) 295-1220

Self-defense, rape and kidnap prevention.

Villari's Studios of Self Defense
7417 Post Road, North Kingstown, Rhode Island 02852
(401) 295-1819

Self-defense, karate, kung fu.

SOUTH CAROLINA

Charleston

Rising Sun, Inc.
1680 Old Town Road, Charleston, South Carolina 29407
(803) 571-2931

Self-defense, karate, other martial arts for women, men, children.

Villari's Studios of Self Defense
342 King Street, Charleston, South Carolina 29401
(803) 577-9008

SOUTH DAKOTA

Aberdeen

Chimera, Inc., c/o Resource Center for Women
317 South Kline, Aberdeen, South Dakota 57401
(605) 226-1212 (days)/226-0680 (evenings) CONTACT PERSON: Jill Stephenson

Self-defense classes for women by women. Students learn effective physical techniques plus warning signals and attacker's tactics. Practice in an atmosphere of cooperation. Emphasis on practical, effective solutions. Women of any age, athletic ability, or previous experience.

TENNESSEE

Nashville

Kong's Tae Kwon Do Institute
2626 Murfreesboro Road, Nashville, Tennessee 37217
(615) 361-1177

Self-defense, martial arts.

Mid-American Taekwondo Centers
4536 Nolensville Road, Nashville, Tennessee 37211
(615) 834-6800

Self-defense and martial arts. Tots' classes (under six).

TEXAS
Dallas

YWCA
4621 Ross, Dallas, Texas 75204
(214) 827-5600

Self-defense classes.

UTAH
Ogden

Errigo's Kung-Fu Studio
1522 Washington Boulevard, Ogden, Utah
(801) 393-6311

Self-defense for women, men, children.

Sunset

O & M's Hop Kwon Do Korean Self Defense
2447 North Main, Sunset, Utah 84015
(801) 776-5526

Women instructors, self-defense classes.

VERMONT
Burlington

Women's Rape Crisis Center
P.O. Box 92, Burlington, Vermont 05401
(802) 863-1236 CONTACT PERSON: Janet

Self-defense classes for women, women instructors.

VIRGINIA

Richmond

Kim School, Inc.
1617 West Broad Street, Richmond, Virginia 23233
(804) 359-6359

Karate and aikido.

Wah Lum Kung Fu
3037 West Cary Street, Richmond, Virginia 23221
(804) 358-0632

Self-defense emphasis, classes for women, men, children.

WASHINGTON

Olympia

FIST (Feminists in Self-Defense Training)
P.O. Box 1883, Olympia, Washington 98507
(206) 438-0288 CONTACT PERSON: Debbie Leung

Self-defense classes for women with women instructors. Developed from a woman's perspective on violence and abuse. Women of all races, ages, and physical abilities. FIST is a volunteer organization that works collectively.

Seattle

Alternatives to Fear
1605 Seventeenth Avenue, Seattle, Washington 98122
(206) 328-5347 CONTACT PERSON: Py Bateman

Self-defense classes for women with women instructors. Classes in self-defense issues for men occasionally have male speakers. Children's classes for boys and girls, parents' classes for both, and senior citizen classes for both. Separate teen classes for females and males.

Feminist Karate Union, c/o Alternatives to Fear
1605 Seventeenth Avenue, Seattle, Washington 98122
(206) 328-5347 CONTACT PERSON: Py Bateman

Classes in traditional karate for women with women instructors.

WASHINGTON, D.C.

Artemis Institute
1940 Calvert St., N.W., Washington, D.C. 20009
(202) 265-2650/966-7783 CONTACT PERSON: Martha Leslie Allen

Martial arts classes (ja-shin-do) with self-defense emphasized. Also a discussion/

presentation class in self-empowerment/self-reliance. Some classes for women only, all women instructors.

D.C. Rape Crisis Center
2201 P St., N.W., Washington, D.C. 20037
(202) 232-0202 CONTACT PERSON: Nicenje Toure

Self-defense classes for women, all women instructors. Community education, self-defense lectures and workshops, and a one-month class for women emphasizing preventive behavior, verbal and physical techniques, and psychological preparedness.

WEST VIRGINIA

Chimera, Inc.
1237 Hampton Avenue, Morgantown, West Virginia 26505
(304) 292-1977 CONTACT PERSON: Kate Brett

Self-defense classes for women by women. Students learn effective physical techniques plus warning signals and attacker's tactics. Practice in an atmosphere of cooperation. Emphasis on practical, effective solutions. Women of any age, athletic ability, or previous experience.

WISCONSIN

Madison

Chimera, Inc.
312 East Wilson Street, Madison, Wisconsin 53703
(608) 255-0076 CONTACT PERSON: Faith Russell

Self-defense classes for women by women. Students learn effective physical techniques plus warning signals and attacker's tactics. Practice in an atmosphere of cooperation. Emphasis on practical, effective solutions. Women of any age, athletic ability, or previous experience.

WYOMING

Casper

Shaw Freestyle Karate
517 West Collins, Casper, Wyoming 82601
(307) 237-7146

Kung fu, karate, jujitsu, tae kwon do, judo.

CANADA

BRITISH COLUMBIA

Vancouver

Crescent Karate-do
#383—1755 Robson Street, Vancouver, British Columbia V6G 1C9
(604) 685-2747 CONTACT PERSON: Lynn Calvert

Karate classes with some jujitsu, self-defense emphasized, for women only, with women instructors. Loose structure, no rank.

Women Educating in Self-Defense Training (WEST)
2349 St. Catherine's Street, Vancouver, British Columbia, VST 3X8
(604) 876-6390 CONTACT PERSON: Alice Macpherson

Self-defense classes for women and children taught by women instructors. Practical mental and physical techniques to help women and children deal with various types of harassment and assault. Awareness, avoidance, and action. Basic, intermediate, advanced, and instructor-level training.

ONTARIO

Toronto

Wen-Do Women's Self Defense

2 Carlton Street, Suite 817, Toronto, Ontario M5B 1J3
(416) 977-7127 CONTACT PERSON: Marilyn Walsh

Self-defense classes for women, all women instructors. Focus on awareness of potentially dangerous situations and development of appropriate responses. Discussion of myths and fears plus physical techniques designed for women. Empowering.

Selected Annotated Bibliography

The books in this bibliography are for those of you who want more information about self-defense or related topics. Entries have been selected for availability and usefulness. We have included a few books we don't recommend so that we can caution against the author's advice, writing style, or bias.

Women's Self-Defense

Atkinson, Linda. *Women in the Martial Arts: A New Spirit Rising.* (New York: Dodd, Mead & Co., 1983).

Extremely supportive of beginning students and women interested in various arts. Includes judo, karate, kung fu, t'ai chi ch'uan, tae kwon do, kendo, and aikido.

Bart, Pauline B. and Patricia H. O'Brien. *Stopping Rape: Successful Survival Strategies.* (New York: Pergamon Press, 1985).

This book details the results of Bart's sociological study of rape avoiders, funded by the National Institute of Mental Health in 1977. Although academic in language, the book includes numerous quotes from interviews of rape avoiders and Bart's fascinating conclusions, which support a variety of resistance strategies.

Barthol, Robert G. *Protect Yourself: A Self-Defense Guide for Women, From Prevention to Counter-Attack.* (Englewood Cliffs, N.J.: Prentice-Hall, 1979).

Barthol is skeptical about a woman's ability to effectively defend herself physically.

Bateman, Py. *Fear Into Anger: A Manual of Self-Defense for Women.* (Chicago: Nelson-Hall Inc., 1978).

Written by a feminist karate and self-defense instructor, this is a good text in karate-style self-defense for women. Includes multiple attacks.

Carmichel, Jim. *The Women's Guide to Handguns: A Guide to Safe Self-Defense*. (Stoeger Publishing Co., 1982).

Davis, Linda J., and Elaine M. Brody. *Rape and Older Women: A Guide to Prevention and Protection*. D.H.E.W. Publication No. (ADM) 78-734, printed 1979, Washington, D.C.

Prevention classes are discussed, with specific suggestions and aids for teachers. A meticulous, thorough handbook put out as a government publication.

Delacoste, Frederique, and Felice Newman, eds. *Fight Back! Feminist Resistance to Male Violence*. (Minneapolis: Cleis Press, 1981).

An excellent source of contemporary history, with abundant success stories throughout. Included are some articles that deal with violence against lesbians, women of color, and the politics of the anti-violence movement.

Elgin, Suzette Haden. *The Gentle Art of Verbal Self-Defense*. (Englewood Cliffs, N.J.: Prentice-Hall, 1980).

————. *More on the Gentle Art of Verbal Self-Defense*. (Englewood Cliffs, N.J.: Prentice-Hall, 1983).

Farkas, Emil, and Leeds, Margaret. *Fight Back, A Woman's Guide to Self-Defense*. (New York: Holt, Rinehart and Winston, 1978).

A good basic book of physical self-defense techniques, presented in a positive way. Exceptionally clear photographs. Arranged in a series of lessons so that the book may be used by teachers.

Fein, Judith. *Are You a Target?* (Belmont, Calif.: Wadsworth Publishing Company, 1981).

A thoughtful, practical, and clear approach to self-defense. Positive and encouraging.

Fighting Woman News: Martial Arts, Self-Defense, and Combative Sports.

A sporadic but interesting publication. Often includes directory of local martial art/self-defense schools from all over the country. Back issues available.

Graff, Sunny, Sandy Dickinson, and Sarah McKinley. Self Defense Teachers' Guide: Proceedings of the National Self Defense Teaching Practicum held March 4-6, 1983, in Columbus, Ohio. (Columbus, Ohio: Intrepid Clearinghouse, 1984).

Both exciting and disappointing. Not a text for teachers, but a summary of workshops. Most interesting are sections on attacks with clubs, multiple attacks, teaching techniques exchange, the Child Assault Prevention Project, and courses on high school women, seniors, battered women, recovering chemically dependent women, fat women, and blind women. Available from Intrepid, P.O. Box 02180, Columbus, Ohio, 43202. Phone (614) 267-4030.

Hudson, Kathleen. *Every Woman's Guide to Self Defense*. (New York: St. Martin's Press, 1978).

Hudson, a martial artist, based this book on techniques adapted from atemi-jitsu, kung fu, jujitsu, and judo.

Kaufman, Doris, Robert Rudeen, and Carol Morgan. *Safe Within Yourself: A Woman's Guide to Rape Prevention and Self Defense*. (Alexandria, Va.: Visage Press, 1980).

Not as good as it sounds. Basic self-defense techniques for a varied set of situations. However, the solar plexus is inaccurately placed on the vital points chart, legal information is misleading, and the language is fairly academic.

Monkerud, Donald, and Mary Heiny. *Self-Defense for Women, Exploring Sports Series*. (Dubuque, Iowa: William C. Brown, 1980).

Written by experienced aikido instructors with interesting things to say about violence against women and the obstacles to learning self-defense. Encouraging and empowering to women. However, many of the physical techniques described are complex, taken directly from aikido, and difficult to learn from a book. An excellent supplement for women enrolled in beginning aikido classes.

Peterson, Susan Goldner. *Self-Defense for Women: The West Point Way*. (New York: Simon & Schuster, 1979).

Author directed self-defense at West Point and her Army philosophy is evident. Many photos clearly illustrate physical techniques. The section on weapons is outstanding.

Peterson, Susan L. *Self-Defense for Women: How to Stay Safe and Fight Back*. (New York: Leisure Press, 1984).

Prevention is a major theme. Physical techniques presented, with understandable instructions and photographs, but author's attitude appears to be one of fear and a conviction that women are not strong enough to successfully resist.

Pickering, Michael G. V. *A Manual for Women's Self Defense*. (North Palm Beach, Fla.: The Athletic Institute, 1983).

Book is positive in attitude and treats all covered subjects with much consideration and common sense. One exception is the section on legal issues, which recommends unequivocally that a woman report an attack to the police and try to have the case prosecuted, with no consideration of the often problematic results of such action to the woman herself. Brevity of instructions may sometimes confuse even an experienced student.

Reimold, Cheryl. *The Woman's Guide to Staying Safe*. (New York: Cloverdale Press/Monarch Press, 1985).

The book devotes five pages to physical self-defense. The rest is a mixed bag—lots of sound advice on surviving danger, from fire in your home to rape. Useful for a woman on her own for the first time.

Sanford, Linda Tschirhart, and Ann Fetter. *In Defense of Our Selves: A Rape Prevention Handbook for Women.* (Garden City, N.J.: Doubleday, 1979). Foreword by Susan Brownmiller.

This excellent book combines practical physical self-defense with psychological preparation. Photographs are clear and realistic. Special sections on older women, teens, disabled women, lesbians, Asian Americans, Black women and other special groups. Currently out of print, but sometimes available in libraries.

Sliwa, Curtis, and Murray Schwartz. *Street Smart: The Guardian Angel Guide to Safe Living.* (Reading, Mass.: Addison-Wesley, 1982).

The Guardian Angels began as a subway safety patrol in 1979, but soon grew. This book is aimed at helping city dwellers deal with small-time street criminals and harassers. Non-threatening attitude, terrific photos of ethnically diverse individuals and groups, neighborhood-based strategies.

Sliwa, Lisa. *Attitude: Commonsense Defense for Women.* (New York: Crown Publishers, 1986).

A no-nonsense, clearly written book by the National Director of the Guardian Angels. Packed with practical and sometimes unique advice for women on surviving in the urban '80s. Chapter titles include "Mental Muscle," "Inside a Subspecies: the Criminal Mind," "Moves Mother Never Taught You," "Street Smarts," and "Suburban Survival." Gives tips on everything from shopping malls to bank teller machines to being safe in your own home.

Smith, Susan E. *Fear or Freedom: A Woman's Options in Social Survival and Physical Defense.* (Racine, Wis.: Mother Courage Press, 1986).

An interesting blend of social and political analysis and practical self-defense advice. Takes an overview of the current climate for women's self-defense, examines common myths held by both men and women, and gives the results of a survey on different kinds of attack and defense. Deals intelligently with different degrees of violence and the best response to a given attack, from verbal responses to "last resort" techniques.

Storaska, Frederic. *How to Say No to a Rapist and Survive.* (New York: Random House, 1975). Reissued in paperback by Warner Books, 1976.

Seriously criticized by feminists. Blames women for rape, says they can't learn to defend themselves, and that they should not use physical defenses. Not recommended.

Tegner, Bruce, and Alice McGrath. *Self-Defense and Assault Prevention for Women.* (Ventura, Calif.: Thor Publishing, 1977).

Although photographs are somewhat old-fashioned, advice and techniques are excellent. Available from: Thor Publishing Co., Box 1782, Ventura, Calif. 93001.

Telsey, Nadia. "How to Say 'NO' to Storaska and Thrive," in *Self Defense Teachers' Guide*. Sunny Graff, ed. (Columbus, Ohio: Intrepid, 1984), pp. 101–103.
   Excellent criticism of Storaska.

Walton, Gerald M. *The Legal Implications of Self-Defense: A Reference Manual for the Martial Arts*. (New York: Vantage Press, 1979).
   Self-defense teachers will find this book helpful.

Women's Self-Defense Law Project. 853 Broadway, 14th Fl., New York, NY 10003, (212) 674-3303.
   Assists attorneys nationwide in providing better representation for women who defend themselves.

Child Safety

Adams, Caren, Jennifer Fay, and Jan Loreen-Martin. *No Is Not Enough: Helping Teenagers Avoid Sexual Assault*. (Impact Publishers, P.O. Box 1094, San Luis Obispo, Calif. 93406, 1984).
   Information-packed guide to recognizing the signs of sexual assault in teens, and helping them to protect themselves. Emphasis on acquaintance rape. Tips on communicating with teenagers.

Adams, Caren, and Jennifer Fay. *No More Secrets: Protecting Your Child from Sexual Assault*. (San Luis Obispo, Calif.: Impact Publishers, 1981).
   Practical, positive information on how adults can prevent or deal with child sexual abuse, with an emphasis on children's rights. How to talk to children about the issue without being scary; how to teach your children good self-defense habits.

Arenberg, Gerald S., Carmella R. Bartimole, and John E. Bartimole. *Preventing Missing Children: A Parental Guide to Child Security*. (Hollywood, Fla.: Compact Books, 1984).
   Steps to take should a child be missing.

Bass, Ellen. *I Like You to Make Jokes with Me, But I Don't Want You to Touch Me*. (Chapel Hill, N.C.: Lollipop Power, 1985), story copyright 1981, book copyright 1985.
   Based on a real-life incident, the story of a small girl who learns, with her mother's support and help, that she can set limits on what she and her grownup friend Jack do together.

Bateman, Py. *Acquaintance Rape Awareness and Prevention for Teenagers*. (Seattle: Alternatives to Fear, 1605 17th Ave., Seattle, Wash. 98122, 1982).

Bateman, Py, and Gayle Stringer. *Where Do I Start? A Parent's Guide for Talking to Teens About Acquaintance Rape.* (Dubuque, Iowa: Kendall/Hall Publishing Co., 1984).

Colao, Flora, and Tamar Hosansky. *Your Children Should Know.* (New York: Harper & Row, 1987).
   Excellent guidebook for parents about helping children defend themselves. Written by two women who pioneered children's self-defense programs, the book includes personal stories by children, information on talking with children, identifying abuse, and practical advice on self-defense.

Fay, Jennifer J., and Billie Jo Flerchinger. *Top Secret: Sexual Assault Information for Teenagers Only.* (Renton, Wash.: King County Rape Relief, 305 S. 43rd, Renton, Wash. 98055), 1982.

Freeman, Lory. *It's MY Body: A Book to Teach Young Children How to Resist Uncomfortable Touch.* (Seattle, Wash.: Parenting Press, 1982).
   A small child speaks up and makes choices about what kinds of touching feel OK with a female babysitter. Since most danger to children comes from men, a parent might want to discuss men also. Available from Parenting Press, 7750 31st Ave., NE, Seattle, Wash. 98115.

Hart-Rossi, Janie. *Protect Your Child from Sexual Abuse: A Parent's Guide; A Book to Teach Young Children How to Resist Uncomfortable Touch.* (Seattle, Wash.: Parenting Press, 1984).
   A book for parents and teachers that accompanies *It's MY Body* (see above). Geared to children ages three to six. Available from Parenting Press, 7750 31st Ave., NE, Seattle, Wash. 98115.

Hechinger, Grace. *How to Raise a Street Smart Child: The Complete Guide to Safety on the Street and at Home.* (New York: Facts on File Publications, 1984).
   Primarily an urban guidebook based on the prevention strategies commonly advised by law enforcement. The approach is careful and considerate of children's dignity and safety. Physical self-defense is not covered.

Moore, Peggy A. *How Not to Abuse Your Child.* (Detroit: Detroit Black Writers' Guild, 1985).
   This book, dedicated to Black parents, presents practical proven tips in an easy-to-read form. Written by a mother of eleven children.

Newman, Susan. *Never Say Yes to a Stranger: What Your Child Must Know to Stay Safe.* (New York: Perigee Books, 1985). Photos by George Tiboni.
   Collection of moral tales in which girls and boys, approached by adult strangers, remember what their parents said, and avoid or escape dangerous situations. Stories realistic, photographs interesting.

Sanford, Linda T. *Silent Children: A Parent's Guide in the Prevention of Child Abuse.* (New York: Anchor Press/Doubleday, 1980).

Tegner, Bruce, and Alice McGrath. *Self Defense for Your Child: Practical Defenses and Assault Prevention for Elementary School Age Boys and Girls.* (Ventura, Calif.: Thor Publishing, 1976).

Excellent book about practical physical techniques for children. Directions and photos extraordinarily clear and easy to understand. Available from: Thor Publishing Co., Box 1782, Ventura, Calif. 93001.

Recovering from Rape

Benedict, Helen. *Recovery: How to Survive Sexual Assault for Women, Men, Teenagers, and Their Friends and Families.* (New York: Doubleday & Company, 1985).

This book is a practical guide to healing after rape that includes sections for women, men, teenagers, older, disabled, lesbian, and gay victims, as well as their friends and families. It also has an extensive resource section that includes rape crisis lines, shelters, counseling for violent men, and a few self-defense programs.

Johnson, Kathryn M. *If You Are Raped: What Every Woman Needs to Know.* (Holmes Beach, Fla.: Learning Publications, 1985).

Practical information for dealing with the legal, medical, emotional and psychological effects of rape. Includes many examples and is a generally positive guide to recovering from rape. Includes information for women who are interested in fighting back via the criminal justice system.

Katz, Judy H. *Fairy Godmothers, No Magic Wands: The Healing Process After Rape.* (Saratoga, Calif.: R. and E. Publishers, 1984).

Chapter on "Counseling the Rape Victim" is included, as well as list of references.

Ledray, Linda Holt. *Recovering from Rape.* (New York: Henry Holt & Co., 1986).

An excellent guide. Although it focuses on the immediate aftermath of rape (with discussions of doctors, the police, the legal system, emotional recovery, and prevention), it deals with long-term consequences as well.

Family Violence

Bass, Ellen, and Louise Thornton, eds. *I Never Told Anyone: Writings by Women Survivors of Child Sexual Abuse.* (New York: Harper & Row, 1983).

Excellent collection of personal accounts.

Bass, Ellen, and Laura Davis. *The Courage to Heal: A Guide for Women Survivors of Child Sexual Abuse.* (New York: Harper & Row, 1987).

A comprehensive, life-changing guide to the healing process and to changing self-defeating patterns in one's present life. Inspiring first-person stories throughout. Excellent resource and bibliography sections.

Bowker, Lee H. *Ending the Violence: A Guidebook Based on the Experiences of 1,000 Battered Wives.* (Holmes Beach, Fla.: Learning Publications, 1986).
An overpriced but useful handbook, aimed at helping women get out of violent relationships. Available from Learning Publications, P.O. Box 1326, 5351 Gulf Dr., 33509.

Browne, Angela. *When Battered Women Kill.* (New York: The Free Press/Macmillan, 1987).
Well-done sociological study of women who have killed the men who battered them. Analyzes the roots of violence, family structures. Interspersed with women's first-person accounts.

Gil, Eliana. *Outgrowing the Pain: A Book For and About Adults Abused as Children.* (San Francisco: Launch Press, 1983).
Written to evoke the pain, explain it, and help the reader through it. Easy to read, useful.

Leman, Lisa G. *Prosecution of Spouse Abuse: Innovations in Criminal Justice Response.* (Washington, D.C.: Center for Women Policy Studies, 1981).
An educational, practical, and sensitive handbook for prosecutors.

Lobel, Kerry, ed. *Naming the Violence: Speaking Out About Lesbian Battering.* (Seattle: Seal Press, 1986).
Anthology of articles ranging from personal accounts to analysis of patterns of abuse, compiled for the National Coalition Against Domestic Violence Lesbian Task Force. Painful and revealing stories, and some perspectives on change.

McNulty, Faith. *The Burning Bed: The True Story of an Abused Wife.* (New York: Bantam Books, 1981).
The book the TV show was based on. The woman burns her abusive husband, and is acquitted of murder.

NiCarthy, Ginny. *Getting Free: A Handbook for Women in Abusive Relationships.* 2nd ed. (Seattle, Wash.: Seal Press, 1986).
Excellent guidebook, packed with a variety of information for women in abusive relationships. Analyzes abusive family patterns, and includes sections on making the decision to leave or stay, getting professional help, living the single life, building a support network. Good bibliography.

NiCarthy, Ginny, Karen Merriam, and Sandra Coffman. *Talking It Out: A Guide for Groups for Abused Women.* (Seattle, Wash.: Seal Press, 1984).
A guide to conducting groups for women who have been abused. As useful and readable for lay women as for counselors. Specific suggestions for dis-

abled women, women of racial and ethnic groups, lesbians. Very good bibliography.

Schechter, Susan. *Women and Male Violence: The Visions and Struggles of the Battered Women's Movement.* (Boston: South End Press, 1982).
This is the leading work on the history of the contemporary battered women's movement, outlining its triumphs, disasters, and future prospects. Schechter warns of problems with increasing bureaucracy, racism and class issues. Essential reading for volunteers and staff of battered women's shelters.

Wheat, Patte, with Leonard L. Lieber. *Hope for the Children: A Personal History of Parents Anonymous.* (Minneapolis: Winston Press, 1979).
Stories of once-abusive parents, and the history of Parents Anonymous, support group for former child abusers.

White, Evelyn C. *Chain Chain Change: For Black Women Dealing with Physical and Emotional Abuse.* (Seattle: Seal Press, 1985).
For Black battered women, this short, readable book defines domestic violence, looks at the psychology of abuse and its effects on children, and gives advice on dealing with the criminal justice system.

Sexual Harassment

Backhouse, Constance, and Leah Cohen. *Sexual Harassment on the Job: How to Avoid the Working Woman's Nightmare.* (Englewood Cliffs, N.J.: Prentice-Hall, 1981). Originally published as *The Secret Oppression* by MacMillan and Co. of Canada, 1978.
Useful, business-like book dealing with legal and business aspects of sexual harassment.

Fighting Sexual Harassment: An Advocacy Handbook. Second edition. (Boston, Mass.: Alyson Publications, Inc. and the Alliance Against Sexual Coercion, 1981).
Intended for social service workers. Available from AASC, P.O. Box 1, Cambridge, Mass. 02139, $4.95.

McCaghy, M. Dawn. *Sexual Harassment: A Guide to Resources.* (Boston: G.K. Hall, 1985). Part of the G.K. Hall Women's Studies Publications, Barbara Haber, ed.
An annotated bibliography of materials on this subject, including audiovisual aids. Both academic and workplace harassment are covered. Very useful.

For Concerned Men

Changing Men magazine, University YMCA Community Center, 306 W. Brooks St., Madison, Wis., 53715.
Journal on the cutting edge of the new feminist men's movement. Deals

with a diversity of issues of concern to men (and women) who are challenging traditional sex roles and male/female dynamics.

McEvoy, Alan W., and Jeff B. Brookings. *If She Is Raped: A Book for Husbands, Fathers and Male Friends*. (Holmes-Beach, Fla.: Learning Publications, 1984).

    This down-to-earth book presents practical suggestions, case studies, and plenty of examples of ways men can deal effectively and sensitively with the rape of someone they are close to. Includes a list of rape crisis centers in the United States.

Sonkin, Daniel Jay, and Michael Durphy. *Learning to Live Without Violence: A Handbook for Men*. (San Francisco: Volcano Press, 1982).

    A handbook for men who are violent in personal relationships. Useful for counselors and group leaders. Available from Volcano Press, 330 Ellis St., San Francisco, Calif. 94102, $10.00.

General Interest

Aegis: Magazine on Ending Violence Against Women. P.O. Box 21033, Washington, D.C. 20009.

    Bi-monthly. Self-indexed. Published by the National Communication Network, Feminist Alliance Against Rape, Alliance Against Sexual Coercion, Washington, D.C. In print. Back issues available.

Bochnak, Elizabeth, ed. *Women's Self-Defense Cases: Theory and Practice*. (Charlottesville, Va.: Michie Co., 1981).

    Invaluable handbook written for attorneys, on how to conduct a defense for a women's self-defense case.

Browne, Susan E., Debra Connors, and Nanci Stern. *With the Power of Each Breath: A Disabled Women's Anthology*. (Pittsburgh, Pa.: Cleis Press, 1985).

    See "Abuse of Women with Disabilities" by Rebecca S. Grothaus, pp. 124–128. This article explores a few of the reasons why disabled women hesitate to use services and makes recommendations for change.

Butler, Pamela E. *Self Assertion for Women*. (New York: Harper & Row, 1981).

    Discusses and evaluates verbal and non-verbal messages women send and suggests changes. Topics include setting limits, dealing with criticism, handling "persecutors." Interesting section on "Androgyny as Power."

Henley, Nancy M. *Body Politics: Power, Sex, and Nonverbal Communication*. (Englewood Cliffs, N.J.: Prentice-Hall, 1977).

    Tremendously useful for women learning to be physically and verbally assertive.

Katz, Judy H. *White Awareness: Handbook for Anti-Racism Training*. (Norman: University of Oklahoma Press, 1978).
  A practical guide to unlearning racism.

Phelps, Stanlee, and Nancy Austin. *The Assertive Woman*. (San Luis Obispo, Calif.: Impact Publishers, 1975).
  Includes all standard assertion strategies. Uses characters such as Doris Doormat, which may be belittling to a woman's self-respect and thus counterproductive. Not recommended.

Saldana, Theresa. *Beyond Survival*. (New York: Bantam Books, 1986).
  A young actress who was attacked and stabbed ten times writes the story of her recovery and the founding of Victims for Victims, a national organization dedicated to helping crime survivors and their loved ones. A very readable autobiographical account.

Smith, Manuel J. *When I Say No I Feel Guilty*. (New York: Bantam, 1975).
  Perhaps the easiest of the assertiveness training books to use: one can learn simply by reading the book.